D0127571

The Story of the CHURCH

PEAK MOMENTS from Pentecost to the Year 2000

Alfred McBride, O. Praem.

Nihil Obstat:
  Rev. Lawrence Landini, O.F.M.
  Rev. Robert L. Hagedorn
Imprimi Potest:
  Rev. John Bok, O.F.M.
  Provincial
Imprimatur:
  +Most Rev. Carl K. Moeddel, V.G.
  Archdiocese of Cincinnati
  November 9, 1995

Scripture citations are taken from the *New Revised Standard Version Bible*, copyright ©1989 by the Division of Christian Education of the National Council of the Churches of Christ in the U.S.A. and used by permission.

Quotations in Chapter 22 from *The Agony and the Ecstasy* by Irving Stone, copyright ©1961 by Doubleday & Company, Inc., are reprinted by permission of New American Library.

Quotations in Chapter 26 from *The Long Loneliness* by Dorothy Day, copyright ©1952 by Harper and Row, Publishers, Inc., are reprinted by permission of Harper and Row.

Quotations in Chapter 27 from *The Seven Storey Mountain* by Thomas Merton, copyright ©1948 by Harcourt Brace and Company, renewed 1976 by The Trustees of the Merton Legacy Trust, are reprinted by permission of Harcourt Brace, Inc.

"And the Children of Birmingham" by Thomas Merton from *The Collected Poems of Thomas Merton*, copyright ©1946 by New Directions Publishing Corporation, 1977 by the Trustees of the Merton Legacy Trust. Reprinted by permission of New Directions Publishing Corporation.

Excerpt from "Barth's Dream" in Chapter 27 is taken from *Conjectures of a Guilty Bystander* by Thomas Merton, copyright ©1965 by the Abbey of Gethsemani. Reprinted by permission of Doubleday & Company, Inc.

Cover design by June Pfaff
Book design by Sandra Digman
Illustrations by Julie Lonneman

ISBN 0-86716-246-5
©1996, Alfred McBride

Published by
St. Anthony Messenger Press

Printed in the U.S.A

Contents

Part One:
Early Church

Part Two:
Middle Ages

Part Three:
Reformation

Part Four:
Modern Church

Introduction

"Will I see before I die the Church of God as in days of old, when the apostles spread their nets to take not gold or silver, but the souls of men and women?" It has been almost a thousand years since Saint Bernard of Clairvaux asked that question, yet his dream of recovering apostolic innocence never dies—even when century after century yields a more sober picture of Catholic behavior. For nearly two thousand years the Catholic Church has housed an unruly family of saints, sinners and ordinary folks. Its history is the record of a boisterous lot of people—inspiring, infuriating, sometimes frustratingly dull and often engagingly charming.

No single volume can contain the whole story of that two-thousand-year history. In this book I have selected what seemed to me the key events, the peak experiences in our history, and knit them together in as reasonable a sequence as I could to give a sense of continuity.

This book is history from a human perspective. I believe that straight narrative history tends to distance the reader from the event. Therefore I have chosen to present thirty key events of the Church's history largely in fictional form: short stories, mini-dramas, interviews, diaries, letters and dialogues. In this way I hope to bring the personal element to life again and let the message of the past assume greater relevance for our own day.

Each event is placed into historical context by the "Looking Back" sections, and the questions "For Discussion/Reflection" in the margins, as well as the "Connecting to Our Times" sections, attempt to relate the chapter's message to some aspect of Church life today. A time line at the beginning of each section relates the secular events of that era to the religious happenings.

Why Study Church History?

The best reasons I can offer to study Church history are the lessons I have learned from the study:

First of all, it seems to me that history does repeat itself. I know that the context makes this repetition less than obvious and that there is never an exact recurrence of any event. But there are, nonetheless, startling parallels. Fourth-century Catholics resisted moving liturgical celebrations from houses to basilicas, just as twentieth-century Catholics raised eyebrows at the "innovation" of home liturgies. The pacifist tendencies of second-century Christians are reappearing in the thinking of some twentieth-century Catholics—even bishops!

At the same time, we are not bound to repeat past mistakes. Heresy-hunting has a long and dishonorable record among us, whether the dissenters be fourth-century Arians, twelfth-century Cathari, sixteenth-century Protestants, eighteenth-century political liberals or twentieth-century theological liberals. Our history in this area is sadly repetitive. We must always disagree with opinions and judgments that seem contrary to orthodoxy, but is it really necessary to oppress those with whom we are not in accord? Today, with the Vatican II documents on religious freedom and ecumenism, we at least have policies of dialogue and tolerance that would have served us well in ages past.

The second lesson I have learned is that a crisis ignored is a crisis postponed. When an institution fails to adapt to historical change, it faces a crisis.

The sixteenth-century Church refused to face the rise of nationalism and the emergence of an educated elite that would not tolerate papal interference or the moneygrubbing associated with the questionable approach to indulgences. This failure to adapt led to the crisis of the Reformation.

A similar failure occurred in the eighteenth and nineteenth centuries when it became clear that monarchy was a dying institution. Altar clung to throne and both tumbled in the chaos of various revolutions.

Crisis does not go away. Eventually, at Vatican II, the Church caught up with the emergence of democratic structures and began to adapt.

Which leads to my third lesson: The Church is remarkably durable and resilient. Despite its failures to adapt and its proverbial resistance to change, despite encountering body blows that have felled empires, the Church is still around. Ultimately the Church does come to terms with change, even if it takes a long time to do so.

Some might argue that adaptation needs to go slowly so that the Church can assess the positive and negative aspects of change, prudently keep the valuable and jettison the useless. What about those who are hurt by unreasonable delay? Ah, yes, but look at those who would be devastated by undue haste. This too is our history, an unresolvable argument between innately conservative and liberal temperaments. Nonetheless, the Church is still here and still very much alive.

The study of Church history offers natural evidence for the Church's durability and continuity and supports our supernatural belief that Jesus abides with us all days. It is our faith that he will not let the gates of hell prevail against us, that he has sent the Holy Spirit to dwell in our midst.

Thus Church history is, in the final analysis, sacred history—a continuation of the salvation history begun with Abraham. It is a record of a people called to faith and aided by grace, a people who have sinned shamelessly and loved God with abandon. I trust that, above all, this is the lesson you will learn in reading and studying this history of the Church.

Part One
Early Church

EVENTS IN THE CHURCH

Pentecost
Peter
Martyrdom of Stephen
Paul

Christian persecution

100	200

EVENTS IN SOCIETY

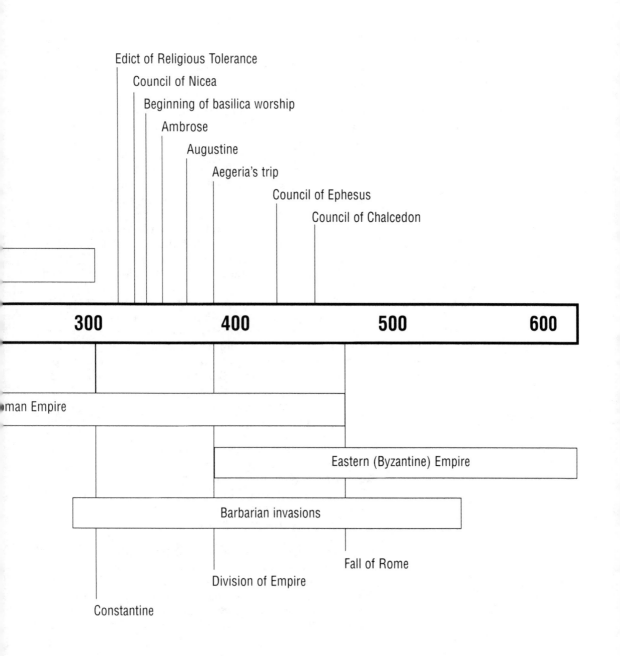

Edict of Religious Tolerance
Council of Nicea
Beginning of basilica worship
Ambrose
Augustine
Aegeria's trip
Council of Ephesus
Council of Chalcedon

300   400   500   600

man Empire

Eastern (Byzantine) Empire

Barbarian invasions

Fall of Rome

Division of Empire

Constantine

1. The Church Begins

Peter Stirs the Crowds in Pentecost Square
(c. 30-33)

FOR BACKGROUND

For the Old Testament background to Peter's remarks about Sinai, see Exodus 19:3-6.

[Y]ou are Peter, and on this rock I will build my church.
(Matthew 16:18)

The Greek traveler stood bewildered in the Jerusalem crowd. What was happening? All about him Jews from many nations milled excitedly and pointed to a group in the center of the square.

The traveler had heard that the Jerusalem holidays were exciting, but he was not prepared for this. The crowd was electrified. What was that group up to? He tried to weave his way closer.

"You are drunk!" someone shouted at the group.

The traveler heard one of them, the big man with the gray-streaked hair, respond: "We are not drunk. We are stunned with joy because we have had an experience like Israel had at Sinai."

The Greek traveler wondered what he meant by that.

"Why not own up," heckled another. "You've been to the wine bottle once too often."

Then the big man raised his hand for silence. The crowd fell quiet.

"Do not judge by appearances," he began. "Listen to our words. At Sinai, God called Israel to be a community of faith. God called our ancestors there to be a holy nation. That meant they should form a community that would worship God and live a worthy life. God also summoned them to be the light of nations, that is, to be a missionary witness helping all people to know God."

"I think I can agree with your first point," ventured a Pharisee in the crowd, "but I don't really believe God wanted us to be missionaries."

"My friend, you have forgotten the meaning of the story of Jonah," the big man remarked. "He was a preacher told by God to go on a missionary trip to Nineveh. Recall that Jonah resisted the call at first until God overcame him. Jonah was an example of how Israel, too, resisted the call."

"Who is that man?" the traveler asked of no one in particular.

"His name is Peter," a tradesman replied.

"He is their leader," said a woman nearby.

A young woman in the crowd, moved by Peter's sincerity, asked, "How is it you were speaking in a language we all could understand when you burst upon us here in the square? How did you manage to unify all of us who speak so many different tongues?"

"Perhaps I can explain this best to you," Peter answered, "by comparing this to the old story of the Tower of Babel. That was a tower of human pride that resulted in a breakdown in communications. The people at Babel could not understand each other.

"Our Master, Jesus, asked us to spend time in prayer to await his Holy Spirit. We followed his word and meditated for nine days in the Upper Room. Into that tower of prayer this day came the Holy Spirit, whose greatest work is to bring all people to unity in Christ. At Babel, people babbled. Here we speak a message that will unify people in mind and heart."

"Is that why you said you've had an experience like that which Israel had at Sinai?" asked an elderly man.

"Exactly," replied Peter. "The difference is that what happened at Sinai was but a shadow of the promise and reality that has happened here today. It is because of Jesus, who died and rose for us, that it has happened. Because of him and his Spirit, we really can be a community of faith and a light for the nations."

"How can we have this experience?"

"Is there any hope for us?"

"Go on, tell us more."

"As I look out over the vast crowd in this square," answered Peter, "I think of a world full of dead bones. I know that my comrades and I must go into this valley of the dead and bring life. Don't you remember the story of Ezekiel and the dry bones?"

> [God] said to me, "Mortal, can these bones live?" I answered, "Lord GOD, you know." Then he said to me: "Prophesy to these bones, and say to them: O dry bones, hear the word of the LORD! ...I will cause breath to enter you, and you shall live. I will lay sinews on you, and will cause flesh to come upon you, and cover you with skin, ...and you shall live; and you shall know that I am the LORD."

The traveler listened to Peter's voice as it carried over the square. It is like a wind, he thought, bearing good news to the world.

On that Pentecost day, Peter asked the people to repent, to change their way of life, to seek a new life in Christ. And they did respond. The Holy Spirit of Jesus moved into the valley of dry bones and brought three thousand to life.

A new Church began!

"Your young men shall see visions and your old men shall dream dreams," Peter exclaimed.

That's what happened. The young let loose a flood of heart-expanding ideals across the earth. The old suddenly realized that their dreams of a happier tomorrow were no longer foolish thoughts, but a reality come true.

FOR DISCUSSION/REFLECTION

Peter converted three thousand people to Christ on Pentecost. There are eighty million unchurched people in the United States. What can we learn from this story of Peter to motivate and help us evangelize the unchurched?

The gifts of the Spirit, outlined in the Pentecost story (Acts 2), are spelled out in greater detail in 1 Corinthians 12—14. Read those chapters and discuss personal applications to your life.

Discuss the seven gifts of the Holy Spirit (wisdom, understanding, counsel, piety, knowledge, fortitude and fear of the Lord) and how they are as important today as in the age of the apostles.

Members of the charismatic renewal prize the gift of tongues—a gift very prominent in the Pentecost narrative. What is the relative value of such a gift in comparison to love and service? (Read 1 Corinthians 14.)

Confirmation is a personal Pentecost for each one of us. What has it meant, practically speaking, in your life?

Prophets have always attributed much of their insight and personal courage to the presence of the Spirit in their lives. Who are some modern prophets who seem to be filled with God's Spirit? If you were to act prophetically, what might you be prompted to do?

FOR FURTHER READING

Crowe, Jerome. *The Acts*. Wilmington, Del.: Michael Glazier, 1979.

Cwiekowski, Frederick J., S.S. *The Beginnings of the Church*. Mahwah, N.J.: Paulist Press, 1988.

McBride, Alfred, O. Praem. *The Gospel of the Holy Spirit*, Our Popular Bible Study Series. Huntington, Ind.: Our Sunday Visitor, 1993.

AUDIO

Acts of the Apostles, by Eugene LaVerdiere. Credence Cassettes.

VIDEO

A.D.: History of the Early Church. Distributed by Ignatius Press (three two-hour videos).

Jerusalem. Educational Video Network (19 minutes).

Jesus of Nazareth. 20th Century Fox (three videos, 371 minutes total).

The Church Begins—Looking Back

The apostles were gathered together in Jerusalem for the observance of the Jewish feast of weeks (Shavuot), celebrated at the completion of Palestine's seven-week grain harvest season in early summer. This season began with the feast of the Passover when the Jews celebrated their historic escape from Egypt.

This harvest festival of fifty days climaxed in the offering of the sheaf of the first fruits to God. At first an agricultural feast, Judaism gradually transformed it into a historical feast with a spiritual meaning. It commemorated for the Jews the revelation of God on Mount Sinai, the giving of the law. By the time of the apostles, this Jewish feast had come to be called Pentecost, the Greek word for "fiftieth," for this was the fiftieth day after the Passover.

It is profoundly significant that on the occasion of this festival, which combined the celebration of the harvest and the memorial day of God's manifestation to the chosen people, a new manifestation of God was made in the dynamic power of the Holy Spirit. As the old covenant was commemorated in the Passover and completed on Mount Sinai, so the new covenant was commemorated in the Christian Pasch and completed on the festival of Pentecost, when the Holy Spirit came upon the disciples.

At this time a new power broke into their lives, manifested in various ways: ecstatic utterance in unintelligible speech ("speaking with tongues"), the power to prophesy, the ability to discern God's manifestation in life. Great enthusiasm and belief urged these followers of Christ to action, giving them the strength to do and effect what apparently was previously beyond them. A new life was born in them.

The evangelist Luke makes Pentecost the birthday of the universal Church. Peter's discourse (Acts 2:14-41) is the first promulgation of the gospel. The gift of tongues for Pentecost is symbolic. The new Church will unify humankind in the one Body of Christ.

Share Your Faith With Others— Connecting to Our Times

On December 8, 1975, Pope Paul VI published his *Apostolic Exhortation on Evangelization in the Modern World*. He wrote, "The tenth anniversary of the closing of the Second Vatican Council seems a fitting occasion for this exhortation. Its teaching can be summed up in this single objective: to ensure that the Church of the twentieth century may emerge ever better equipped to proclaim the Gospel to the people of this century" (#2).

Peter's first sermon at Pentecost was a call to conversion to faith in Jesus and initiation into his Church through Baptism. Both Paul VI and John Paul II continue Peter's ministry of evangelization for our own times. They challenge each of us to share our faith with others. Studies show that Catholics are bashful about doing this. Only two percent of Catholics are willing to witness their faith to others and invite them to faith in Jesus and communion with the Church. Contrast this with evangelical Protestant Christians, who are far more enthusiastic about sharing their faith.

The New Testament Church grew because the apostles and disciples responded to the graces of the Holy Spirit and gladly proclaimed Jesus in word and deed, in faith and love. It has been said, "The only thing we take with us in death is what we gave away in life." Let us give the treasure of our faith especially to those who are seekers for truth, joy and authentic self-fulfillment.

Pentecost—the fiftieth day—was a time in Judaism to visit the temple in Jerusalem. The city was teeming with visitors when the Holy Spirit arrived.

2. First-Century Adjustments

Paul the Troubleshooter
(c. 52)

"What is going on down in Jerusalem?" Paul of Tarsus was always easily annoyed, but now he was furious. The Christians in Jerusalem were setting up entrance requirements for Church membership that Paul judged to be absolutely wrong.

"Think of it," said Paul to some of his Galatian friends. "They want to force the old rules onto Gentile candidates for the Church. They're demanding that Gentiles agree to be circumcised before entering the Church and, when they become Christians, to abide by the Jewish dietary laws, such as not eating pork."

"From what you've told us, Paul," said one of his friends, "they're missing the point of what Christ required of those who would join the Church."

"Exactly," replied Paul. "Jesus was interested in a new way of life, not ancient religious customs. He invited people to embrace a new life and to celebrate this decision with Baptism and the Breaking of the Bread."

"It's strange," remarked another friend, "how they've forgotten that Abraham, the father of all people of faith, was not circumcised, nor did he observe the dietary laws."

"Of course," said Paul, "Abraham pleased God by his faith and his good life. The Jerusalem group is making a mistake by forcing these old practices of piety on the newcomers."

"It's easy to see how that would happen," replied an old man in the group. "Those venerable religious practices have meant so much to the Jewish people."

"True enough," Paul went on, "but we must show them that these things are not essential to the religion Jesus taught. I'm going down to Jerusalem immediately to stop this development. Let the newcomers develop their own practices of piety to suit their mentality."

Paul did go down, and he won the day. (Read the story as told in Acts 15:1-21 and Galatians 2:1-21.)

This was but one of the many problems Paul faced. It is important to recall that Paul's concern for the problems of his people grew out of his idea of Christian love. "If I speak in the tongues of mortals and of angels, but do not have love, I am a noisy gong or a clanging cymbal.... If I give away all my possessions, and if I hand over my body so that I may boast, but do not have love, I gain nothing" (1 Corinthians 13:1, 3).

It is the love of Christ that urges Paul on. Each human

problem with which he deals in his letters is an example of how this love can be made real in daily life.

Had Paul written a modern newspaper question-and-answer column, he might have given advice in this way:

'Dear Paul': A First-Century Advice Column

Q: I am a Christian homemaker, and I am concerned about the contaminated meat [meat previously offered to idols] that I find at the meat counter. Can I in good conscience buy such meat for my family?

A. Don't worry, the meat really isn't contaminated because the gods in question do not exist. Still, if you think you would scandalize a fellow Christian by buying and eating it, you might, for that person's sake, decide to pass it up for a time.

Q. Our house liturgies have degenerated beyond belief. During the supper part of the liturgy, people are dividing into cliques. The rich eat expensive dinners and some of them get drunk. The poor often go hungry. How can we possibly call this the meal of friendship?

A. If anything could be called sacrilegious, it is what you describe. The people who do what you say are ridiculing the Eucharist. All those who eat the bread and drink the cup had better examine their behavior and improve. Otherwise they will incur God's judgment on themselves.

Q. Lately, we've been experiencing an abuse of the gift of tongues. The "tongue-speakers" prattle on endlessly. We have no interpreters in our congregation. At least if we understood what the tongue-speakers were talking about, we might be able to tolerate it. As it is, the whole thing is more a nuisance than a gift of God.

A. I couldn't agree more. Certainly the gift of tongues is a gift of God, but it is not exactly the most important one. Teaching, nursing and governing are far more useful gifts. Faith, hope and love are better yet. Tongue-speaking doesn't have to be a nuisance if you put a time limit on the speakers and are sure to have an interpreter. If you can't do this, then I suggest you maintain a respectful silence.

Q. I'm a widow and would like to remarry. How do you feel about that?

A. I rather wish you wouldn't, so you could spend most of your energies on the things of God.

Q. Since the end of the world, the second coming of Christ, is so

FOR BACKGROUND

The martyrdom of Stephen (see Acts 7:54-60) touched off a general persecution of Christians. It is at this time that Paul steps into New Testament prominence as Saul, chief of the persecutors in Jerusalem.

Paul (Saul) was born in Greek-speaking Tarsus in Cilicia, in ancient Asia Minor, modern-day Turkey. A member of the Diaspora (Jews dispersed throughout the empire), Paul was by birth a Roman citizen. He was a Pharisee, a man of the temple. When he was fifteen or sixteen his parents sent him to Jerusalem to study in the school of Rabbi Gamaliel, where he became a rabbinical scholar.

After his conversion to Christianity, Paul spent much time explaining his change of heart in the synagogues of Damascus. Then he passed some years in meditation in the Arabian desert. Thereafter he went to Jerusalem, where Barnabas, a Gentile convert, convinced the apostles of Paul's good intentions. From Jerusalem Paul began his mission to the Gentiles and Greek-speaking Jews. Eventually he became the apostle to the non-Jewish world, the answer-man and chief adviser on the new religion.

near, I've quit my job. I figure there's no point in working if the end is so close. I must admit I'm having trouble with my family. Our food supplies are low.

A. I never meant my teaching on the second coming to be an excuse for idleness. You may recall that when I visited you I paid for whatever I ate and did some part-time work during my ministry with you. A real Christian does not act irresponsibly. I don't think Christ is coming to find shiftless people, let alone reward them for their idleness.

GOSPEL AUDIENCES

Our lesson demonstrates how Paul responded to the pastoral problems of his day. More broadly, we should understand that New Testament books were directed to specific audiences with their needs and interests in mind. We can see this best in the gospel audiences, the local Churches.

The Church of Matthew's Gospel was originally composed of Jewish Christians, but Gentile Christians had come to predominate. His Gospel treats the fundamental question of how obedience to God's will can be expressed in the new age created by the death and resurrection of Jesus.

Mark's Gospel speaks to Gentile Christians unfamiliar with Jewish customs. The author shows them how to have Christian courage in the face of persecution.

Luke does not know the details of Palestinian geography. This suggests that Luke was not a Palestinian and that he wrote for a non-Palestinian audience largely made up of non-Palestinian Christians.

According to the introductions in the *New American Bible*, John's Gospel is more than history. The narrative serves his theological purposes. He writes to an audience experiencing the division between the Church and synagogue. He extols the equality of women. The Samaritan Woman is a prototype of a missionary. The first witness of the resurrection is a woman.

Paul's preaching of Christ was not Good News for everyone. He spent two years

First-Century Adjustments—Looking Back

This chapter conveys some of the problems the early Church faced as it tried to get off the ground. It's one thing to present the teachings of Jesus to a Palestinian culture, but what happens when you try to adapt the gospel to a very different Greco-Roman mentality?

Paul and others had to try to get the gospel across to city people—both the "man in the street" and the more sophisticated. Read his sermon to the Athenians in Acts 17:16-34.

To preach effectively to the Athenians, Paul had to know the city and its people. Here, in modern language, is how Paul might advise missionaries to familiarize themselves with the city in which they will preach:
- Walk around the city. See what's going on. Get the feel of the city and its people. Books may help, but shoe leather is better.
- Look at the "gods." What do the ads say? What's playing at the movies and theaters? What's going on at the stadiums? Who's performing at the night clubs?

Using this kind of strategy, Paul was able to present the gospel in a way that would make sense to people. The teaching of Jesus is timeless. But the presentation and application must be timely.

The introductory episode and the "Dear Paul" column take up the timely topics Paul had to face. The scriptural reference for each of the problems is given below along with some commentary:

1) *Entrance requirements:* Practically all the first Christians came from the Jewish faith. It was only natural for them to want Gentile converts to agree to circumcision and the Jewish dietary laws, for these were cherished and venerable customs of piety in the Jewish community of faith. But Paul's experience taught him that these customs didn't mean much to Gentiles and sometimes served as an obstacle to conversion. Paul concluded that these customs were not essential to the "new way" of Jesus and argued successfully that they not be required for Gentiles. (See Acts 15:1-21 and Galatians 2:2-21.)

2) *Contaminated meat:* Note the delicacy Paul employs:

"The meat is really all right, but don't scandalize your neighbor." (See 1 Corinthians 8.)

3) *House liturgies:* It would be nice to believe that the early Christians were a community of saints. Actually, they were just as subject to faults and misemphases as we are today. Paul knew how to "rap knuckles" when needed. (See 1 Corinthians 11:17-34.)

4) *Tongues:* Groups of charismatic Catholics, people trying to capture an awareness of their personal relationship with the Spirit, have sprung up throughout our country. Paul's words are of special interest to them. Read 1 Corinthians 12—14. Chapter 12 tells of the variety of gifts from the Spirit. Chapter 13 says that love is the greatest gift. Chapter 14 tells how to deal with the "gift of tongues."

5) *Remarriage of widows:* Paul is here stating an opinion, not a law. He encourages widows to spend their new free time working for the gospel. But, should they wish to marry, they are certainly free to do so. (See 1 Timothy 5.)

6) *Second coming:* The Thessalonians were treating the second coming with lazy abandon. They were literally giving up on life. Read the whole Second Letter to the Thessalonians for the full picture. Paul's corrective measures are contained in 3:6-13.

The problems taken up in this chapter required from Saint Paul the timely application of the gospel. He exercised his pastoral role in applying the principles of Christ to the daily life of Christians.

Our own time has its own set of problems (such as the peace issue, celibacy and questions of authority). These problems also demand the heat of love and the light of truth, which is the fire of the gospel. Here is our common fellowship with the first Christians, inasmuch as we follow the same teaching of Christ and try to use it to solve our own religious problems today.

The Challenge of Inculturation— Connecting to Our Times

Saint Paul's response to the pastoral needs of the churches he founded and served is a model of what we would today call "inculturation." While the gospel message is the same for all nations, it needs to be adapted and applied to a particular culture and the pastoral needs of a people. For example, Christ's teaching about the indissolubility of marriage requires one approach in the United States, where divorce is a major problem, and a different one for tribal Africa, where polygamy is still practiced. The gospel goal in both cultures is the same: a stable, permanent, monogamous Christian marriage. How this is achieved in a pastoral setting requires respect for the positive aspects of different cultures as well as an appropriate way of solving the challenges they present.

in Ephesus, where his ministry began to take a toll on the local silversmiths, who had enjoyed success selling miniatures of the Temple of Artemis to pagan worshipers. The silversmiths' protest in support of their jobs and the temple (Acts 19:23-41) became a near riot. City officials had to intervene. Paul, realizing that his presence was a liability for the Christian community, moved on to Macedonia.

FOR DISCUSSION/REFLECTION

Saint Paul is credited with bringing Christianity to the entire known world. He made several journeys to convert all to Christianity, not just Jews. Could Christianity have remained a Jewish sect as opposed to an international religion today without Paul?

Saint Paul spent much of his life in travels throughout the known world. He encountered many cultures and customs. Yet he seemed to welcome everyone into the Church. He felt Christianity was for everyone. Do you think Christianity fits in everywhere in the world today? Do you feel welcome in a parish different from your own? Do you make visitors feel welcome in your church?

Read about other countries and see what customs are practiced by the Catholic Church there. Would those customs fit in here?

Why was Paul so successful? Could someone do the same today?

FOR FURTHER READING

Becker, Jurgen. *Paul: Apostle to the Gentiles.* Louisville, Ky.: Westminster/John Knox Press, 1993.

Fitzpatrick, Joseph P., S.J. *Paul, Saint of the Inner City.* Mahwah, N.J.: Paulist Press, 1990.

AUDIO

Praying with Paul, by Eugene LaVerdiere. Credence Cassettes.

VIDEO

A.D.: History of the Early Church. Distributed by Ignatius Press (three two-hour videos).

Paul, Apostle to the Church Today. Teleketics, Franciscan Communications (six 30-minute segments).

Quo Vadis. MGM (122 minutes).

I pray that the sharing of your faith may become effective when you perceive all the good that we may do for Christ. (Philemon 6)

New cultures and new eras of history pose new moral challenges such as nuclear war, population growth, *in vitro* fertilization ("test tube babies"), cloning, world poverty and hunger, and so on. These would be the questions facing Paul today.

Finally, liturgy and prayer will take on the expressiveness of a given culture. African-American liturgies often include clapping and swaying, while Hispanic-American ones include many aspects of popular devotion, such as processions with statues of Mary and the saints. There are many beautiful mansions in our Church where diverse cultures may pour out their hearts to God in ways familiar to their history and customs.

As Catholics in a multicultural Church, we should have hearts open to the splendid diversity of God's people. We should be enriched by it and work patiently to solve the challenges that it presents.

Paul's Travels

First Journey
Second Journey
Third Journey
Fourth Journey

3. More Than Martyrdom

Early Christian martyrs were buried in caves outside of the walls of the city of Rome. These caves were called the "catacombs." They remain today: underground cemeteries for many who suffered and died for Christ.

Real religion is not only worth living for, it is also worth dying for. The whole history of our Church is filled with stories of heroic Christians who chose martyrdom to witness their belief in Christ. Christ himself led the way as the king of martyrs. Stephen followed his master to death and became the first Christian martyr.

In the first three centuries of Church life, thousands of Christians paid with their lives for their belief in Christ. Certain Roman emperors became famous for terrorizing Christians and brutalizing the Church. Men like Decius, Diocletian and Nero established the ancient equivalent of the World War II death camps in stadiums where Christians faced lions instead of gas.

The roster of Christian martyrs is lengthy and impressive. Ignatius of Antioch, Cecilia, Lawrence, Agnes, Clement and Lucy are but a few of those who displayed magnificent courage in standing against those who would lure them away from their religious conviction about Jesus and his way.

Countless thousands of Christians were deprived of their civil rights, went to jail, endured torture and exile, the loss of property and the hostility of the non-Christian community because they were strong and loyal to their faith.

What made them do it? The love of Christ urged them on. What was the result? The firm planting of the Church. The blood of martyrs proved to be the seed of the Church.

The faith, hope and love which Jesus asks of every

I am the wheat of God. I must be ground by the teeth of wild beasts to become the pure bread of Christ.

—Saint Ignatius of Antioch

Christian is sometimes illustrated in acts of heroism, as in the lives of the martyrs. The training ground of such heroism, however, is the practice of these virtues in the simple things of daily life. Like people in any age, the early Christians also had to solve plain, everyday problems in the light of their religious convictions. Such is the theme of the playlet that follows.

Coffee Break: Ordinary Life in the Second-Century Church

The characters:

    Mark, a 35-year-old Christian
    Maria, a newlywed and convert to Christianity
    John, a Christian father of two teen-age sons

Maria: It's strange, you know, to be called an "atheist" because I don't believe in the pagan gods.

Mark: As long as we are on names, you'll be hearing them scorn us Christians as the "third race." We're neither pagan nor Jew, but a race apart.

John: I can understand it to some extent. A friend of mine once wrote me, "I feel like a stranger in my homeland."

Maria: I suppose things would be somewhat easier if we lived off by ourselves. But here we are right in the midst of city life and forced to come to terms with it. I never thought a meat counter would be a problem for me till I became a Christian. Paul's advice comforted me somewhat, but I am still uneasy about buying meat.

John: One of my secret ambitions was to be a sculptor. I love working with stone. But my Christianity would limit the opportunities for work in that profession. The profitable contracts are for statues of pagan gods. So I settled on being a tailor instead.

Maria: What did you do about schools for your sons?

John: I found a Christian tutor. The teachers at the pagan schools were teaching the myths as though they really happened. They were turning the literature class into a pagan religion class.

Mark: If you think schools are a problem for a Christian, John, you should have a week's "rest" in a city hospital. I was in for surgery last month. I tell you I couldn't help feeling nervous every time the hospital chaplain came brushing by my bed chanting a litany to one of the pagan gods.

Maria: John, you married a non-Christian, didn't you? I thought the Church discouraged that.

John: That's true, Maria, but I loved her so. I thought one day

FOR DISCUSSION/REFLECTION

Many martyrs from the early Church can still have an impact on our lives today. Read a short biography of an early saint and reflect on this person's courage and faith:

    Peter
    Paul
    Perpetua
    Agnes
    Any other person that you admire.

Ignatius of Antioch was an early Church Father. He wrote important letters which tell us of life in the early Church. Why are Church writings so important? Is the Bible the only important book for Christians?

Write a letter to explain Baptism, Confirmation or the Mass to a friend. Give a detailed account.

FOR DISCUSSION/REFLECTION

"Coffee Break" attempts to show the challenges to Christian practice that came from the milieu in which the early Christians lived. How do the following contemporary experiences serve as a challenge to Christian behavior today?

Sex and violence in films and TV

Lack of discipline and value orientation in schools

The prospect of nuclear war

High divorce rates

Poverty at home and in the Third World

Students are asked to participate in many activities in addition to getting an education. How can the following help you as you try to fit your Christian values into the modern world?

Habitat for Humanity

Pro-Life Movement

Amnesty International

Local soup kitchens

Big Brother/Big Sister

What in "Coffee Break" do you find striking about the Christians' response to problems of their time?

she might "come around," as they say, but she remained a pagan to her death.

Mark: In any case, there's no doubt yours was a beautiful marriage. Just to move to a new topic, you should have heard our priest deliver another of his blistering sermons last Sunday against the gladiatorial combats.

John: I know from experience it's hard to resist those contests. As a young man I once agreed to attend the games to please a friend. I resolved to keep my eyes shut. But when the shouting began, my eyes popped open and I was yelling louder than the rest.

Maria: There's so much violence in our society! I met a man the other night who turned down a judgeship because, as a Christian, he would not want to pass the sentence of death.

Mark: You have the further question of war. What is a Christian to think of that?

John: Our first Christian theologian, Tertullian, said that when Christ told Peter to put down the sword, he thereby disarmed every soldier.

Mark: What would happen if we laid down our swords and the enemy was at the gate?

John: He said we should leave the outcome to God. Even if things got rough, it would only last a short time. Of course, he thought the second coming was soon to happen, so naturally the time of troubles would be short.

Maria: Do you remember when Origen gave that lecture series here last year? He forecast that when Christianity became widely accepted, it would so change the quality of society that war would vanish.

John: But in the meantime, what am I to do with my two sons who will soon be eligible for the army? I'm not inclined to recommend they serve in the army of a state that thinks nothing of terrorizing Christians.

Mark: On the other hand, I have Christian relatives on the northern border where skirmishes with the barbarians are common. Their young sons have joined the local militia. Every able-bodied man is needed just to assure mere survival.

John: Yes, there are no easy answers to these questions.

Maria: You know, one of the things I've missed since I've become an "atheist" is the use of makeup. I always enjoyed using mascara, rouge and perfume.

Mark: I hope you've thrown away your wigs, too. Our priest asked whose hair he would be blessing if he laid his hand in blessing on a wig.

John: I don't know if it's any comfort to you, Maria, but I think you're beautiful the way you are. Still, I wonder sometimes if we haven't pushed this rejection of personal adornment too far.

Mark: I'd like to talk more about this, but my wife is waiting for me at the fish market.

Maria: I must be going, too, or my husband won't have any dinner on the table tonight.

John: Good-bye for now. We'll take this up again.

More Than Martyrdom—Looking Back

During the first two centuries after Christ, the Christian people were subjected to ten major persecutions or reigns of terror. Subsequent histories of that period have tended to concentrate on the cruelty of the Roman emperors and the heroism of Christian martyrs. Little attention has been paid to the periods of repose between persecutions—the majority of the time in which Christians found themselves. They were indeed a beleaguered minority, but most discrimination was at the level of minor irritations. In other words, life did go on. "Coffee Break" describes this dimension of early Christian experience.

The following material describes the imperial policy and the public attitude of the Roman state towards Christians. But, in practice, this became a critical issue mainly during periods of active persecution.

Hostile Roman imperial policy against Christians began around 60 and continued for the next two hundred years. Nero charged Christians with anarchy and hatred of civilized society and, thus, with being political agitators. In the Roman theory of government, the state was central. Religion was a branch of the civil service and was linked with the safety of the state. It was a matter of patriotism to honor the national gods, the emperor and the state itself. To refuse to do this was considered a sacrilege, and one was accused of being a nonbeliever, an atheist.

Christians, who refused to acknowledge the gods, were at once both anarchists and atheists in the eyes of Rome. In time they became scapegoats for many of the troubles that afflicted the state. Ten major persecutions unleashed the fury of the Roman government against Christians.

As the episode "Coffee Break" indicates, it was not always easy for Christians to achieve reasonable and peaceful coexistence with Roman society. The army put young Christian men in a conflict-of-conscience situation. For those who were pacifists (not all were), the army was out of the question altogether. For those who went into the army (and many did), there was a further problem: The Roman army was especially devoted to the god Mithra; it spread his cult in their campaigns. The Christian soldier had to disassociate himself from this cult. But if he did, he was martyred.

Christian encouragement of celibacy was seen as an attack on Roman family life. Christian fasting irritated the orgy-minded, banquet-loving Romans. The Christian practice of severe restraint in dress and cosmetics offended the fashion-conscious Romans. Such habits set Christians apart from the Roman state, family and religion. Christians saw Jesus as their real leader. Rome saw them as a third race that had to be destroyed.

FOR FURTHER READING

Bainton, Roland. *Christendom: A Short History of Christianity and Its Impact on Civilization* (two vols.). New York: Harper Torchbook, 1966.

Donaghy, Rev. Thomas J. *Lives of the Saints II.* New York: Catholic Book Publishing Corp., 1990.

Hoever, Rev. H., S.O. *Lives of the Saints.* New York: Catholic Book Publishing Corp, 1990.

VIDEO

A.D.: History of the Early Church. Distributed by Ignatius Press (three two-hour videos).

An Empire Conquered. Brown-ROA (three 16-minute segments about six early martyrs: Clement, Cecilia, Apollonius, Agnes, John and Paul).

A Time to Build. United States Catholic Conference (60 minutes).

Maximilian Kolbe. Daughters of Saint Paul (21 minutes).

The Catacombs—A Walk Through the Past. Vatican Press Release (15 minutes).

The Scarlet and the Black. 20th Century (156 minutes).

Becoming a Martyr-Witness Now— Connecting to Our Times

Martyrdom for the Christian faith has become as common in our century as it was for our brothers and sisters in the early days of the Church. During World War II, Saint Maximilian Kolbe died at Auschwitz in place of a fellow prisoner who was thus able to survive the death camp and return to his family. In later years, millions of believers in Iron Curtain countries suffered in many ways for their faith. Some were deprived of higher education and satisfying employment and some endured harassment. Others were sent to gulags (concentration camps).

Our secularized society offers many challenges to believing Catholics. Consumerism, individualism and sexual permissiveness confront Catholics with a call to simplicity of life, a concern for the community and society, and sexual self-discipline. Perhaps we are not called to endure beatings, jails and executions, but we face subtler forms of opposition which require courageous living. A martyr is a witness. A martyr does more than pay lip service to Jesus. A martyr-witness practices what he or she believes.

Many persecutions have occurred in history. We have looked at the persecution of Christians by the Romans. The Nazi regime put many people to death during World War II in the death camps. Over six million Jews perished. Many Christians suffered, too. Four million Gentiles died because they resisted Nazism or simply because they were Gypsies, homosexuals, communists, or were mentally or physically "defective."

FOR BACKGROUND

Like his father, who was eventually beheaded during a persecution under the Emperor Septimius Severus (193-211), Origen (c. 185-c. 254), the great biblical scholar and speculative theologian, was ready to offer himself for martyrdom as a teenager. His mother, however, saved his life by hiding his clothes. This forced him to stay home, where instead he wrote a famous treatise on martyrdom addressed to his father in prison.

4. Early Liturgy

Simple warmth and hospitality marked home worship in the early Church. The home atmosphere conveyed the meaning of Eucharist as "the holy in the common." It illustrated the unity of Christians gathered in one Lord around the table. The following story about the quality of a liturgical leader catches the spirit of their effort.

Come to the Welcome Table
(c. 200)

Claudia had finally lulled her baby to sleep when she heard her husband come in.

"How did the meeting go, Richard?"

"We elected Martin to preside over our house liturgies."

"He's a good choice. I don't know of any man in our neighborhood who can make you feel more at home. He seems to have the word *welcome* engraved on his bones. What kind of procedure did you follow?"

Richard kicked off his sandals, poured himself a glass of wine and stretched out on the couch before replying to Claudia.

"The retiring president, Julian, took charge of the meeting. He started by reading us a quotation from the First Letter to Timothy. It went something like this:

> Now a bishop must be above reproach, married only once, temperate, sensible, respectable, hospitable, an apt teacher. He must manage his own household well."

"I'm sure he stressed the word hospitable in the reading," Claudia stressed.

"Yes, he did. He added another short reading from the ancient *Teachings of the Apostles*:

> When a poor man comes to liturgy, whether from your own neighborhood or from a strange place, if he is old and weak be sure, O Bishop, with all your heart to provide a place for him, even if you must sit on the floor."

"I assume Julian gave a little speech after the readings."

"Certainly. He reminded us that since our worship takes place at home, it should naturally reflect the virtues and styles

EARLY EUCHARISTIC PRAYERS

As far as concerns the Eucharist, give thanks in this fashion. First in respect to the cup: We give you thanks, our Father, for the holy vine of your servant David, which you made known to us through your servant Jesus; yours is the glory forever and ever!

Then, in respect to the broken bread: We give you thanks, our Father, for the life and knowledge that you made known to us through your servant Jesus; yours is the glory forever and ever!

As this broken bread was scattered on the mountains and, having been gathered together, became one, so may your Church be gathered into your kingdom from the ends of the earth, for yours is the glory and power through Jesus Christ forever and ever! (*Didache*, 50-150)

And when he delivered himself to a voluntary passion, to loose death and to break asunder the bands of the devil, and to trample hell and to enlighten the righteous and to set up the boundary stone and to manifest the resurrection, he took a loaf and gave thanks and spoke, "Take, eat, this is my body which is given for you." Likewise also the cup and said, "This is my blood which is poured out for you. As often as you do this, you make my commemoration."

Remembering therefore his death and resurrection, we offer to you the loaf and the cup and give thanks to you and do you priestly service. (Hippolytus, *Church Order*, 31, 11:21, c. 236)

of home life. We aren't going to have big crowds like the impersonal throngs at the pagan temples."

"All the better," Claudia reiterated, "since that allows us really to know each other and be a fraternal gathering of friends."

"Precisely, Claudia, and he added that we should not overlook the value of the informality that our home setting brings to worship."

"I do enjoy the fact the we have so much conversation at our liturgies. I enjoy the discussions and get a lot out of them. Still, I wish our catechist would not refer to these discussions as the 'word service.' I think he's being too stuffy. He's spoiling a good thing."

"I'm not going to argue with you over that, Claudia, but Julian did say we must elect a man who is skilled in the art of conversation. You know how some of our discussions have been a crossfire of conflicting testimonies. Julian advised us to choose a man who knows how to help people talk to—not at—one another."

"He's right there. Our Jewish neighbors call their house liturgy the meal of shalom, which means a meal of peace and friendship. And we are reliving the Last Supper, where Jesus reassured his apostles for one last time that he regarded them as his dearest friends."

"Julian feels very much the same way," Richard continued. "He reminded us that our home liturgy is one place at least where we can have one brief and shining hour of peace. He talked at length about the sense of leisure, informality and friendship as hallmarks of our gatherings."

"Was there really much difficulty in selecting Martin?"

"Not really, Claudia. We all just knew that Martin was the man. We know he will hear the command God has always given to his leaders, 'Fashion me a people.'"

Their baby awoke and began crying.

"Our son is calling, Richard. I'm delighted with the outcome of the meeting. If you see Martin before I do, give him my love. I'll see his wife tomorrow and congratulate her."

FOR DISCUSSION/REFLECTION

What values about worship are more easily taught by a home liturgy than one in a church?

Our Jewish brothers and sisters retain the ritual of the Passover meal, which they celebrate at home. Why do you think they have synagogue services as well?

Jehovah's Witnesses gather for worship in Kingdom Halls that are kept deliberately small. Why do you think they follow such a policy?

How often would you want a Eucharist to be celebrated in your home?

Why was it natural for the first Christians to have all their Eucharists at home?

Prayer is an important aspect of our daily lives. In addition to the liturgy many other forms of prayer exist. Meditation is a good way to slow down in an otherwise hectic schedule. Silence is a good way to focus on prayer and God. Family prayer is a good way to bring unity to a group within the same household, even if it is just a short petition to begin the day. Thankful prayer is a good way to remember that God is always there for us. There are many other types and methods of prayer. Discuss how many can fit into our busy lives.

Other than a Mass, what forms of prayer are likely to be found in your home?
— Family rosary
— Prayer before and after meals
— Evening prayer
— Advent wreath
— Lenten devotions

Early Liturgy—Looking Back

The early Christian "Welcome Table" has been described for us by Justin Martyr. He put into writing the first full account of Christian liturgical celebration and the duties of the liturgical president about 150. The following is an excerpt:

> ...And on that day which is called after the sun, all who are in the towns and in the country gather together for a communal celebration. And then the memoirs of the Apostles or the writings of the Prophets are read, as long as time permits. After the reader has finished his task, the one presiding gives an address, urgently admonishing his hearers to practice

these beautiful teachings in their lives. Then all stand up together and recite prayers. After the end of the prayers,...the bread and wine mixed with water are brought, and the president offers up prayers and thanksgivings, as much as in him lies. The people chime in with an Amen. Then takes place the distribution, to all attending, of the things over which the thanksgiving had been spoken, and the deacons bring a portion to the absent. Besides, those who are well-to-do give whatever they will. What is gathered is deposited with the one presiding, who therewith helps orphans and widows....

History of the Eucharist

By the time of Christ, a custom had grown up among the Jews for fellowship groups to meet together for a sacred meal, *Chaburah*, where the things of God would be considered. It was at such a meal that Jesus celebrated with his apostles on the night before his death. For about the first twenty years after Christ, Jewish-Christians continued to worship in the temple, to pray in the synagogue, as well as to meet for the breaking of bread at the Lord's Supper. We have no idea how often they met for this meal, but it was always in a home large enough to hold the community. As time went on, Christians were excluded from the synagogues, but they continued to develop a form of worship modeled on the Jewish synagogue service: a reading from Scripture with interpretation, preaching, prayer and praise. As in the synagogue anyone, even a boy of twelve, could be called on to read and interpret. The assembly was presided over by an apostle, a prophet or a member specially gifted by the Holy Spirit, who preached after the Scripture reading and invited other members to demonstrate their gifts by taking part in the service.

Even as the Liturgy of the Word began to develop from the synagogue service, the Liturgy of the Eucharist emerged from the Lord's Supper. In larger population centers, private homes became inadequate, so sectional meals were tried. This contributed to a period of strain, confusion and friction in the later part of the first century and the beginning of the second. The danger of disunity and lack of deference to authority led to the adoption of the ceremonial eucharistic meal instead of the community supper.

In early worship, prayers were completely free. Then prominent leaders began to write "pattern prayers" to be used as models for worship in the various Churches. Prayers grew in substance and length. Usages developed by slow degrees into rites, and rites expanded into ceremonies. Solid, standard ground was reached by the time Justin Martyr wrote the above description about 150.

It appears that, by the time of the apostles' deaths, Christian society had already developed a hierarchy of three grades who ministered to all Christians: deacons, *presbyteri* (or priests) and *episcopi* (or bishops). Each town was under a chief bishop, who soon exclusively held the title *bishop*. As a rule, the community chose the individual for each minister-

Why is it important to pray together at home and in other small groups? Would it make you uncomfortable to practice your religion in front of your friends? Why?

From earliest times, the fish has symbolized Christ because the letters forming the Greek word icthus, *meaning "fish," are the initial letters of the Greek words:* Jesus Christ God's Son Savior. *The fish is also used as a symbol of Baptism because a fish can only live in water, and the Christian comes to life through the waters of Baptism.*

ial position (see 1 Timothy 3:1-13 for the criteria used), but investiture was made by the local bishop or by superior ecclesiastical authority representing the succession of the apostles. Gradually the organization of Churches in a territory took place and some leading Church was given authority over those in surrounding areas.

FOR FURTHER READING

Nardone, Richard M. *The Story of the Christian Year.* Mahwah, N.J.: Paulist Press, 1991.

This is the Word of the Lord, arranged by William J. Freburger. Notre Dame, Ind.: Ave Maria Press, 1984.

VIDEO

How to Pray as a Family, by Gaynell Cronin. Ikonographics (20 minutes).

Let Us Pray, by Gaynell Cronin. Ikonographics (two 25-minute segments).

As Christianity continued to grow, many Christian communities needed more than one worship service. In order to preserve and symbolize unity, the practice arose in some places of sending a piece of consecrated bread (the fragmentum) from the bishop's church as an addition to the Communion bread in the other churches of the city.

The Feeling of Family Worship— Connecting to Our Times

In the years just after Vatican II, many parishes initiated liturgies in people's homes. These worship services did not replace parish church liturgies. These home liturgies generated a sense of intimacy with the Mass as well as a feeling for family and neighborhood worship. These events advanced the understanding of the renewed liturgy and helped the participants to appreciate what the new liturgy was all about. They introduced a personal, communal and human dimension to the worship experience.

While home liturgies are no longer as common as they were several decades ago, the message remains relevant. For one thing, they help us identify with the Last Supper, where the first liturgy took place in a home setting. Second, they evoke within us a family feeling for worship, one that should prevail at our parish celebrations. We gather as God's family around the Table of the Word in Scripture and the Table of the Supper of the Lord at the altar. Finally, we will come to parish liturgy with a sense of intimacy with Christ who is indeed Lord, but who is also the dear friend who speaks to us in Scripture and the homily and who draws us into his mystery at Eucharist.

A home setting invites us to family and community, to abandoning our individualistic ways and becoming concerned for one another. The same should be true of our parish liturgies. The setting is larger and more people attend, but the call to community in Christ remains the same. The shrines of Scripture and the altar remain two forms of one reality, the "welcome table," where Father, Son and Holy Spirit preside, through the ministry of the priest, to love us, bless us and give us food for the journey of life, both here and hereafter.

5. From House to Basilica

Worshiping God in Grandeur:
A Fourth-Century Challenge

"Have you heard the news, Bishop Thomas? The government is donating a local courthouse to us for use as a church."

"Yes, Deacon Philip, but I never thought I'd see the day when we would be using a basilica, of all things, as a place to worship God."

"Our young liberals are quite excited by the idea. They say it is about time we had a way of introducing pageantry and glory into the worship of God."

"That's true, Philip, but you can expect some trouble from the old guard in the Church. They have been worshiping God at home all their lives. They are not going to be too thrilled by this new way of doing things."

"Some of it can hardly be avoided, Bishop. Ever since Constantine granted freedom of religion, there has been a massive increase in our Church population. Sheer numbers alone demand some larger gathering place."

"I'm with you on that, Philip, but I can foresee that something beautiful will be lost if we move completely away from the old-fashioned home liturgies. Once we get into the basilica, we are going to get more formal. The old sense of intimacy and friendship will fade away. I'm sorry to say it, but the new worship will be an event in which most of the participants will be strangers to one another."

"But everybody will be united in the same belief."

"Granted, but believing the same gospel is not the same as knowing the person beside you."

"Bishop, you said something beautiful would be lost, but won't you admit something magnificent will be gained by moving to public liturgy?"

"Well, yes, Philip, that's true. In that great hall, with an immense throng before the high altar, all of us will be inclined to sense the grandeur of God. The basilica gathering will teach us about God's majesty."

"I think it will also help Christians experience themselves as part of a larger gathering. The narrow confines of a home liturgy have a way of obscuring the universal character of Christianity."

"No quarrel with that, Philip. With home liturgy, people tend to close in on their own little groups. Basilica worship should help them identify with the whole Church. Remember that we, the 'light of nations,' must not hide our lamps

Floor plan of basilica

FOR BACKGROUND

Basilica was the name for a style of Roman buildings used as courts of justice and places of public assembly. This secular architectural form played a large role in shaping the common Western view of what a church building should look like.

Another meaning of the word *basilica* is a place known for its historical importance, architecture and its contribution to the growth of the faith. The "major" basilicas represent sites important from the early centuries of Christian history. There are thirty "minor" basilicas in the United States. Can you name the one closest to you?

The Church is God's and it must not be pledged to Caesar.... For the emperor is in the Church, not over the Church; and far from refusing the Church's help, a good emperor seeks it.

—Saint Ambrose

under a bushel."

"Bishop, this move to the basilica looks like it will give a good boost to the compulsory celibacy movement."

"I can see, Philip, where it's not going to hurt the movement. As long as house liturgies were our normal practice, it was natural to pick a married man for president of worship. Basilica worship will make the 'sacred' central. And 'sacred' will mean whatever is unworldly. There is a growing feeling that an ordained man will be expected to withdraw as much as possible from worldly concerns."

"Probably house liturgies will die out within a few generations."

"I hope they don't. The home liturgy preserves something the Church will always need, the feeling of personal friendship that is central to the Eucharist. I think the Church is big enough for both kinds of liturgy. One highlights the value of the human. The other extols the grandeur of God.

"Without home liturgy, we may lose the message of friendship implicit in the Eucharistic celebration. Without basilica liturgy, we could lose our sense of identity with the faith of millions. Each form of worship has a role to play. God grant that our future allows for both kinds.

"There is a time for everything, a time for hearthside warmth, a time for breathtaking majesty. Our God is both friend and Lord. The two styles of liturgy, Philip, will help you and me remember that."

From House to Basilica—Looking Back

All over the Western world, the Christian population rose from an insignificant minority, to a respected minority, to a majority, to a vast majority of the whole population. Christianity's growth went through these phases at different times in different places. Communities of increasing size needed larger churches.

In the early days of the Church, Christians did not consider it important to possess temples; they celebrated Eucharist wherever the community could assemble—a home, a lecture hall. The *gathering* of the faithful took precedence over the *place* where they gathered. In the second century, Gnosticism began to raise its head in the Christian communities. It claimed all material things to be evil and held material creation, including the human nature of Christ, in contempt. In order to offset this, the Church had to defend material creation and the goodness of Jesus' humanity.

The effect of this emphasis could be seen in the change in Christian worship in the third century. The material element of the sacrifice, the gifts of bread and wine, was now stressed, thus developing the Offertory of the Mass. Previously, the gathering point at the liturgy had been the *cathedra* (the chair of the bishop) or the bishop himself. In the third century, the altar became the center of attention, evolving from a simple wooden table to a fixed and more elaborate table of stone.

The Church and its liturgy were considerably affected by Constantine, who ended the political oppression of Christians. In 313 he issued an Edict of Tolerance that gave freedom of religion to Christians (see Chapter 7). A large number of people joined the Church. Bishops, especially the Bishop of Rome, were granted positions of precedence among Roman officials. The formal court ceremonials of the imperial household had an important effect on pontifical functions. The emperor and his family erected for worship in Jerusalem, Bethlehem, Constantinople and Rome great buildings after the fashion of imperial buildings, palaces and halls. The basilica became the model for churches.

Development of the liturgy continued throughout all of Christendom until about the fourth century. A definite framework used by all developed through tradition. As the Christian population grew, stricter regulations became necessary. Liturgical texts were gradually prescribed. At first these regulations came from the synods of the leading cities: Alexandria, Antioch, Byzantium and Rome. By the seventh century Rome, long the site of a rich liturgical development, had become the dominant model for Christian worship in the West. The Roman liturgy eventually became the liturgy of the whole Western Church.

Liturgy Is Poetry in Motion—Connecting to Our Times

As we saw in our chapter on home-based liturgies, such experiences summon us to family and communal sensitivity in our worship. They also lead us to loving concern for others and a commitment to justice in our neighborhood, city, country and the world itself.

This chapter, which describes the move from house liturgies to church buildings, introduces another aspect of liturgy. If home worship reminds us of the human dimension of liturgy, church worship draws our attention to the divine side of this experience.

Liturgy is an action. It is poetry in motion. The visible side of liturgy focuses on the action of the assembly and the presider. This, of course, includes the acts of the lectors, servers, deacons, eucharistic ministers, ushers, choirs, musicians, hospitality teams and so on.

But there are invisible actions at liturgy as well. The Father is present, pouring out the blessings of creation and providence. The Son, through the ministry of the priest, is present, communicating the graces of his saving work, his paschal mystery, in the Consecration and in Communion. The Spirit is present, transforming the gifts of bread and

FOR DISCUSSION/REFLECTION

What values about worship are more easily taught in a church Eucharist than in a home Eucharist?

Why did Christians of the fourth century abandon house liturgies for worship in public buildings?

How do the following elements offset the potential loss of personal involvement in worship in a large church?
— Congregational singing
— Lectors
— Eucharistic ministers
— Choir
— Music ministers
— Hospitality ministers
— Ushers
— Liturgical preparation committee

What other suggestions would you have to increase involvement of the people in church worship?

Why is it important to preserve a sense of the divine grandeur and awesomeness as well as God's nearness and intimacy?

wine into the Body and Blood of Christ, teaching us the word of God and its meaning for us. The Spirit also conveys to the assembly the power of being a community and the realization of the Body of Christ. Finally, the Spirit gives to each of us the graces of being a temple of the Spirit, a child of the Father and a companion of Jesus.

The majesty of a parish liturgy, the awe evoked by ceremonial and the sense of mystery unfolded in the rituals are positive ways to help us experience the divine side of what happens at liturgy. Divine love is being poured out through the Holy Spirit, who broods lovingly over the assembly in the liturgical event.

All this does much to strengthen our faith, nourish our hope and increase our love. It offers us "God-consciousness." Yet the more this happens the more we become sensitive to concerns of love and justice because those are God's concerns, too. To benefit best from liturgy we should be conscious of both its human, familial, communal aspects and of the divine mystery and acts of the Trinity that occur there.

FOR FURTHER READING

Deedy, John. *The Catholic Fact Book.* Chicago: Thomas More Press, 1986.

Farra, Harry. *The Little Monk.* Mahwah, N.J.: Paulist Press, 1994.

VIDEO

Cathedral. Unicorn Projects (60 minutes).

My Father's House. Teleketics, Franciscan Communications (ten minutes).

The Story of the Cross. Doko (26 minutes).

The Easter Controversy

As liturgy became standardized, so too did feast days. There was disagreement for some time, however, over the celebration of Easter. Some Christians in Asia Minor celebrated Easter on Passover, the fourteenth day of the Jewish month of Nisan, which usually fell on a weekday rather than Sunday, the day of the resurrection. Victor, Bishop of Rome from 189 to 198, threatened to break off communion with those who continued this practice. In 325 the Council of Nicea decreed that Easter be celebrated on the first Sunday after the first full moon in spring, the practice today.

6. Development of Ritual

Aegeria's Travel Diary
(c. 390)

Saturday, March 8

I had a miserable time on the boat coming from Rome. It was bad enough that the Mediterranean decided to be stormy the whole trip, but the least I could have expected was a comfortable bed. After all, I did pay for first class. I won't book passage on that line again!

Fortunately, springtime in Jerusalem more than makes up for my discomfort. The hillsides are covered with the "lilies of the field." The sun is warm but the air is dry with a slight edge of crispness to it.

I've heard so much about the famed baptismal candidate school here. Yesterday my porter was praising the talks that the candidates receive from Bishop Cyril. "That's where they hold the classes," he said, pointing to a church that boasted two large domes on the roof. "They call the church the Martyrium, or the Church of the Resurrection. It's built over Calvary and the empty tomb."

There was an announcement on our hotel bulletin board that the enrollment ceremonies begin tonight, before the First Sunday in Lent. Since I know that amounts to little more than handing in your name, I'll wait until morning to see how the candidates begin Lent.

Sunday, March 9

The church was crowded for the morning liturgy. Up near the altar I saw about two hundred people standing and looking a bit nervous.

"What's that they're standing on?" I asked my neighbor.

"They've been instructed to take off their shoes and stand barefoot on an animal skin rug," she replied.

"What's the point of all that?" I questioned.

"Well, you know very well that only slaves go in bare feet. And Bishop Cyril says that Adam wore an animal skin tunic after he sinned. It was a sign of his shame. The meaning here is that the candidates are presently slaves to sin and Satan."

Everyone grew quiet as Bishop Cyril came forward and quizzed the candidates. If I didn't know he was a bishop, I would have said he was a Bedouin tribesman. He has their bronzed skin and coal-black eyes. After he spoke to the candidates, he turned to their sponsors: "Tell me if you know any reason why I should not admit these people to bap-

FOR BACKGROUND

At the end of the fourth century, a woman named Aegeria attended the Easter celebrations in Jerusalem. The impressions she recorded in her *Peregrinatio* have long provided liturgists with insight into early initiation rituals. Her observations are presented here as fictionalized diary entries.

FOR DISCUSSION/REFLECTION

Aegeria's diary and our current RCIA raise some questions for us:

Why is it important to involve the Church community in the baptismal process?

How does this "adult focus" on our faith journey affect our appreciation of the role of continuing education in the Church?

How would this approach affect our understanding of infant Baptism?

What do we learn from having special liturgical ceremonies accompany the stages of initiation into Christ and the Church?

RCIA candidates have a sponsor from the parish. What is the role of the sponsor?

Discuss the important things that a convert should learn about the Church.

tismal school. Will you give the pledge that these are honest people who sincerely seek God? If so, I will inscribe their names in the Book of Life."

No one objected. The candidates overcame their first hurdle.

A singer came forward and chanted the Gospel story of Jesus overcoming the tempter in the desert. Then the candidates filed out and we celebrated the Eucharist.

Monday, March 24

Today I went down to the Martyrium to see what classes were like. They certainly started early enough—seven-thirty in the morning! As usual, the sexes were separated. They began, as they did each morning, with the ceremony of exorcism.

Later, in my audience with Bishop Cyril, I asked him if he seriously thought exorcism was really all that useful.

"I know you think it smacks of magic, my dear Aegeria," he replied, "and you have a point. But it won't if you see it as a ceremony that dramatizes a quiet and persistent shedding of old habits and ways that would mar the new Christian way of life."

"In that sense, I can agree with you, Bishop Cyril, but I would be happier if you said that as clearly to them as you do to me."

"Point well taken, Aegeria. I will try."

The rest of the candidates' time was taken up in studying the Scriptures, the story of the Church and the meaning of the sacraments. I liked the way they took the stories of the Bible and used them to unite the whole story of human relationship to God, from Adam to Bishop Cyril. Even better, I thought, the teachers were especially good in linking up the material to the moral issues of our day.

Tuesday, April 15

The last few weeks have been full of sightseeing as both a tourist and a pilgrim, visiting the places associated with Jesus and his life. Consequently, I've had little time to write about the progress of the candidates in Bishop Cyril's school—just these scribbled notes of their activities:

Fifth Sunday—Candidates receive personal copies of the Apostles' Creed and the Our Father.

Sixth Sunday—Candidates receive a copy of the Gospels.

Holy Week—Exams. They look worried.

Easter afternoon, April 20

Bishop Cyril and I have become quite friendly, so he made sure I had a good place to witness the long-awaited baptismal ceremony at the Easter Vigil.

Exactly at sundown, when the shades of night were falling, the candidates faced the west and shouted: "We renounce Satan!" Then they proceeded to the baptistry, an eight-sided building modeled after the Roman bath houses.

I loved the wall paintings inside the baptistry. They were mostly garden scenes depicting shepherds and sheep.

One thing that puzzled me was the drawing of a deer chewing on a snake.

"An old legend says," Cyril told the assembly, "that if a deer eats a snake, he incurs an unbearable thirst. This deer will be saved by drinking from the paradise waters." Indicating the two hundred, he said, "And our new candidates...."

The candidates then stripped off their old clothes, and Cyril addressed them. "You are now, in a sense, restored to primitive innocence. Adam clothed himself because he was ashamed. You will not be ashamed before God."

Next they were rubbed down with oil. "You are anointed with oil," Cyril continued, "to tone you up for the great contest with the evil spirit, who would still try to keep you back from Christ. In the old days your ancestors believed a monster dragon lived in the sea. In the depth of this baptismal sea is the diabolical dragon against whom you must fight. We've oiled you up for the battle.

"You will descend into the pool and be completely immersed three times in the name of Father, Son and Holy Spirit. Like Jesus in the tomb, you will be buried, but you will rise again as he did."

The candidates stepped into the pool and Cyril baptized them. As they stepped out, they slipped into white robes as Cyril told them, "Wear this new white garment as a sign of your new way of life.

"You know that Roman soldiers wear a tattoo to show which general they belong to. You have heard that pagan priests brand their arms with hot needles to show which god they worship. Some of you brand cattle to let the world know they are yours.

"This sign which I trace on your forehead with holy oil is the final seal of your Baptism. This is a confirmation that you belong to the Christian God now. As Jesus bore the scars of his passion even at Easter, so you bear the sign of the cross upon you this holy night."

I liked the ceremonies. They had plenty of meaning. I was impressed by the dignity with which they were carried out. As I saw the newly baptized wearing their white robes, carrying palm branches and walking in procession to attend their first Mass and make their first Communion, I felt I was witnessing the procession of the redeemed as described in the vision of John:

> After this I looked, and there was a great multitude...robed in white, with palm branches in their hands. They cried out in a loud voice, saying,
> "Salvation belongs to our God
> ...and to the Lamb!" (See Revelation 7:9-10)

This has been a Lent I'm not likely to forget. I must talk with my pastor about it when I get back to Rome.

FOR FURTHER READING

Danielou, Jean. *The Bible and the Liturgy.* Notre Dame, Ind.: University of Notre Dame Press, 1966.

Penock, Michael Francis. *This is Our Faith.* Notre Dame, Ind.: Ave Maria Press, 1989.

Turpin, Joanne. *Catholic Treasures New and Old.* Cincinnati: St. Anthony Messenger Press: 1994.

See also *The Rite of Christian Initiation of Adults* in *Rites of the Catholic Church* (Collegeville, Minn.: The Liturgical Press, 1990).

AUDIO

Authentic Spirituality, by Michael Downey. Ave Maria Press (75 minutes).

The New Catechism: A Comprehensive Overview, by Alfred McBride, O. Praem. Alba House Communications (five audiocassettes, five hours total).

Development of Ritual—Looking Back

Aegeria's diary is a picturesque presentation of the well-developed initiation ritual of fourth-century Christianity. Many of those ceremonies have endured to this day, though in less dramatic form. In their original form they were superb educational tools—nonverbal communicators in the best sense. Happily, our revised liturgy is recapturing this spirit. Let's go over the ceremonies Aegeria observed.

1) *Standing on the skins.* The candidates stood barefoot on animal skins, combining the cultural idea of "barefoot slavery" and the biblical shame of Adam and Eve. Baptism will celebrate the Christian decision to leave the bondage of a meaningless, sin-darkened life.

2) *The exorcism.* Sin lies not only in deeds but in the evil and invisible attitude of the heart. The ceremony of exorcism calls for a purification of inner attitudes.

3) *Receiving copies of the Gospels, the Creed and the Our Father.* We cannot move to the new way of life unless we have been called by God. The Gospels are the call, the Creed our yes, the Our Father our prayer of embracing friendship.

4) *Exams.* The Christian community questions those who would enter its midst to see if they are sufficiently prepared for reception. This also symbolizes the constant testing of Christian life in the years ahead.

5) *Facing west; renouncing Satan.* The east is where the sun rises with all the poetic overtones of a new day and a new beginning. The Church often called for "orienting" the altar; that is, placing it so the priest faces east. Prayers frequently compared the resurrection of Christ to the rising of the sun.

Conversely, the west is where the sun sets, the region of darkness and nighttime fears. Darkness brought with it the prospect of demons (in modern cities, the prospect of mugging). Hence, the night became the symbol of the power of the devil and the life of evil. Since the baptismal candidates were about to renounce Satan, it was quite natural for them to address their renunciation in the direction that symbolized night and Satan.

6) *Eight-sided baptistry.* The first formal baptistries were Roman bathhouses, which were usually eight-sided buildings. Since Christians of the first four centuries were fond of symbolic meanings, it isn't surprising that they saw a spiritual meaning in the very eight sides of the building in which the ceremony was performed. They spoke of celebrating the eighth day—Easter.

Easter Sunday was not so much the first day of a new week as the day that stood above and beyond the usual groups of seven. Hence, it stood for the extraordinary and, in fact, the eternal. "Enter into the eighth day" meant joining Jesus in his Easter life. This, of course, is exactly what was happening in Baptism, since the candidate was entering into the new life of grace and union with the risen Jesus.

7) *The anointing with oil.* Greek and Roman culture abounded in what we know today as health clubs. They

were as muscle-minded and sports-minded as we are. When a contest of strength was upon them and they needed to be limbered up for the struggle, it was common to give them a rubdown with oil.

What greater struggle can there be than with the power of evil that shuts off union with God? Evil must be overcome and put down. Furthermore, it is a struggle to suppress the bad habits and sins that have resulted from succumbing to evil. Hence, the oiling represented the new Christian's preparation for the battle with the forces of evil both from within and without. If an athlete needed oil to down an opponent, how much more would baptismal candidates need limbering up to contend with the spiritual enemy that kept them back from God!

8) *The triple immersion.* The great mystery of Christianity is the Trinity's self-communication. Early Christians were deeply conscious of their profound relationship with Father, Son and Spirit. In Baptism the candidate was being introduced into the very life of God, and that life was mediated in a rich Trinitarian fashion.

The sacramental act insisted on a special immersion in the name of each Person of the Trinity to symbolize the union of the candidate with each and thereby urge the newborn Christian to live by the amazing richness of God's self-communication. To this day Christians are baptized with water in the name of the Father, the Son and the Spirit.

9) *The white garment.* Once again remember that we are dealing with a symbol-loving community. Even for many Americans the white suit or white robe symbolizes goodness. The virginal bride wears white on her wedding day. The sheriff in the old Westerns was the man in the white hat. Aegeria quotes the Book of Revelation, which describes the redeemed wearing white robes in the procession that follows Christ, the true Lamb. All of these are examples of the innocence symbolized by the white garment.

10) *The sealing.* The confirming seal of God is set upon the candidate's brow. The newly baptized now join the company of the redeemed and proceed to take part for the first time in the whole Mass, receiving Communion.

VIDEO

Adult Baptism: Exploring Its Meaning. Catholic Update Video, St. Anthony Messenger Press (31 minutes).

RCIA: The Journey Through Easter. ROA (31 minutes).

How to Benefit From Our Initiation Rites— Connecting to Our Times

The early Church wisely created a substantial initiation rite to incorporate candidates into the Body of Christ. The process contained elements of ritual, community involvement and instruction. It included a number of steps whereby the candidates advanced over a period of a year to the Easter Vigil, when they received Baptism, Confirmation and Eucharist.

That ancient practice has been revived by our Church today and richly transposed for our needs in the light of pre-

At the Last Supper, on the night he was betrayed, our Savior instituted the eucharistic sacrifice of his Body and Blood.

—Saint Augustine

FOR BACKGROUND

Today's Rite of Christian Initiation of Adults (RCIA) echoes Aegeria's description of baptismal customs in the early Church. The major stages of the new rite are:

— *Conversion* to Christ and Church as a result of evangelization.
— *Catechesis:* The candidates for Baptism (catechumens) are prepared for the sacrament by a series of liturgical ceremonies, training in prayer and in spiritual and moral living, and instructions in the fundamentals of Christian belief.
— *Illumination* (normally ritualized on the Sundays of Lent): The candidates formally elect Christ and the Church and seek purification as they move more deeply into their faith journey, surrounded by members of the Church community who encourage them. This stage concludes at the Easter Vigil, when the candidates are baptized and confirmed and celebrate their first Eucharist.
— *Easter reflection:* The newborn members of the Church consciously seek to assimilate the meaning of the sacraments and the Church community they now experience.

sent cultural awareness and numerous valuable liturgical studies. We call this process the *Rite of Christian Initiation of Adults*. The value of this development has deepened our appreciation of Baptism, Confirmation and Eucharist, which we now call the Sacraments of Initiation. (New converts receive all three. Those already baptized into Christian Churches receive Confirmation and Eucharist for the first time.)

Still, we must acknowledge that the majority of us do not go through this process. Normally we receive Baptism when we are infants, Eucharist as young children and Confirmation most often in early adolescence. Hence most Catholics do not *experience* these three sacraments as one rite of initiation in the same manner that adult converts to our Church do.

Nonetheless, these sacraments still call us to a more profound union with Jesus and our parish community and the universal Church. Every Easter, we renew our baptismal promises. This is more stirring when we join our parish on Holy Saturday evening and participate in the Easter Vigil with those who are receiving these sacraments for the first time.

We should keep the date of our Confirmation on our calendars and renew our pledge to be active Catholics and to be more responsive to the call of the Holy Spirit in our lives on every anniversary. Finally, we should seek ways to make our participation in the celebration of the Eucharist always more living, conscious and active. A daily time set aside for interior prayer is an excellent way to prepare for the eucharistic celebration.

In these ways we can bring alive for ourselves the sacraments of initiation and so benefit more from their intended impact on our lives.

7. Constantine

With the Edict of Tolerance in 313, the Emperor Constantine freed the Christian Church from the state of a persecuted minority, and Christian people soon moved toward a privileged status in society. Among the many benefits that came from this change was a certain leisure that enabled the Church to enrich its liturgical practice and deepen its religious ideas (especially about the Holy Trinity, the divinity and humanity of Jesus, and the role of Mary as mother of God). The following playlet deals with these themes.

Exciting Times
(325)

The characters:
> Martial, retired commander of Constantine's expeditionary forces
> Jerome, young bishop freed from prison after the edict of religious tolerance
> Diana, young society woman

The scene: The garden of Diana's villa in suburban Constantinople. The year is 325, twelve years after Constantine gave freedom to the Christian Church.

Martial: The mist was never heavier on the English plains than when Constantius, the father of Constantine, died. None of us were sure that young Constantine would ever amount to anything.

Diana: Why didn't he automatically become emperor of the western half of the empire?

Martial: Because too many others wanted the job and were willing to plunge us into civil war to get it.

Jerome: Did you persuade Constantine to take a gamble and risk his army to gain control?

Martial: I did. Frankly, I was amazed at how well he turned out. He was a master strategist, a born warrior and organizer. Step by agonizing step, he overcame all his enemies.

Jerome: Do you believe he really had a vision of the cross at the Milvian Bridge?

Martial: Who knows? It may have been a dream. It doesn't matter. He thought it was a vision in which the Christian God promised him victory. He had stunning conquests to prove

FOR BACKGROUND

As a Roman emperor, Constantine was a pagan. His mother was a convert to Christianity. She is a saint today, remembered for finding on a pilgrimage to Jerusalem what is believed to be the true cross. Saint Helena is pictured with the cross in art.

As a young soldier, Constantine had a vision of the cross. He then adopted the cross as his standard. Constantine stopped the persecution of Christians in the Roman Empire by signing the Edict of Milan in 313.

FOR DISCUSSION/REFLECTION

Early Church councils such as Nicea, Ephesus and Chalcedon struggled for ways to express the mystery of God. They produced statements on the Holy Trinity and on the divinity and humanity of Jesus that have served us ever since. What would happen to our approach to Jesus if we saw him only as God, with nothing human about him? How would we relate to Jesus if we thought of him as God dressed up in human form?

How would we view Jesus if he were thought not to be the Son of God at all? Suppose he were not divine, only human. Would we pray to him? Would we think he could possibly be our Savior?

Why is it important to us that Jesus be really human and really divine?

The mystery of God induces in us sentiments of awe, reverence and modesty of expression when speaking of God (no one statement says it all). We also say that there is a mystery about the human being. What are some sentiments that arise from this approach to the human? How can we come to appreciate the uniqueness of each person?

Constantine considered himself a colleague of the bishops. What are some advantages and disadvantages that arise from this union of Church and state? Do you think the United States separation of Church and state is better? Why or why not?

Constantine was the Roman emperor, yet he was very much involved with the leadership of the Church. He attended councils and influenced the selection of

it after that. Who can fight success? He was only twenty-four, and master of the West.

Jerome: When I look at the scars left by the chains on my arms and legs from prison days, I will never cease to bless him for the edict of religious tolerance.

Diana: I know! Just think, a short time ago we Christians were put to death for our faith. Now, Christianity is fast becoming the state religion. Furthermore, I like what Constantine has done for our old fortress town of Byzantium. Since he moved the royal court here to the East and transformed our Byzantium into Constantinople, a young woman has enough parties to keep her going all the time.

Jerome: The Church has lots more going for it now. Our slogan during the "age of martyrs" was "The world does not love us." What will religion do now that the world loves and accepts us?

Martial: From what I can tell, Bishop, the new era gives you leisure time to develop a thoughtful theology and a rich liturgy.

Diana: Oh, I can see a great change in the Church since freedom day. Look at how the ecumenical council is speaking so deeply about the Trinity and the divinity of Jesus. What's more, I'm fascinated by your new liturgy. I can tell you've been borrowing freely from the court ceremonials. My parents don't like that one bit. They prefer the simplicity of the home liturgies that they've known all their lives.

Jerome: You really seem to know what's going on, Diana. As Martial says, the emperor has made it possible for the Church to ponder spiritual realities with greater ease. However, that is only true here in the East. Our brethren in the western half of the empire must use whatever energy they have to save the tottering world around them.

Martial: Yes, Constantine has abandoned the West. The empire there is falling apart because of the power vacuum.

Jerome: And hence the Church there is occupied with the task of preventing total disorder.

Diana: Tell me, Bishop, a little about the background of your ecumenical council over at Nicea.

Jerome: As you know, Diana, Arius has challenged the Church about the divinity of Jesus.

Martial: Is this a new problem?

Jerome: No. Ever since New Testament days we've had questions about the meaning of Jesus. Some said he was only God; hence, the body that people saw was only a mirage. Others claimed he was just a man.

Diana: Arius spoke at one of our women's forums. He came on very strongly in denying the divinity of Jesus. I found him such a compelling speaker that I began to wonder if he wasn't right.

Martial: Bishop, I'm a soldier, not a theologian. Nor am I a Christian. Can you put the problem in plain terms for me?

Jerome: Well, it's not that easy; but, briefly, I would put it this way: God has come near to us in a new way. He did this through the Son, Jesus. We call this event salvation.

Diana: But why make such a fuss about the divinity and humanity of Jesus?

Jerome: Diana, the mission of the Christian Church is to announce the event of salvation. We must make sure that people do not forget that its origin is from God. It comes through Jesus. Our fear is that if Jesus is not understood as God, then salvation will not be seen as a divine act.

Diana: Is that why the Nicene Creed speaks of Jesus as "one substance with the Father"?

Jerome: Yes, this was the way the Council of Nicea chose to speak of Christ's divinity.

Martial: Do you think you will have any trouble now with speaking of Jesus as human?

Jerome: I wouldn't be at all surprised. Let me play the prophet and forecast that another council will speak out on the humanity of Jesus.

Diana: What is the importance of thinking of Jesus the man?

Jerome: Diana, it is one thing for God to love people. It is another matter to make that love known and available. God loves people, but people must have a human brother from whom the saving love will be experienced. Jesus is that brother. He is the humanity of God. Because he is a man as well as God, he is the perfect bridge between God and humanity.

Martial: Bishop, in the army we are forced to live on a practical level. We must beware of any final solutions. Smugness is the soldier's greatest enemy. Will Nicea and your forecasted councils close the door on this matter?

Jerome: A very important objection, Martial. The more we deal with the discussions about the meaning of Jesus and the Trinity, the more we are awed by a sense of the mystery of God.

Martial: Well now, if you see God as holy mystery, won't that stop you from trying to understand him?

Jerome: By no means! We will always search out the meaning of God.

Martial: You're looking at one old soldier whose head is swimming. The emperor is having a party tonight for the veterans of the great campaigns. I must tell him of our conversation.

Diana: It's an exciting time for us all.

Jerome: I hope we have enough sense to make the best of it.

popes, but was not baptized until he was on his deathbed in 337. Should secular leaders participate in Church business? Why should the Church remain independent from the government?

FOR BACKGROUND

In the history of the Church, there have been twenty-one Church councils. The first of these was the Council of Nicea, called to formulate a creed.

The Nicene Creed was written in two stages. The first part was written at Nicea I in 325 and the last section was added at Nicea II in 787.

Most of the early Church councils were held in the eastern part of the Roman Empire. Constantine had moved the capital to the city of Byzantium, which he renamed for himself: Constantinople. The city of Rome was about to be besieged by the barbarians.

Constantine—Looking Back

Constantine, an able general (though only a modestly talented administrator), rebuilt Byzantium as Constantinople, the capital of his empire. Although he deferred Baptism until just before his death in 337, he was attracted to Christianity as early as 312, a year before he issued the edict of tolerance that legalized the practice of Christianity. He himself called the Council of Nicea to restore unity when the Arian heresy divided the

FOR BACKGROUND

Heresy is teaching a false belief. As the Church Fathers were organizing the early Church, some individuals as well as some groups wanted to change the beliefs of Christians.

Three heresies affecting the Christian church from the third to the eighth centuries all dealt in one way or another with Christ's humanity versus his divinity:
— *Arianism* taught that Christ was not divine or equal with the Father.
— *Nestorianism* taught that Mary was mother of the human nature of Christ only; thus, not Mother of God.
— *Monophysitism* went to the other extreme, emphasizing Christ's divinity and minimizing his humanity.

Church, an action which influenced Church-state relations for centuries to come.

Early Church Councils

Council of Nicea (325). Arius, a priest of Alexandria in Egypt, taught that Christ was not truly divine or equal to God the Father. Arius and his followers believed that Christ had not always existed but that the Father had created the Son in order to save the human race.

Athanasius, Bishop of Alexandria, was Arius's great foe. His conflict with Arius was a difficult one and Arian pressure sent him into exile five times.

In 325 Constantine called the Council of Nicea in order to end the controversy. Nicea condemned the teaching, banished Arius for a time and formulated a creed to safeguard true Christian teaching. The Nicene Creed (the creed familiar from the liturgy) states that Christ is divine and equal in all things to the Father. The phrase chosen to express this was "of one substance with the Father."

Council of Constantinople (381). Called by Emperor Theodosius I, this council reinforced Nicea's decisions and declared the equality of Father, Son and Spirit. Despite repeated condemnation, Arianism continued as a religious belief until the end of the eighth century, largely among barbarian tribes.

Council of Ephesus (431). Nestorius, Patriarch of Constantinople, emphasized the humanity of Christ but remained unclear about his divinity. He criticized the term *Theotokos* (God-bearer) as applied to the Virgin Mary. He refused to call Mary the "Mother of God." Cyril of Alexandria opposed Nestorius and the ensuing conflict became both religious and political.

The Council of Ephesus, summoned by Emperor Theodosius II, condemned Nestorius's position and declared that no one should alter the decisions of Nicea. In the course of seven sessions the Council Fathers defined the union of divine and human natures in the one person of Christ, and also declared Mary Theokotos, the Mother of God.

Council of Chalcedon (451). The Emperor Marcian summoned the largest of the general councils at Chalcedon in 451. The bishops defined doctrines by reinforcing the documents of Nicea and Ephesus. They insisted upon the unity of person in Christ, approved the term *Theotokos* and spoke of the two natures of the Incarnation. They drew up a profession of faith which read, in part:

> Jesus Christ is one and the same Son, the same perfect in Godhead and the same perfect in manhood...begotten from the Father before the ages as regards his Godhead...and from the Virgin Mary, the *Theotokos*, as regards his manhood;...made known in two natures without confusion, without change, without division, without separation, the distinction of natures being by no means taken away by the union.

Vatican II Is More Than 'History'— Connecting to Our Times

Constantine caused a turning point for Christians by changing their status from a rejected and persecuted minority to a socially accepted religious body. One of the immediate outcomes of this change was a surge in theological discussion and reflection. The change brought about the "age of the councils"—events that gave us remarkable and enduring new understandings of biblical teachings about the Trinity, the meaning of Jesus Christ and the divinity of the Holy Spirit.

by all accounts the greatest religious event of the twentieth century was the Second Vatican Council. It takes a distinguished place along with the great ancient Councils of Nicea, Ephesus and Chalcedon. But since today's youth are born after Vatican II, they may not see it as vividly as adults who lived through those exciting times. Vatican II is as much "history" for today's young people as World War II— and the councils of Constantine's age.

This is the dilemma always posed by the passing of time, even so brief a time as thirty or forty years. Television does help in making recent history seem more real, as seen in the fiftieth anniversary of the Normandy invasion or in retrospectives about President John F. Kennedy. Still, there is no way of ignoring the fact that Vatican II is not creating the vivid impression on youth today that it did for those present to the experience.

But councils are peak experiences of faith for the Church. Just as we properly bring alive biblical events that happened thousands of years ago, so we must do the same with the powerful events of Vatican II. Its teachings about reading the "signs of the times"; the Church as People of God, Body of Christ and Temple of the Spirit and hierarchical institution; the need for ecumenism and interfaith relations; the nature of liturgy and priesthood, and many other rich insights have only begun to be appreciated. In fact, it will be the joy and privilege of today's youth to explore intelligently and faithfully as adults what these teachings mean for the twenty-first century.

FOR FURTHER READING

Marthaler, Berard L. *The Creed*. Mystic, Conn.: Twenty-Third Publications, 1987.

The Imperial Church From Constantine to the Middle Ages in *History of the Church*, Vol. II, ed. Hubert Jedin. New York: Seabury, 1980.

VIDEO

Rome—In the Footsteps of Peter and Paul, Part One. Brown-ROA (50 minutes).

Thine Is the Kingdom. Films for the Humanities (52 minutes).

8. Western Church as Servant

'Fill the Power Vacuum': A Fifth-Century Imperative
(c. 476)

FOR BACKGROUND

In 395 the sons of Emperor Theodosius divided the empire between them for administrative purposes. The two divisions functioned as independent states and, since their boundaries coincided closely with the divisions based on language and culture, the separation became permanent. In the West invasion and settlement by Germanic peoples continued to weaken the power of succeeding emperors. In 476, when Odoacer the Rugian deposed Romolus Augustulus from his puppet throne, the history of the Roman Empire in the West was closed.

The barbarians sacked the city of Rome in 410 and the West was never the same again. The Huns arrived at the gates of the city of Rome in 452, only to be met by Pope Leo I, who turned them back. The popes remained in Rome throughout the Dark Ages even after the government fled.

"Frank? Why, it is you! Whenever did you get back from Rome? How are you? You look so different!"

"Hi, Laura. Yes, I just got back. I—"

"Oh, Frank, it's good to have you home again. When you were gone so long, we thought.... Well, things are so dangerous over in western Europe."

"Much more than you could ever imagine, Laura."

"We hear the whole society is crumbling."

"Yes, it's very sad, Laura, to see the West in such a mess."

"What in the world caused it all, Frank? I mean, Rome was such a strong and well-ruled empire."

"Well, you know when Constantine came here to the East a century ago, he pretty much left a power vacuum in the West. The ruling families who were left soon died out. And the new wave of barbarians, who had no respect for the world they were invading, didn't help matters."

"Is there any hope for the West, Frank? Isn't there any force or group that could help build society?"

"It's a funny thing, Laura, but there is hope. Oddly enough, the political hope of the West lies with the Church. The Church seems to be moving into the power vacuum. I say 'funny' because we are so accustomed here to a Church that works mainly at developing new forms of liturgy and at thrashing out problems of theology. But in the West the Church is now involved in such questions as what to do with schools, farms, unsafe streets, food distribution and price controls."

"Well, good for the Church! I agree it seems a bit odd, doing that kind of work. But if that is the need, then the Church is certainly performing a great service. How does it come to have the talent for this kind of administration?"

"Well, all during the centuries of persecution, the Christians lived in a kind of shadow society. They weren't able to take part in public life, so they lived an 'underlife' that imitated the superb administrative skills of the Roman rulers. They were like understudies waiting in the wings to take the lead if it were ever offered to them."

"Frank, do you really believe the Church was planning

a sort of takeover as it watched Rome fall?"

"No, no, Laura. I didn't mean that at all. Christians never consciously plotted to replace their masters. It was just a happy coincidence for the West that, at the time when people with administrative skills were needed, the Church was there—able and willing to answer the need."

"I still can't imagine the Church there not being all wrapped up in liturgical concerns or dogmatic questions. But things being what they are, I suppose it does not have the time."

"Exactly, Laura. Bishops there are more like secular governors. They worry about the price of fish, salary complaints, tax evasions, grain supplies—you name it. They get involved with the merchant marine, wills, cheating landlords and border disputes."

"One thing is for sure, Frank, a Church like that is going to have a strong sense of order and organization, if for no other reason than that it will have had so much practice."

"That's right, Laura, the Church in the West is moving toward an orderly system of moral teaching and Church law."

"That's no surprise, Frank, for a Church that deals so closely from day to day with social problems and moral behavior."

"But I have one major fear, Laura, for our brothers and sisters in the West. There can be too much of a good thing. The Church has assumed the exercise of political power because there is a great need. This is in answer to the Spirit's call to be a servant to that society. But will the Church give it up when the secular society is strong enough to go out on its own?"

"The Church has been at it for a century now, and probably will have to wield power for at least a century more. The Church is creating a new civilization. I guess my concern is based on the axiom, 'No one surrenders power willingly.' My hope is that when the time comes, the Western Church will prove an exception to that rule."

"Frank, I really have to run now, but I'm having a few people over tonight, some of your old friends. Could you come? I know they would love to see you. We are all hungry for news about the West."

"I'd love to."

"Say about eight?"

"Wonderful, see you then."

FOR DISCUSSION/REFLECTION

When the western part of the Roman Empire collapsed, the Church used the administrative skills of its bishops and pastors to bring order out of chaos. These religious leaders became the secular governors and mayors of leaderless states, cities and towns. Their work of service brought hope to a despairing world and created the basis for a new civilization.

One of the major reasons that the Church was so successful in taking over in Europe was that the clergy were educated. Universal education is a modern phenomenon. One hundred years ago the average person did not read or write. Imagine how few were educated in the early Church! What would it be like if only one in a thousand persons could read, write, count?

Culture in the West suffered during these years. In the East the culture flourished. This brought about a feeling of superiority in the East. How did this affect the Church?

Should the Church become involved in the secular society? How should priests, brothers and sisters relate to politics? Should they demonstrate for causes, get involved in other countries' domestic problems, or should they just do "Church" duties?

Western Church as Servant—Looking Back

The material in the above episode falls into three parts: (1) how a power vacuum occurred; (2) why and how the Church could fill it; (3) the values and disadvantages of filling the power vacuum.

FOR FURTHER READING

Baus, Karl. *Handbook of Church History: From the Apostolic Community to Constantine.* New York: Herder and Herder, 1965.

Bokenkotter, Thomas. *A Concise History of the Catholic Church.* New York: Doubleday Image Books, 1977.

Dawson, Christopher. *The Making of Europe.* Kansas City, Mo.: Sheed and Ward, 1945.

1) *Rome's fall.* As mentioned in Chapter 7, Constantine moved to the East, an action which had its most severe effects a century later when barbarian invasions coupled with weak leadership left the West in chaos. This absence of strong leadership developed a power vacuum and the Church stepped in to fill it.

2) *Church rule.* During the centuries of persecution, Christians formed a "community within a community," observing and absorbing the managerial policies of their Roman overlords. The years of experience that the Western Church thus gained in administrative work influenced the kind of theology that would develop later, namely, a concern for human behavior (moral theology) and a concern for an efficient institution (canon law).

3) *Servant Church.* Europe owes a remarkable debt to a Church that stepped into the fourth-century chaos and helped bring to birth a new civilization. Not until the seventh century was Europe beginning to gain sufficient strength to go out on its own again. The Church had indeed been midwife to the making of Europe.

In doing this for Europe, the Church was fulfilling its role as servant of God. Just as faith calls for love and service at the individual level, so also it summons the institutional level of the Christian community to reflect the same love and service in the broader public dimension. The task may be secular but the motivation is divine, whether it be a neighbor sitting with a sick person or the organizational Church administering the parceling of land to barbarians newly arrived from the North.

Eastern Church

By contrast, the Eastern Church lived within the confines of a prosperous and stable empire. This cultural situation freed the bishops to concentrate on their pastoral role in the areas of sacramental life, spirituality and theology. It afforded theologians the leisure to develop in-depth understandings of major doctrines such as the Trinity and the Incarnation and to present defenses against heretical aberrations. This explains why the great Church councils of Nicea, Ephesus and Chalcedon were held in the East: not only because the heresies were more localized there, but also because the Church there had the talent to deal with them.

This also accounts for the rich development of spirituality and mysticism that are characteristic of the Eastern Church. There the Church had the time and the freedom of several centuries of imperial support and protection. This was aided and abetted by the monasticism of the East, which was oriented much more to prayer and meditation than that of the activist farmer-monks of the West. Eastern monks were not obliged to clear wildernesses and play the frontier roles of their Western counterparts. Basically subsidized by the wealthy, they could take time to mature the mystical bent to which they had given themselves.

A Church That Serves People Today—Connecting to Our Times

In this lesson we see how the Church of the West ministered to the people of Europe, who faced the chaos caused by the fall of the Roman Empire and the barbarian conquests. Law and order had collapsed and basic needs like food distribution, public safety, health care and fundamental commerce required able leaders to oversee their fulfillment.

Because so many of the Catholic bishops were members of the old Roman leadership families, they were able to bring the skills of their family training to roles of administration—not only for the Church's religious needs, but also for the basic human needs of a society in chaos. In doing this the Church's leaders were fulfilling a command from Jesus to be "servants" of all peoples. Many bishops and popes were thus required to exercise both political and religious leadership to make this happen.

Today our Church no longer needs to occupy political roles such as king, president or prime minister. But the Church still is called to be a "servant" to the basic needs of people whose human dignity demands it. In the United States, for example, the Catholic Church is the largest non-governmental provider of social services. Catholic charities provide services to the poor, people with AIDS, the indigent, unwed mothers and their children, those suffering from substance abuse, hungry people and many others in need.

Worldwide, the Church's missionary organizations bring the gospel as well as education, health care and food to millions. In addition the Church's social teachings call for "development" for the world's impoverished nations. This includes: (1) education for girls in countries where only boys are schooled; (2) new technology for farms; (3) new roads so food can be properly distributed to the hungry as well as to ports for marketing; (4) clean water programs both to avert disease and provide irrigation; (5) advanced health care and hospitals; (6) encouragement of loans from rich nations to poor ones—loans which respect the moral, cultural and spiritual values of these peoples.

Under the principles of justice and the highest regard for human dignity, the Church has found a new way to practice its old role of being a "servant."

FOR BACKGROUND

Symbolic of the Church as servant was the preferred title of Pope Gregory the Great (590-604), "servant of the servants of God." He saw as the duty of the Bishop of Rome to do anything necessary to maintain the communion of Churches.

Theodosius ordered all of his subjects to "rally to the faith brought to the Romans by the apostle Peter."

9. Saint Augustine: Remarkable Christian

In any ranking of the ten most influential men in the history of the Church, Augustine will always be included. During his seventy-six years (354-430), he witnessed the emergence of the Church as a powerful force in society. He also beheld the decline of Roman political power and the waves of barbarian invasions from the North. More and more he dwelt on the otherworldly "city of God" as he observed the collapse of the "city of man." The forces that created that catastrophe finally succeeded in 476, the date historians assign to the fall of the Roman Empire.

In the following imaginary interview, a biographer questions Augustine about his life and times.

An Interview With Augustine
(c. 420)

Interviewer: Bishop Augustine, did you receive a Christian upbringing?

Augustine: My mother, Monica, was a Christian. My father, Patricius, was a pagan. It was customary to raise children in the religion of their father. Officially, I was a pagan, but my mother determined to make me a Christian. I was an independent spirit and resisted my mother's wishes.

Interviewer: Did your mother control your education?

Augustine: Mother may have been an ardent Christian, but she also believed I should have a sound classical education in the pagan schools. She saw no contradiction between her efforts toward my Christian character development and a first-class education.

Interviewer: Is it true that your mother was a battered wife?

Augustine: In my childhood days it was common for North African husbands to beat their wives. But my father never laid a hand on Monica. She knew how to control him. I heard her speak of other wives as "slave girls of their husbands." In their quarrels I watched her wait out his anger and then coolly take charge of him and even convince him how she had been right in the first place. Monica was a formidable woman.

Interviewer: Do you think your mother was overbearing to you?

Augustine: There is no doubt I thought she tried to make me a mother's boy. She insisted on following me everywhere, even when I grew into manhood. I shook her off briefly in

You have made us for yourself, O Lord, and our heart is restless until it rests in you.

—**Saint Augustine**

my twenty-eighth year, when I traveled to Europe. I had to lie to do it. I still feel bad about that. You know that in my *Confessions* I tell that story and express my remorse. "Thus I lied to my mother—and what a mother." I see now more clearly that her main motive was to make me a Christian.

Interviewer: Why did you convert to Manichaeism?

Augustine: I was feeling some guilt about my moral life. I had taken a mistress and sired an illegitimate son. I sought relief in religion. I studied the Bible and was disappointed. How could anyone accept the contradiction of a vengeful Old Testament God and a New Testament merciful Christ? Worse yet, I judged the stories in the Bible to be too coarse and unreal after being immersed in the refinements of the Latin classics.

I was pleased to find that the Manichaean religion repudiated the value of the Old Testament just as I did. Not feeling very good about myself, I identified with the Manichaeans, who also held a low opinion of the goodness of human nature. I needed a religion that emphasized severe self-discipline. Manichaeism suited my ascetic bent of those days.

Interviewer: How then did you come to be a Christian?

Augustine: I think my mother had the most to do with it. I could not deny her personal influence upon me year after year. And think of those powerful prayers of hers. Of course circumstances also played a role. I am by nature a restless searcher, a questioner. I am not easily satisfied with soft responses.

I had taken a teaching position in Milan. The most celebrated speaker in the city was Bishop Ambrose. I began attending cathedral services and listening to Ambrose's persuasive sermons about the Old Testament. He cleared away many of my objections and presented me with a challenge to become a Christian.

I spent many hours with Ambrose discussing the possibility of my conversion. He advised me to study Neo-Platonist philosophy. I now see why, for my Manichaean outlook concentrated my attention on my body and on physical matters. Neo-Platonism woke me up to the values and reality of the life of the spirit.

Nevertheless, I was cautious. It took well over three years of such study and thinking to turn me around. And then it happened. I was sitting alone in my garden and relaxing from my study of the New Testament. I thought I heard a child call out playfully, "Take and read." Startled, I looked at the biblical text in front of me:

> [L]et us live honorably as in the day, not in reveling and drunkenness, not in debauchery and licentiousness, not in quarreling and jealousy. Instead, put on the Lord Jesus Christ, and make no provision for the flesh, to gratify its desires (Romans 13:13-14).

In that moment my doubts dissolved. I was filled with

FOR BACKGROUND

Augustine spent his youth as a pagan. He went to study in the city of Milan in Italy, where he was converted under the inspiration of another great saint, Ambrose. Ambrose was a renowned orator, a well-known scholar and composer of many early Christian hymns.

As the barbarians invaded the Roman Empire, the Church and the office of the pope gained power and filled the power vacuum left when the government moved East.

Another movement founded in Northern Africa was that of monasticism. Saint Anthony of Egypt founded a group of monks who lived what is referred to as the "desert experience." Augustine spent time in the desert after his conversion.

▼
━━━━━━━━━━━━━━━━

FOR DISCUSSION/REFLECTION

One of the most celebrated controversies Augustine engaged in was a debate with a theological genius named Pelagius. This Pelagius argued that people were in full charge of their own moral destiny. No matter what the impact on the human condition caused by Adam's fall, human beings could choose the good from the font of their own resources. Is there something "Pelagian" about popular self-help theories such as "pulling your own strings"; "looking out for number one"; "I must take charge of myself"?

Augustine was profoundly impressed by the moral weakness of people and the deeply rooted character of human evil tendencies. He believed we were much more affected by Adam's fall than Pelagius would allow. People could not avoid sin without the help of grace. Augustine believed we are free, but that we need the impulse of God's grace to choose the good. We cannot save ourselves. We need the grace of Christ to motivate us and see us through. How do we at one and the same time experience ourselves as fully in charge and yet be responsive to God's grace? How can we avoid being fatalistic about God's role in life as well as resist the temptation to go it on our own?

Who are some of today's theologians? What are they saying? Do you find that today's theologians have the pastoral spirit of Augustine? Do you think it is possible for an academic theologian to be involved in parish work and still be able to do theology? Would scholarship suffer?

Explain in your own words what grace is, where it comes from, and so on, as if

light. I became a Christian.

Interviewer: You have become a celebrated Christian theologian. What has made you so successful?

Augustine: I will leave my fame and so-called success to you and others who may care to reflect on my career. I frankly see myself less as a theologian and more as a pastor for my people. I have been bishop of this small North African diocese of Hippo for nearly thirty-five years. I view myself as a small-town pastor. I know practically everyone by name. I am involved in their weddings, funerals, family tragedies and triumphs. I am outspoken—some would say too vocal—about the public issues that affect my people.

I believe my job is to nourish the faith, hope and love of my people. You know what my sermons are like. Two to three hours of give and take with them. Yes, there is a bit of the philosopher in me. What else would you expect of the self-important young intellectual I once was? I love the impact when my people and I interact. They teach me as much as I teach them. In my solitude at the monastery in Hippo my writings soar because of my pastoral experience.

Interviewer: Don't you think your debates with the Donatists influenced your writings?

Augustine: Yes, I thrive on controversy. The Donatists were fair game. They were too clean, too rigid for the rest of us Christians. They never forgave the collaborationist bishops during the persecution of Diocletian. Even when those bishops were reconciled to the Church, the Donatists refused to acknowledge they were real bishops or that the priests they ordained were real priests. Only the successors of the martyred bishops were genuine. To join them you had to be rebaptized.

Actually they helped me understand that the sacraments work even when administered by sinners. Not that priests should be sinful, of course. The Donatists had the problem of all religious elites. They had the self-righteousness of the self-chosen. Too pure. I could not ignore them when they drew away whole towns and cities from a proper understanding of the Church.

I was not always temperate in speaking about them. I recall preaching, "The clouds roll with thunder so that the house of the Lord shall be built throughout the earth. And these frogs sit in the marsh and croak, 'We are the only Christians!'"

I still like those lines.

I argued that innocence is only one side of the Church. Christians must become holy. Christians also must coexist in the same community as sinners and correct the sinners.

Interviewer: Is it true you are bitter about the way Jerome treated you?

Augustine: Unfortunately, I never met Jerome except in letters. I was young when I began writing to him. He was already an established giant in biblical studies. I admit I was arrogant then and treated him without due respect. He was quick to correct me: "You are still young. Do not challenge an old man in battles about the Bible."

I was wounded. I wrote him, "How can we engage in discussion if you have made up your mind to offend me?" When Jerome decided to bury the hatchet, writing, "Come let us play together harmlessly in the fields of the Scriptures," I was not amused.

Very seriously, I wrote back, "If you used the word *play* to imply that what we do is easy, I expect more of you. It is your duty to help those engaged in exacting study. Examining the Bible is not a matter of romping round on level ground or puffing and panting up a mountain."

No wonder Jerome ignored many of my letters. No, I am not bitter at all. I would love to have known him personally and jousted with him.

Interviewer: Why did you write *The City of God*?

Augustine: Some people think I did it to explain the sack of Rome and the other indignities the barbarians are inflicting on the empire. They are wrong. Never forget I was trained as a classical scholar in the Roman tradition. I spent over thirteen years writing *The City of God*.

That book was not one of my raging pamphlets against one or another of the heresies I have fought. I wrote it with all the self-conscious skills that Roman literary tradition demands. What prompted me? I admired the history and glory of the empire. But I also saw the propaganda and self-service, the conservatism that created a myth. That's why I wrote, "Away with the vain screen of common opinion. Away with the whitewash." I was both debunking Roman tradition and at the same time cherishing the genuine moral values I uncovered.

My audience was a small group of leisured aristocrats, trained in my tradition, puzzled by the great transition going on in culture. I gave them my interpretation of human events today. I drained the glory of Rome and projected it onto the glorious city of God. I demonstrated that the virtues of Roman heroes would only be realized in the citizens of this other city. It is in the heavenly Jerusalem that the essence of the Roman Republic will find true realization.

Interviewer: Do you think the barbarian invasions mean the end of the world?

Augustine: No, I do not. Any reader of history knows that empires rise and fall. I am not at all certain that what we see is the end of Roman dominion. Perhaps this is a political adjustment, a purification. Or maybe we are seeing the passing of an old order. I regret and mourn the death and devastation. The barbarians are preparing to invade North Africa. Soon enough we will see women raped, men slaughtered, homes burned. We have not the will nor the military might to withstand them. But the end of the world? I don't think so.

In the last ten days of his life, the Augustine who spoke and wrote hundreds of thousands of words asked that he be left alone and in silence. He ordered four psalms that dealt with

you were talking to a young child.

Augustine's mother, Saint Monica prayed for her son's conversion for her whole life. Why is prayer effective? What is the value of praying for others?

It is said that in the conversion of Augustine the pagan empire died. His becoming a Christian began the new empire which was to be Christian. How can we contribute to the Christianizing of culture today?

In *The City of God*, Augustine tells how this world is not as important as the world to come. How can we balance our contribution to the earthly city and the city of God?

Augustine was named Bishop of Hippo in Northern Africa by Pope Siricius in the late fourth century penance to be copied out and posted on his sickroom walls. In prayer and quiet he died on August 28, 430.

FOR FURTHER READING

Brown, Peter. *Augustine of Hippo*. Berkeley, Ca.: The University of California Press, 1975.

Hamman, A. *Early Christian Prayers*. Kansas City, Mo.: Sheed and Ward, 1961.

Saint Augustine. *The City of God*, trans. Marcus Dods. Modern Library Giants series. New York: Modern Library, 1950.

Van der Meer, F. *Augustine the Bishop*. Kansas City, Mo.: Sheed and Ward, 1961.

Saint Augustine and Manichaeism— Looking Back

The belief Augustine embraced before becoming a Christian was a "materialistic dualism." It taught that the world is the end product of a battle between forces of light and darkness.

According to Manichaeism the soul was an element of light imprisoned within the darkness of the body. Manichaeans claimed to be the true Christians, preaching Christ as the one who could free the imprisoned light. Believers generally divided into two levels: the "elect" and the "hearers."

Augustine joined the "hearers" because this lower group was allowed marriage as a concession to the weakness of the flesh.

Monica—Giving New Meaning to Motherhood

As mother of Augustine, Monica possessed what we would today call a wholistic vision of her maternal calling. She certainly looked after the physical needs of her son. And like any ambitious, upwardly mobile woman she spared no money or energy in seeing that her bright young boy received an excellent classical education. She was the first to notice that her son had an exceptional mind. To assure his intellectual training she brought him to the best available teachers.

Luckily, the North Africa of her day was more than a backwater colony of Rome. The empire of Carthage, of which her hometown of Hippo had been a part, once rivaled Rome in political and economic power. Its descendants knew the value of education, trade, military strength and classical culture.

But Monica wanted more than a physically able, intellectually agile son. She wanted him to become a Christian and a man of faith. Her husband, Patricius, was not much help to her in this regard. She was the one who valued the Christian faith. She was both mentally and spiritually strong. When she was young, she was accused of drinking too much wine. Strong-willed already, she resolved never to let alcohol get the best of her. And it didn't.

While many African wives suffered beatings from their husbands, Monica made it clear to Patricius she would never put up with it. He learned how to contain his violence. She told her friends (with some hint of sarcasm) that "they were slave girls of their husbands. It was not for them to rise up against their lord and master." She had no intention of being a battered wife.

Monica was a woman of large emotions, easily expressed. She was furious with Augustine for taking a mistress when he was a young man. She refused to let him live at home or eat at her table. But she put great stock in her dreams and the wisdom that might come from them. She had a dream in which she met a "radiant being" who questioned her about her anger and grief. She told him about Augustine's mistress and his cynical remarks about the Church. The being assured her she had little to fear: "Your son is with you." Monica took this to mean that Augustine would eventually see things her way. After that she welcomed him (and, presumably, his mistress as well) home. She grew in patience in the middle of her vexing impatience for her son's conversion.

She decided she had to be a vital presence in Augustine's adult life until God brought him to faith. When he went to Italy to pursue his career as a teacher, she followed him. He could not escape the brooding and insistent presence of his mother. He wrote, "She loved to have me with her, as is the way with all mothers, but far more than most mothers." When he sailed to Italy, he lied to his mother about it, hoping to escape her. "I lied to my mother—and such a mother!"

Monica followed him to Rome and then to Milan, where she found the remarkable Ambrose, who would be God's agent in bringing her son to Christianity. Ambrose's cultivated and faith-filled sermons appealed to the spiritually starved Augustine. Moreover, Ambrose composed music for learning the truths of faith, melodies that melted Augustine, who was always fond of music.

Augustine became a candidate for entrance into the Church and took lessons about the faith. Monica loved Ambrose for the influence he had over her son. Augustine writes, "She hastened to Church more zealously than ever and drank in the words of Ambrose as a fountain of water.... She loved that man as an angel of God."

Ever thinking about her son's financial as well as his faith future, she forced him to give up his mistress of fifteen years as she eyed some rich prospects for a wife for him. What happened to the nameless mistress? No one knows, but some believe Augustine financed her entrance into a community of "virgins and widows" in Carthage.

As things turned out, Augustine was never to marry. After his entry into the Church, he embraced a life of celibacy. During the first three years of his conversion he (and his mother) lived with a group of students and intellectuals in northern Italy. Finally, he and Monica resolved to go back to Africa. While they were at Ostia waiting for a ship, Monica contracted a fatal illness and died.

Before she died she told him, "Son, as far as I am concerned, nothing in this life now gives me pleasure. I do not

AUDIO

St. Augustine (Rome: 354-430 A.D.), The Giants of Philosophy: The Audio Classics Series, narrated by Charlton Heston (Knowledge Products).

The Confessions of Saint Augustine. Distributed by Ignatius Press.

VIDEO

The City of God. Films for the Humanities (52 minutes).

Late Have I Loved Thee, written and narrated by James J. O'Donnell, Ph.D. Santa Fe Della Productions.

know why I am still here, since I have no further hopes in this world. I did have one reason for wanting to live a little longer: to see you become a Christian before I died. God has lavished his gifts on me in this respect."

When she died, Augustine was so stunned by the absence of her formidable presence that he did not weep. Only several weeks later did her death really hit him.

And he released a flood of healing tears.

PROFILE: SAINT AMBROSE

Saint Ambrose (340-397), who converted Augustine, was Bishop of Milan and one of the great Church doctors. As an imperial governor, he was stationed in the imperial city of Milan with the duty of keeping peace when Auxentius, bishop of the city, died. During the ensuing election Ambrose was unanimously acclaimed by the people. He became bishop and thereafter an uncompromising foe of Arianism and resurging paganism. It is recorded that, at one point, he barricaded himself and his parishioners within a church in order to prevent an Arian takeover.

Ambrose was friend and adviser to three emperors; nevertheless, he consistently fought to keep the Church independent of civil power. During his career he also composed hymns and wrote commentaries on Scripture and treatises in theology.

What Do Conversion Stories Teach Us?— Connecting to Our Times

The conversion of Augustine is one of the most powerful narratives of its kind in Church history, ranking in influence with that of Paul. Of course it helped that Augustine was one of history's most talented literary writers, hence the account of his conversion remains a classic and one of the best-read conversion stories ever written.

Conversion accounts such as those of Augustine, Paul, Thomas Merton, C.S. Lewis or Dorothy Day tell about their journey to Christian faith. What value do they have for us who are already Christian? We can see how they motivate seekers for truth and God to embark on a path to Catholicism. But we are already Catholics. So what can they teach us?

Conversion narratives enrich us in many ways. We may be Catholics but tend to take our faith for granted. Our eyes are clouded over with what Coleridge calls the "film of familiarity." We become jaded in the faith and fail to see its freshness and originality. We lose excitement about our religion.

Converts share with us their bouncing and unmitigated enthusiasm for Jesus and the Church. For them it is all new. Their stories lend us their "eyes" so we can see afresh what we have forgotten. Someone has said that life's greatest problem is "forgetfulness of being." That is also religion's dilemma. The membership forgets how wonderful is the gift of faith.

C.S. Lewis asks us to be as "surprised by joy" as he was. Augustine charms us to fall in love again with God as he was privileged to do. Paul excites us to be so close to Jesus that we can say as he did, "For to me, living is Christ" (see Philippians 1:21). Thomas Merton invites us to a contemplative faith and a meditative life—a dimension of faith obscured by the noise of daily life. Dorothy Day inspires us to a conversion of sympathy and empathy for the poor and oppressed.

We read conversion stories to regain an enthusiasm for our religion and to stimulate our own personal conversion, which must occur again and again as we go through life's many stages and passages.

Part Two
Middle Ages

EVENTS IN THE CHURCH

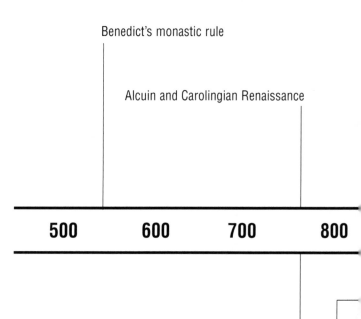

Benedict's monastic rule

Alcuin and Carolingian Renaissance

| 500 | 600 | 700 | 800 |

Charlemagne
Einhard

EVENTS IN SOCIETY

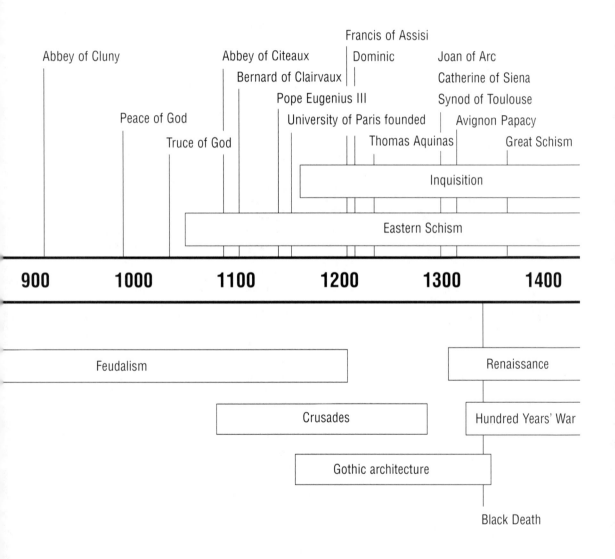

Francis of Assisi

Abbey of Cluny   Abbey of Citeaux Dominic   Joan of Arc

         Bernard of Clairvaux   Catherine of Siena

           Pope Eugenius III   Synod of Toulouse

  Peace of God   University of Paris founded Avignon Papacy

     Truce of God   Thomas Aquinas   Great Schism

Inquisition

Eastern Schism

| 900 | 1000 | 1100 | 1200 | 1300 | 1400 |

Feudalism

Renaissance

Crusades

Hundred Years' War

Gothic architecture

Black Death

10. Charlemagne: The Second Constantine

Charlemagne's ambition was to do for the western part of Europe what Constantine had done for the eastern section: namely, to bring the whole area into political unity. Constantine had created the Roman Empire of the East and established his capital at Constantinople. Charlemagne dreamed of uniting the West in a similar way.

Two obstacles stood in his way: the Church and a number of warlords who controlled various territories.

We have already noted that the Church filled the power vacuum left after the fall of the western Roman Empire in 476 (see Chapter 8). By the time Charlemagne came along (771) the Church had, for three centuries, been supervising commerce, agriculture, law and other civic functions in addition to serving spiritual needs. Yet the Church had never gained total control of western Europe. Roving tribes and their warlords held vast power. If anything, the Church had staved off total chaos and created islands of civility in what might otherwise have been reversion to barbarism.

Charlemagne's first task, therefore, was to convince the Church, now grown accustomed to political power, to relax and let politicians take care of the secular realm. The Church could then minister to the spiritual. Charlemagne's other task was to subdue the warlords and create one vast empire from the north of France to the southern tip of Italy, from the Atlantic in the west to the Elbe in the east.

He was hugely successful in his military conquests. In the years between 771-800 he subdued the tribal chieftains. He also appears to have attained his goal with the Church. In 800 Pope Leo III crowned Charlemagne Emperor of the West, and the Church seemingly yielded political control into his hands.

A harmonious relationship between Church and state, pope and emperor had apparently been established. Subsequent history was to prove differently. Church and state soon vied with one another in power struggles, each seeking to control the other. That tension exists to this day, though it has been vastly modified in democracies where Church and state are separate.

A Love of Learning in Brutal Times

Charlemagne's love of learning led the way for the founding of the great universities. As a lover of the arts, he inspired the growth of Romanesque architecture and sculpture. His interest in farming is said to have led to the three-field system of agriculture (rotating crops and letting one field lie fallow).

The world of Charlemagne was a place of rugged living. Early castles were like the log forts of the Wild West in America. In time stone castles were built and the peasants lived near them for protection. The same was true for the monasteries. Eventually, villages and cities grew up around these citadels of God and humanity. Still, a good deal of brutality prevailed.

Justice had its superstitious side. Take, for example, the trial by water. The accused was thrown into the water. Sinking proved innocence. Of course, one could sink by expelling air and then hope the accusers would effect a rescue before it was too late.

Less easy to overcome was the trial by hot iron. The accused had to grab a hot iron. If the hand showed no signs of festering after three days, the accused was declared innocent. A person whose hands were toughened by hard work might succeed in displaying innocence, but if not...?

Sometimes complaints were settled by judicial combat. Parties to an argument fought with picks and wooden shields until one gave up. The loser was judged guilty and sometimes sent to the gallows.

One refuge from this brutality was the monastery. The life of the monks disciplined the barbaric behavior of those who came to it. Poverty controlled the desire for goods and the ruthless ways used to get them. Celibacy brought the passions under the curb of self-mastery. Obedience restrained the wild and vulgar ways of former days.

The principle was: Subdue the body and let the spirit grow. The motive was: Do this for God's glory and the good of humankind. The result was the civilizing of semi-barbarians and the growth of culture.

The light of the Church had always been the strongest hope for the making of Europe after the fall of Rome. Now, in the monasteries, the reserve of spiritual power was to become a medieval form of atomic energy.

Needed: Man of Genius

Charlemagne repeated, to some extent, the military achievements of Constantine, but had to cope with a different kind of Church. Constantine had encountered a Church that was still suffering outcast status. Charlemagne came upon a Church that was practically lord of the West in secular as well as spiritual matters.

It would take the military genius of a man like Constantine to subdue barbaric tribes like the Saxons, to remove the Church diplomatically from political power, to introduce a semblance of political unity and peace in the West. Charlemagne was that amazing man. The sketch that follows was written by Charlemagne's friend and biographer, Einhard.

FOR DISCUSSION/REFLECTION

From the fall of the Roman Empire in 476 to the pope's crowning of Charlemagne in 800, the Western Church was virtual political and religious ruler of territories under its control. With Charlemagne power was divided; the emperor took charge of secular matters and the Church oversaw the spiritual realm. That neat division did not last too long. Subsequent popes and emperors intruded on each other's powers, causing strife and wars. There is a saying, "No one surrenders power willingly." Why is this so? Why would this especially be harmful for the mission of the Church?

Charlemagne believed in the value of education. He had a personal teacher who accompanied him wherever he went, a monk named Alcuin from the city of York in Northern England. Why would an emperor need to have further education? Why would he choose a monk for his teacher? Was religion of major importance to Charlemagne?

Do we value religious education? At what point if any in our lives have we learned all there is to know about the faith? How can we help to educate others?

Einhard's Portrait of Charlemagne
(742-814)

FOR BACKGROUND

Einhard impressed Charlemagne with his talent and industry. Thus Charlemagne placed him in charge of the royal building program and entrusted him with important diplomatic missions. In his later years he wrote his *Vita Karoli Magni*, one of the finest biographies to come from the early Middle Ages. The excerpts in the "Portrait" are taken from this *Life of Charlemagne*.

Charlemagne was probably six feet, four inches tall. Considering that the average male height of the time was five feet, two inches, he was tall indeed.

Charlemagne made the city of Aachen in Northern Germany his capital. His father, Pepin the Short, also ruled from Aachen. The Frankish Kingdom stretched through part of modern-day Germany and France. Charlemagne was buried in the cathedral at Aachen.

Charlemagne means "Charles the Great" and he did indeed have a great reign.

The learned English monk, Alcuin, served as Charlemagne's teacher and, at times, his conscience. In 778, after an uprising of Saxons in his territory, Charlemagne decreed that all Saxons, under pain of death, had to be baptized and give one-tenth of their income to the Church. Alcuin expressed his disapproval of Charlemagne's methods: "A man can be drawn to the faith, but he cannot be forced. A man may be forced to receive Baptism, but it does not follow that he will thereby receive the faith."

Charles was large and strong, and of lofty stature.... His height is well known to have been seven times the length of his foot. The upper part of his head was round, his eyes very large and animated, nose a little long, hair fair, and face laughing and merry. Thus his appearance was always stately and dignified, whether he was standing or sitting; although his neck was thick and somewhat short and his belly rather prominent.... In accordance with national custom, he took frequent exercise on horseback and in the chase.... He often practiced swimming, in which he was so good that none could surpass him.

He used to wear the national, that is to say the Frank, dress—next his skin a linen shirt and linen breeches, and above these a tunic fringed with silk; while hose fastened by bands covered his lower limbs and shoes his feet, and he protected his shoulders and chest in winter by a close-fitting coat of otter or marten skins. Over all he flung a blue cloak and he always had a sword girt about him, usually one with a gold or silver hilt and belt.

Charles was temperate in eating and particularly in drinking, for he hated drunkenness in anybody, much more in himself and those of his household.... While at the table, he listened to reading or music. The subjects of the readings were the stories and deeds of olden times. He was fond, too, of Saint Augustine's books, and especially of the one entitled *The City of God*.

Charles had the gift for ready and fluent speech and could express whatever he had to say with the utmost clearness.... He was such a master of Latin that he could speak it.... He cultivated the liberal arts, held those who taught them in great esteem and conferred great honors upon them. He took lessons in grammar from the deacon Peter of Pisa.... Another deacon, Alcuin, a man of Saxon extraction who was the greatest scholar of the day, was his teacher in other branches of learning.... He also tried to write, and used to keep tablets and blanks in bed under his pillow, that at leisure hours he might accustom his hand to form letters; however, as he did not begin his efforts in due season but late in life, they met with ill success.

He cherished with the greatest fervor and devotion the principles of the Christian religion, which had been instilled into him from infancy. Hence it was that he built the beautiful basilica of Aix-la-Chapelle, which he adorned with gold and silver and lamps and with rails and doors of solid brass.

He was very forward in aiding the poor.... He not only made a point of giving in his own country but, when he discovered there were Christians living in poverty in Syria, Egypt and Carthage, he had compassion on their wants and used to send money over the seas to them. He died at the age of seventy-two and was buried at Aix-la-Chapelle.

Charlemagne—Looking Back

Three items of interest surface in this chapter: Church-state conflict, the Carolingian Renaissance and the cruelty of judicial methods.

1) *Church-state conflict.* We have already seen that in filling the power vacuum, the Church was acting as a genuine servant to the West. As Christopher Dawson put it, the Church was a midwife for the making of Europe—a task that was naturally self-destructive because secular power would in time reassert itself.

The task of religion is paradoxical. Religion stands both inside a culture to create and build up and outside to criticize and purify. Now the Church had been inside for three centuries. It was time to step back to allow the culture to unfold on its own strength, while the Church tested the spiritual mettle of the new creation.

Unfortunately, this did not happen. The Church held on to as much political power as possible, thus becoming embroiled in the perennial intrigues among the leaders of England, France and the Holy Roman Empire. Charlemagne had hoped to ease the Church away from this position and to provide a protective atmosphere for the Church as Constantine had done in the East.

Charlemagne was only slightly successful. In fact, he alerted the Church to a change it would not accept. The result was the beginning of Church-state conflicts that have lasted even to our own day. If the Church wasn't busy making and unmaking kings, the state was busy making and unmaking popes and bishops. Even as late as the election of Pius X (1903), the emperor of Austria attempted to intrude an imperial veto.

2) *Carolingian Renaissance.* With the able assistance of Alcuin, Charlemagne cooperated wholeheartedly with the Church in preserving an interest in learning that might otherwise have disappeared in this barbaric period. (The Church's influence in education will be discussed in Chapter 13.)

3) *Cruelty of judicial methods.* The cruelty of administrative justice illustrates the barbarity of the times. In spite of the civilizing influence of the Church, much brutality lingered. It would take a good deal longer to introduce more civilized procedures.

FOR FURTHER READING

Clark, Kenneth. *Civilization.* New York: Harper and Row, 1969.

Ganshof, Francois Louis. *Feudalism,* trans. Philip Grierson. London and New York: Longmans, Green, 1952.

VIDEO

Charlemagne. Series for the Humanities (60 minutes).

Pippin. 20th Century (120 minutes).

Support for the Dialogue of Religion and Society—Connecting to Our Times

With Charlemagne we see the revival of independent lay political leadership in the West. Popes and bishops are expected to return more to their spiritual leadership roles. Both then and in the ensuing centuries there remained struggles for control.

Sometimes the kings wanted to control the Church for political purposes. Other times popes and bishops intruded into the political realm for their own purposes. Church-state conflicts appear again and again.

In the United States, our founding fathers created a country in which there would be an explicit separation of Church and state. No religion would be established by the government. On the other hand, the state would see that no laws prevented the exercise of religion.

As American history unfolded, especially in the mid-twentieth century, the separation of Church and state became what was known as the "wall of separation." In practical terms this has meant eliminating prayer in public schools, preventing religious exhibits on public property and studying the Bible purely as literature, not as a text of faith. It has also resulted in the state's enacting laws about certain moral issues which radically offend the beliefs of many faiths. The *Roe vs. Wade* decision of the Supreme Court on the right to abortion is one such example.

Catholics in the United States approve the separation of Church and state. But Catholics, here and worldwide, do not agree to the separation of religion and society. Yes: there should be no established Church. No: religion should not be excluded from a voice in the culture and in the political process. Yale professor Stephen Carter eloquently defends this position in his book, *The Culture of Disbelief.*

As young people prepare to be active citizens in our society, they should be aware of their responsibility to apply their religious and moral beliefs to the issues of the day. This should be done in an environment of freedom, respect for everyone's human dignity, debate, persuasion and the vote.

Charlemagne taught us to be aware of the differing responsibilities of Church and state. He and his culture solved the problem within their lights. We must do it within our contemporary insights.

11. Monks

The monks provided the Church with a first-class contingent of missionaries for the conversion of Europe. They not only preached the gospel, they also cleared swamps, started schools, experimented with farming techniques and built monasteries around which grew towns such as York and cities such as Paris.

In scriptoriums—the monastic equivalent of research labs—they wrote out enduring copies of the books of Greece and Rome, thus preserving that heritage of human knowledge for us. They did all this in the conviction that God's Spirit willed the civilizing of the people.

Saint Benedict was the father of the monks of the West. He founded the first monastery, Monte Cassino, in the middle of the sixth century. His *Rule* has remained a monastic guide to this day. (The chart on pages 64 and 65 shows how this fits into the overall development of monasticism in the Church.)

Since even the best groups get ragged at the edge, monks faced two major reforms in the Middle Ages. The first reform came with the founding of the Abbey of Cluny in 910.

William I of Aquitaine and his wife gave the monks the town, manor house, waters and revenues of Cluny so they could build a monastery. This economic windfall meant the monks could leave manual labor to the serfs. Now they could concentrate on the development of an elaborate liturgy and cultural pursuits such as the preservation of Greek and Roman classics and the conducting of schools.

FOR DISCUSSION/REFLECTION

"I reprove and discipline those whom I love" (Revelation 3:19a). This biblical admonition reminds us of the link between love and constructive criticism. We see in Bernard's advice to Pope Eugenius III an application of the principle. Since Vatican II public criticism of popes and other Church leaders by Catholics has increased. Discuss some of these criticisms. How valid are they? Do you think they are delivered in the loving spirit of Revelation 3:19?

Is our relationship with Church leaders healthier now that we feel more free to articulate such criticisms? Do we have a better Church in which not only the leaders rebuke the flock, but also the flock rebukes the leaders?

What are some practical guidelines for public criticism of Church leaders?

What are the opportunities and dangers in our relationships with one another for constructive and destructive criticism?

True or false: Most criticism and confrontation is usually made impulsively in anger or annoyance. This does more to increase confusion than to bring enlightenment. Discuss.

How do we avoid arrogance in criticizing others?

Cluny, the remaining transept of the medieval church.

FOR BACKGROUND

Saint Bernard of Clairvaux (1090-1153) "was so famous a preacher that he became known as "Doctor Mellifluous," for the words coming from his mouth were said to be like honey. He had such an extensive influence on the thinking of his age that he has been called "the conscience of all Europe." Pope Eugenius, a friend of Bernard's, asked him to comment on the pope's role as head of the Church.

In his letter Bernard explains that the pope is to be a man of service. He has been given the responsibility of serving others, not a position of kingly power; Bernard therefore takes the opportunity to suggest changes—although gradual—in the external trappings of papal practice. Among these are a kind of taxation of the people to support the papacy, the practice of throwing coins to the crowds during papal processions (a gesture designed to gain political favor), majestic dress and pageantry.

Bernard's counsel, presented as a "letter" to the pope, is actually drawn from a treatise, *De Consideratione*, written at the pope's request.

The second reform began with the founding of the abbey of Citeaux in 1098. The new monks, called Cistercians, owed their thinking to Stephen Harding, author of their "Charter of Charity." The playlet that follows deals with concerns and issues of this period.

The Cistercians wanted none of the worldliness of Cluny. They wanted withdrawal from the world and a return to manual labor. They refused land grants. They took swamps and "useless" property and turned it, by their manual labor, into "golden meadows."

Their most famous monk, and the greatest churchman of the twelfth century, was Bernard of Clairvaux. But, as Bernard's letter to the pope (page 59) shows, it was still possible for a monk to have concern for events in the larger Church and the world.

From Swamps to Golden Meadows
(c. 1115)

The characters:
    David, abbot of Cluny
    Stephen, monk of Citeaux
    Eleanor, a visitor at Cluny

The scene: Guest house at Cluny about the year 1115. The Benedictine abbey, now two hundred years old, boasted one of the largest churches in the world and a guest house big enough to accommodate forty men and thirty women.

David: Well, Stephen, how's the reform going at Citeaux?

Stephen: Quite well, thank you, Abbot David. I must say I was spoiled by life here at Cluny. I did love being at the crossroads of the world, welcoming the continual stream of visitors and lounging in the human splendor of the abbey.

David: It's strange that in less than two centuries we, who were the reforming abbey, now suffer the indignity of being told we are out of date.

Stephen: Your abbey served a great purpose. It freed hundreds of men to learn the art of prayer and to preserve the cultural heritage of the West. You achieved the impressive feat of merging religious and secular concerns in a satisfactory way for over a century and a half. You Benedictines literally reshaped the spiritual life of people all over Europe with your daughter houses.

Eleanor: Every good thing has its day. Eventually, you began to collapse under the huge weight of the possessions that mounted with each passing year. As a young girl, I visited your Benedictine Abbey of St. Alban's in England. They had a stable big enough for three hundred horses.

Stephen: You're right, Lady Eleanor, about the weight of secular responsibilities. I used to be guestmaster here. It was my job to provide clean towels, uncracked cups, silver spoons, blankets and sheets for the guests. In winter I was supplying candles and candlesticks, a fire that did not smoke and writing materials on demand.

David: Yes, and don't forget how you had to brush away the spiders' webs and put clean straw on the floor.

Eleanor: I recall that the guestmaster checked to see whether my father removed his sword when we first arrived at the abbey. Somewhat more embarrassing, when we were leaving, he went through our baggage to see whether we had taken along any of the linen or silver of the house.

Stephen: I felt more like an innkeeper than a monk.

David: Look at my white hair—it didn't come from age. I was formerly abbot at St. Edmond's, where they had an enormous debt. It took me twelve years to pull them out of bankruptcy, but I paid for it with a prematurely white head.

Eleanor: Tell me, Stephen, why do you Cistercians insist on moving into swamps for your new houses? I know you want to get away from the distractions here, but aren't you going a bit too far?

Stephen: One easy answer, of course, is that the land is cheap. Another is that it forces us to return to the ideal of manual labor as favored by Saint Benedict. We must work to clear the marshes and lay good foundations for the buildings.

Eleanor: I suppose a common task like that does a lot to improve your community spirit.

Stephen: It seems to. I've rarely felt such a bond with my brothers as when we put our shoulders together to change the swamps into golden meadows. At least it beats chasing spiders' webs.

David: What are you going to do about prayer? I should hope you won't reject that tradition of Cluny.

Stephen: Not at all. We're just as devoted to prayer as you are. But we are less interested in the pageantry, ceremonies and wordiness of your prayer life. We believe your way of praying is too stuffy, too formal and without meaning. It seems too much like theater. I sometimes wondered if the services were meant to please people rather than to honor God.

Eleanor: I can appreciate, Stephen, that you people have moved toward a more authentic prayer life. What bothers me, though, is the austerity of your buildings. You have no stained glass. I've heard that some of your houses forbid the image of Christ on the cross. And I believe all of your houses exclude any statuary or sculpture.

David: I worry about that too, Stephen. Our monasteries became the one place in a barbaric society where the arts flourished. Doubtless, prayer has a way of humanizing. But the arts also soften the animal and brute instincts of people.

Stephen: I know just what you mean. No one loved the soaring Gothic beauty of this abbey more than I. I know how much

As the monastic ideal spread some began to exaggerate its ascetic character. One such person was Simeon Stylites. He gained fame because he spent the last part of his life on the top of a pillar.

A tragic love story comes from the annals of monasticism. It involved the brilliant young monk, Abelard, and his young student, Heloise. Hired by her uncle and guardian, Abelard was to tutor his young student but, by his own words, the study sessions soon involved "more kissing than teaching." Heloise eventually became pregnant, which led to their secret marriage. After the child's birth Abelard placed his young wife in a convent near Paris. Heloise's uncle, in an act of revenge, castrated Abelard, and these ill-fated lovers spent the rest of their lives in the shadow of their love affair.

FOR DISCUSSION/REFLECTION

Today we normally think of monks in terms of prayer, as witnesses to contemplation. The monks of the early Middle Ages also devoted themselves to prayer. Less known is how the Benedictines—and later the Cistercians—laid a firm economic base for Europe by creating a network of cultivated land and well managed farms. These farmer monks acted as internal colonizers of Europe's frontiers, much like American pioneers pushing out into the prairies. How do today's Trappists reflect and repeat this historic tradition of the monks?

Explain this monastic irony: the more monks attended to social, economic and political affairs, the more their impact diminished.

For many people monasticism is a bygone or antiquated expression of Christianity. What is its value in this day and age?

In an attempt to give people an understanding of the monastic life, many communities allow people to live temporarily at a monastery. Would this possibility ever interest you? Why or why not?

If Bernard of Clairvaux was seen as the conscience of the Church during his day, who might be seen as fulfilling this role today? Mother Teresa, Pope John XXIII, Dorothy Day, Martin Luther King, Pope John Paul II or someone else?

Imagine you were asked by the present pope to comment on his role as head of the Catholic Church. How would you respond?

peace it brought me and how often it calmed the growling tensions within me.

Eleanor: Then why don't you speak up about this matter at Citeaux?

Stephen: I did, as a matter of fact. Several times I brought it up at community meetings. I even braved a showdown with Bernard himself on the matter.

David: Apparently they weren't impressed.

Stephen: True enough. But I realize that this is all part of the reaction against the excesses of Cluny. You know how reforms have a way of going to the opposite extreme.

Eleanor: I sense you believe that they will get over being so strict.

Stephen: Certainly. I wouldn't be surprised that, before I die, a new flowering of the arts will be associated with the Cistercians.

David: Actually, I'm not worried about the arts. What Europe needs is some advanced thinking about agriculture, animal husbandry, milling and weaving. We need some practical breakthroughs. There's hardly been any progress since the days of Charlemagne.

Stephen: On that score, I can forecast a bright future. We are attracting some people incredibly skilled in these areas. The techniques we learned draining marshes were only a beginning.

Eleanor: And this isn't going to hurt the economy of northern Europe.

David: So the cycle may begin again. The day you make more wool than you need, you'll be at the market selling. And then you'll be right back where you started—involved again with the very world you now run away from.

Stephen: That's already come up at our community meetings. Typically, the conservative wing doesn't want to think about that. They hope to keep our reform intact, refusing to see that such a course inevitably leads back to the business world they hope to escape.

David: Well, you've done away with the extravagances that have crept in up to now. If the time comes when another reform is necessary, there will be men around to see that it's done.

Eleanor: You mentioned Bernard a little earlier. How is he doing at Clairvaux?

Stephen: He's as busy as ever. I understand he's just written a rule of life for the Knights Templar monks at Jerusalem.

David: Where did they get such a name?

Eleanor: My cousin, who's just back from the Crusades, says that they were lodged in quarters next to what they believed to be Solomon's temple. So they consider themselves "knights by the temple."

David: Stephen, did Bernard say anything special in his rule for the Templars?

Stephen: One passage did startle me: "The soldier may securely kill, kill for Christ and more securely die. He benefits himself if he dies—and Christ if he kills. To kill a malefactor is not homicide, but malicide (the killing of the bad). In the death of a pagan, the Christian is glorified because Christ is glorified." So Bernard said.

Eleanor: I know Bernard is the greatest churchman of Europe, but those words make me shudder a bit.

David: It is an unusual statement. I must think about it.

Stephen: One thing is certain. He speaks the mood of our times.

David: No quarrel with that. It catches me up short to realize that this is the mood of our times. The tower bell rings for vespers. Let us pray for our world and our people—and God's reign of peace.

AUDIO

Love Casts Out Fear, In the Image of God, Pure Love, all by Thomas Merton. Credence Cassettes.

Monastic Spirituality/Citeaux, Monastic Spirituality, Part II, Meaning of Monastic Spirituality, all by Thomas Merton. Credence Cassettes (three audiocassettes; 60 minutes, 60 minutes and 90 minutes).

Bernard Confronts His Age: A Letter to the Pope
(c. 1150)

Dear Pope Eugenius,

That you have been raised to the pinnacle of honor and power is an undeniable fact. But for what purpose have you been so elevated? Here is a question that calls for your utmost consideration. It was not, as I suppose, that you might enjoy the glory of lordship.

For when the prophet Jeremiah was similarly exalted, he heard the voice of the Lord saying to him:

> See, today I appoint you over
>   nations and over kingdoms,
> To pluck up and to pull down,
> to destroy and to overthrow,
> to build and to plant. (Jeremiah 1:10)

What is there here suggestive of pomp and glory? Have we not rather the imposition of toilsome administration poetically expressed in the language of agriculture?

Therefore, that you might not think too highly of yourself, bear always in mind that a duty of service has been imposed upon you, and not a dominion conferred. Surely, you are not greater than Jeremiah? And although you are perhaps equal to him in power, in merit of life he is immeasurably your superior.

Learn from him to use your position of eminence, not to show your authority, as to do the work the time demands. Learn that you have more need of a hoe than a scepter to do your job.

What is to be thought of the practice of purchasing the applause of the crowd, and paying for this with the plunder of the churches? The poor find their living sown in the streets of the wealthy. Silver coins are seen to glitter in the mud.

There is a rush from all sides. But it is not the neediest who secures the prize. Rather, he who has the advantage in bodily strength or fleetness of foot surpasses his competitors. I cannot

Due to his prestige, Bernard became one of the most traveled and active Church leaders of the twelfth century. His advice was sought on a variety of issues: doctrine, Church policy, monastic reform and especially questions having to do with the spiritual life and human relations. Bernard once wrote to Pope Eugenius III: "People say that I am the pope, and not you. They come to me from all sides, weighted down with their cares. It would be scandalous and sinful to refuse my help to so many friends."

▼

FOR BACKGROUND

Martin of Tours

Martin of Tours added to the popularity of monasticism in the West. Born around 355, he spent most of his life in Pavia, a city in Northern Italy. At a young age Martin, going against his parents' wishes, sought to become a Christian. In an attempt to free him from Christian influence, Martin's father entered his son in the army.

While in service under Julian the Apostate, Martin was approached by a beggar seeking alms. Having no money, Martin took the cape off his back, cut it in two with his sword and gave half to the beggar. Later, in a dream, Martin saw Jesus approach him and say: "Inasmuch as you did it to one of the least of these my brethren, you did it to me."

Within two years Martin was baptized and left the army. He traveled for a while and even visited the popular and saintly Bishop Hilary of Poitiers, who became a close friend. Martin settled just outside of Poitiers and began to live the monastic life.

Because of his sanctity, the people of Tours wanted Martin as their bishop when that see became open. Some bishops protested that, as poorly and ragged as he was, the prestige of the office would be damaged. In the end, though, Martin was chosen Bishop of Tours. He did not abandon his monastic ways, however. Next to his cathedral he built a cell where he spent as much free time as possible. When demands on his time left him no peace, he moved to the outskirts of the city, where he continued to minister to the people of Tours. Martin's very

say that this usage, or better, this crying abuse, began with you. But in God's name, let it end with you.

I must go on to speak of another matter. In the midst of these depressing scenes I behold you, the supreme shepherd of the flock, advancing majestically "in gilded clothing, surrounded with variety" (Psalm 45:12-14).

Tell me, what profit does the flock derive from such magnificent pageants? If I may venture to say it, they are better calculated to provide food for the wolves than pasture for sheep.

Do you think that Saint Peter loved to surround himself with this pomp or display, or Saint Paul? No. In all things that belong to earthly magnificence, you have succeeded not Peter, but Constantine. However, I would counsel you to tolerate this splendor at least for a time, yet without falling in love with it, or regarding it as essential to your state.

Ever cordially in Christ,
Bernard

Monks—Looking Back

The life of the monks was central to the development of medieval spiritual, cultural and technical life. Their own ability to reform themselves was a sign of their dynamism and imagination. The play underlines these points:

1) *Reform for a spiritual purpose.* The Abbey of Cluny had been a reform movement in which the art of prayer, especially its liturgical form, was developed. It also was involved in copying manuscripts and salvaging the general cultural heritage of the ancients. The arts flourished and a civilizing impact was felt in Europe. But after two hundred years the abbey declined in spiritual vitality because of its wealth. The energies of abbots and monks went into keeping up the buildings, managing the large estates and dealing with vast numbers of people—tourists, businessmen and local gentry—coming in to pass the time.

Under Stephen Harding and Bernard of Clairvaux a new reform took place. It originated at the Abbey of Citeaux; hence the monks were called Cistercians. They deliberately chose secluded places for their monasteries, both to recover the spirit of manual labor and to get back to a life that allowed them to concentrate on continuous attention to God.

Like the Puritans of a later date, the Cistercians stripped their churches of all ornament—stained glass, statues, sculpture and even, in some cases, the image of Christ on the cross. Their ceremonies were severe and their life starkly simple. The purpose was to recover the spirit of prayer.

They not only succeeded in achieving monastic simplicity but also contributed technical advances in agriculture that aided the growth of Europe's economy. In time, they passed beyond their "puritan" stage and inspired a new flowering of the arts.

2) *Integration of religion and life.* Even though the Cistercians "fled the world," they fled more from its baggage than from its people. Jesus had told the apostles to travel light in order to announce the gospel; so it was with the monks. They taught people how to pray. They also taught people to re-create the earth for the sake of human concern.

3) *The Knights Templar.* This subject picks up the theme of war introduced in "Coffee Break" (see page 14). Bernard, the greatest of Cistercians, wrote the rule for the Knights, illustrating how religion and war can get mixed together and how the spirit of the times influences the rationale of even one so saintly as Bernard.

We will be seeing the phenomenon of holy war again in the episode on the Crusades (Chapter 14). It may be helpful to keep in mind that this theme occurs again and again in religious history. In the Old Testament it is especially evident in the Book of Judges and in 1 and 2 Maccabees. Noble religious figures such as Gideon and Judas Maccabaeus killed ruthlessly for the protection of religion, the glory of God and (not to be forgotten) their own political purposes.

Popes have fought wars. Luther backed a cruel repression of the Anabaptists during the peasants' rebellion. It is impossible to render a judgment on these people from so great a distance. There is nothing to stop us from disagreeing with what they did and asserting that we do not personally believe in such behavior for ourselves.

life and example gave support to the monastic ideal.

FOR FURTHER READING

Johnson, Paul. *History of Christianity.* New York: Macmillan, 1976.

Saint Bernard. *Sermons on Conversion,* trans. Marie Bernard Said. Kalamazoo, Mich.: Cistercian Publications, 1981.

Nuns, Monks and Religious: Finished or Starting Over?—Connecting to Our Times

The small seed of monasticism planted in the early centuries of the Church flowered into the male and female Benedictine and Cistercian monasteries of the Middle Ages. The seed became a garden as time went on, with the arrival of male and female Franciscans, Dominicans, Norbertines, Augustinians, Carmelites—also such exclusively male orders as the Jesuits, Redemptorists, Oratorians, Christian Brothers and many others.

Vast numbers of religious women outstripped their male counterparts in congregations such as the Ursulines, the Visitations, Mercy Sisters, St. Joseph Sisters, Sisters of Notre Dame and a bewildering number of other communities. Religious women constitute the world's largest number of Catholics committed to the religious life.

The history of religious orders and congregations has often followed the cycle spoken of by an old monk: "Diligence begets abundance. Abundance begets laxity. Laxity begets decay." The life-cycles of religious life often illustrate the bittersweet wisdom of this saying. Today, the religious life is flourishing in the developing nations, but is facing a

VIDEO

Merton. Mass Media Ministries (60 minutes).

membership crisis in Europe and North America. Sometimes the reason for this is due to what the wise old monk predicted.

But other reasons have something to do with it as well. Times of radical cultural change in the past also witnessed a temporary decline of religious life, followed by a remarkable resurgence. The arrival of print technology with Gutenberg, coupled with global expansion triggered by Columbus' discovery of America, at first shook the monasteries and convents to their foundations, only to see new orders (such as the Jesuits) founded and a second spring of religious life.

Today, the computer-driven culture, the communications revolution in information and transportation again is causing a cultural upheaval. It is reflected in the religious life as everywhere else. If history is prologue, then we can anticipate that, when the smoke clears, we will see a resurgence of religious life as well as new congregations.

Saint Bernard of Clairvaux

Bernard, a Cistercian, became a member of Citeaux. After his entrance, the monastery took on renewed life and vigor. At the suggestion of Stephen Harding, he and twelve monks founded a branch of Citeaux at Clairvaux. This foundation proved highly successful.

In investigating the life of any saint it must be remembered that saints, like anyone else, are affected by the social conditions and thoughts of their age. Bernard's advocacy of the Second Crusade and his composition of a rule for the Knights Templar (a group of soldiers formed to protect pilgrims in the Holy Land) indicate the militant nature of his Christianity. His concept of faith left little room for inactivity. He chided popes, decided agendas for councils, fought corruption at Cluny, became consultant to kings, popes, bishops—the powerful elite of his time. Regardless of how one views his zeal, one notes his profound influence upon the peoples and events of his age.

Bernard died in 1153 and was declared a saint of the Church in 1174.

Development of Monasticism

ESSENES: The location of this community was discovered in 1947 at Wadi Qumram. The Dead Sea Scrolls were found here. It is thought that a community composed of a priestly class and laity lived here prior to Jesus' ministry. Some consider John the Baptist to have been a member of the Essenes.

EARLY CHRISTIAN COMMUNITY: "All who believed were together and had all things in common; they would sell their possessions and goods and distribute the proceeds to all, as any had need" (Acts 2:44-45).

ANTHONY OF EGYPT (c. 251-356), a hermit in the Egyptian desert about 313, was later joined by others after the Edict of Milan ended persecution of Christians.

ANCHORITE: One who withdraws from the world.

CENOBITE: One who lives a community life.

HERMIT: One who lives alone.

SAINT PACHOMIUS, who lived in upper Egypt about the fourth century, wrote the earliest monastic rule. The monks lived in various monasteries, but all under one head. By the end of the fourth century this order had over five thousand members. Pachomius was a layman; the monastic movement has essentially remained a lay movement in Eastern churches.

SAINT ATHANASIUS brought the monastic idea to the West about 337. His book, *The Life of Anthony*, influenced monastic development.

IRISH MONASTICISM: Monks from Ireland exerted profound influence on Gaul and Italy.

RULE OF SAINT AUGUSTINE (354-430) developed the common life, later to be adopted by some mendicant groups.

SAINT BASIL (c. 329-379) wrote the rule for the East. He was to eastern monasticism what Benedict was to the West.

JOHN CASSIAN (con't. on next page)

JOHN CASSIAN: His writings greatly influenced monasticism.

BENEDICT founded Monte Cassino (c. 529). He wrote the rule for the legislation of the monastic family. He allowed the monks to do no work for society other than charity.

CASSIODORUS founded a monastery in Calabria (c. 537). His monks copied manuscripts in an effort to preserve Roman culture.

BENEDICTINE CENTURIES: Approximately the sixth to the tenth centuries. Until this time, the monastic life had been a search for Christianity in an "evil" world. Withdrawal seemed the best means of attaining sanctity. Under the influence of Pope Gregory the Great, a monk and follower of Benedict, missionaries were sent to England. Monasteries developed a diversity in observance and wealth. Charlemagne tried to reform them by enforcing universal observance of the Rule of Saint Benedict.

CLUNY: The formation of this monastery in 910 was the first real reform. The monks observed the Rule of Saint Benedict, which called for a life of prayer and useful work. Liturgy was carried out with as much perfection as possible. Over a thousand monasteries under the direction of Cluny were founded in western Europe.

CITEAUX, founded in 1098, was the second reform of those following the Rule of Benedict. They chose to be called Cistercians rather than Benedictines. The elaborate pomp and ceremony of Clunic worship was rejected for simplicity. Saint Stephen Harding, author of *Charter of Charity*, led the reform, stressing literal interpretation of the Rule as well as total avoidance of political and social entanglements. The monks did much field work, adding tremendously to the agricultural knowledge of the times. In 1115, Bernard joined Citeaux.

CLAIRVAUX was an outgrowth, rather than a reform, of Citeaux founded by Bernard and twelve monks at the suggestion of Stephen Harding. The concept of penance done for the expiation of sin became a stronger notion. Cistercians today are more commonly known as Trappists.

12. Gothic: Architecture of Faith

'Men of Chartres': A Call to Build a Cathedral
(c. 1145)

▼

FOR FURTHER READING

Daniel-Rops, Henri. *Cathedral and Crusade.* New York: E.P. Dutton, 1957.

The town crier leaped atop a barrel in the center of the marketplace, silenced the few men gathered about him and called out to gather more. "Men of Chartres, listen. Our bishop wants us to build a cathedral. He wants it to be so magnificent that our neighbors in St. Denis will stand in awe of our work. Those men whose purity of life befits them to work on this, step forward. All those men who wish to put coins in the purse, step forward. The rest of you stand in awe of work for the glory of God."

The crowd rustled. No one would be the first to come forward. There would be days of talk and soul-searching. Only then would the guilds come forward one by one to volunteer workers.

Louis, a young stonecutter and native of Chartres, held his breath in wonder. If only I could work on it, he thought to himself. If only my work could be part of this town's

When you look at the Cathedral of Chartres you notice that the steeples do not match. One is quite simple and the other quite ornate. The reason for this is that one was destroyed by fire and replaced. The more ornate one is the newer.

praise of God.

Little did he know that soon his guild would choose him to work on the cathedral. Many like himself would spend a lifetime on this work, passing the completion of it along to their children. Workers would spend years carving a small but elaborate detail high atop a spire, unseen by human eyes but done in the belief that such a deed honors God.

These cathedrals were the visible evidence of medieval faith.They were buildings that towered toward heaven to "touch" their God.

Centuries later, in our own day, we see these masterpieces and marvel at the faith which produced them.

VIDEO

Cathedral. Unicorn Projects (60 minutes).

Exeter. International Films (29 minutes).

Gothic Architecture—Looking Back

Gothic architecture is a nonverbal communication of faith. The great European cathedrals stand as an art form of faith.

The period of Gothic architecture began sometime between 1137 and 1144 with the reconstruction of the royal Abbey Church of St. Denis. This particular church, the shrine of Saint Denis, the apostle of France, and also the site of several kingly coronations, represented the alliance of the Church and the kings of France. It combined architectural characteristics never before brought to one building. The objective was to make it both a site of religious pilgrimage and a symbol of French patriotism.

The new spirit in architecture originating here was twofold: an emphasis on geometric planning and the quest for interior illumination. Both of these reflected religious significance. Geometric exactness and proportion resulted in harmony, which exemplified the unity of the universe as created by God. The light flooding the interior represented the divine light, the Spirit of God.

In northern Europe where sunlight is scarce, Romanesque buildings—heavy, hooded, columned—were too dark. Architects were asked to devise a building that could support huge windows to let in light. Their solution was to use the pointed arch, locked by a keystone and supported from the outside by flying buttresses. The result was a building that resembled two soaring hands, locked in prayer and pointing to God.

Once this was done, the glassmakers and the sculptors came to the forefront. The glassmakers used colored glass in order to soften the light, present a jeweled effect and offer the viewers Bible stories in living color. They were wildly successful, so much so that we are unable today to match the extraordinary coloring they achieved. This is above all true of the matchless windows of Chartres.

The sculptors brought life to stone, creating an army of saints, kings, guildsmen, angels, demons, witches and ani-

Detail of Gothic Cathedral showing flying buttress (shaded) and pointed arch.

FOR DISCUSSION/REFLECTION

It often took a century or more to finish a cathedral. What motivation do you feel a person would need in order to devote years to working on one small section of a building? Could you find the same motivation anywhere today?

The liturgy is the basic determining element in the construction of church buildings. Until most recent times congregational participation was at a minimum, so there was no architectural concern with bringing the congregation into the act of worship. The current emphasis on participation and community is chief among the reasons for a departure from traditional architectural styles. What is the outstanding message of modern church architecture? Does it reflect the spirit of our times? If so, what is the spirit?

Churches of the Middle Ages focused on the tabernacle and altar, emphasizing faith in Christ's Real Presence in the Eucharist. Many churches today have Blessed Sacrament chapels. Their worship spaces focus on the altar, the lectern and the baptismal font to show our faith journey from Baptism to Eucharistic celebration, which includes both Liturgy of Word and Liturgy of Sacrament. How does the present emphasis help us participate more effectively in the Mass?

Which type of church do you prefer for worship—Gothic or modern? Why?

If you were able to design a church, what would it look like? How would you express the fundamentals of Christianity through design? Is that possible?

mals. Even the rainspouts on the roof shared in the world of beauty formed by the sculptors. With boundless fancy, gargoyles—wide-mouthed beasts—fed rainwater from the drainage pipes onto the ground below.

In 1145 the Gothic style moved from the rural abbey of St. Denis to the urban centers with the beginning of the construction of Chartres Cathedral under the supervision of the bishop of Chartres, a friend of the abbot of St. Denis. But Notre Dame of Paris, begun in 1163, follows the original Gothic style of St. Denis much more closely than does Chartres. Bourges and Reims were begun about 1200.

The cost of the cathedrals was met by donations from all ranks of society and from all over the country, which brought to the projects a merger of religious fervor and local civic pride.

Many of the cathedrals were dedicated to the Virgin Mary. *Notre Dame* ("Our Lady") graced the names of the major cathedrals at Paris, Chartres, Rouen, Reims and Beauvais. Jesus was the king of glory and Mary was the queen of heaven. Medieval people loved legends about our Lady, and they were delighted to see these stories depicted in stone and glass.

Friendly rivalry played a part in the building of the cathedrals. Each town wanted to have a bigger and more splendid church than the next. This rivalry reached absurdity in Beauvais, where the builders reached too high and the roof caved in. They tried several more times with the same result.

The prize for the most beautiful of all cathedrals goes to Chartres. Incredibly balanced, boasting dazzling windows and nearly ten thousand figures in its windows and statuary, it survives as a testimony of human skill and Christian faith that rarely fails to touch anyone who makes a visit to its halls. American writer Henry Adams has memorialized it in his classic work *Mont-Saint-Michel and Chartres*.

Cathedral: The Center of Beauty and Faith—Connecting to Our Times

All world religions have striven to embody their faith in structures of surpassing beauty. Israel boasted of Solomon's temple. Muslims celebrate their mosques. Hindus rejoice in their shrines. Babylon prided itself on its step-like ziggurats, similar to the monuments constructed by the Aztecs, Incas and Mayans in our southern hemisphere.

Christianity has created cathedrals of towering beauty. From the awesome, sixth-century Byzantine church of St. Sophia in Istanbul to the medieval Gothic cathedrals to the Romanesque and baroque basilicas, to the contemporary architectural wonders, there always arise buildings of beauty to express the exuberant faith of Christians.

In a unique way, especially for northern Europeans, the Gothic cathedral seems to have spoken most eloquently about the meaning of faith. But what is truly relevant to this discussion is the intrinsic relation of religion and beauty. Our bodies hunger for food. Our minds thirst for ideas. Our emotions reach out for affection. Our souls want faith and God.

But what seems to integrate all these hungers is our innate esthetic craving for beauty. Keats said, "Beauty is truth, truth beauty." Philosophers often note that the one, the good, the true are all summarized in the beautiful. There is something about beauty that establishes all the hidden connections we look for when we want to make what is precious to us fit together. Love is certainly one way to do it. Another tried and true method is beauty. That is why we will always have poets, artists, musicians, sculptors, novelists, glassmakers and architects.

All their talents converge in a given cathedral—and in our parish churches. All the beauty of our worship spaces is meant to draw us to deeper faith in God.

Medieval churches...responded to the needs of an age when books were scarce, and there were not many who could read them. Church buildings thus became the books of the illiterate, and an attempt was made to set forth in them the whole of biblical history, the lives of great saints and martyrs, the virtues and vices, the promise of heaven and the punishment of hell. Today it is difficult for us to read these architectural books. But those who worshiped in them knew their most minute details, in which their parents and grandparents had read for them stories and teachings that they in turn had learned from earlier generations.

—From *The Story of the Church*, **Volume I,**
by Justo Gonzalez
(San Francisco,
Harper & Row, 1984),
pp. 329-331.

13. Friars

Francis of Assissi

The thirteenth century saw the introduction of a new kind of religious order. Its members were called friars. Unlike the monks, who confined themselves to the monastery and its surroundings, the friars went out among the people.

One religious order, the Franciscans, worked at popular preaching and did so with immense success. Their emphasis on the human side of Jesus signaled the rise of Christmas cribs, the Stations of the Cross and other dramatizations of Gospel stories.

Their founder, Francis of Assisi, with his love of gospel poverty, the beauty of nature and every person he met, is a saint who is universally appealing. Many say he is the saint who has most perfectly imitated Jesus.

A second order of friars, the Dominicans, became especially noted in the field of education and scholarship. Their most famous member is Thomas Aquinas. He was a radical theologian for his time, daring to use the thoughts of Aristotle to help explain the meaning of the gospel. Like any innovator, Thomas lived a tumultuous career. But even though he battled his opponents with vigor, he did so with a sense of modesty, balance and human understanding.

The following stories are about two friars: Francis and Aquinas.

Francis: A Turning Point for Poverty
(c. 1228)

"It's hard to believe, Francis, that you didn't get along well with your father when you were a young man. You seem so much at peace with yourself that I can't imagine you in conflict with anyone."

Francis, the revolutionary friar from Assisi, stopped playing his musical instrument and paused before replying.

"This peace was not always with me, Luke. I was quite wild, a leader among my friends, always anxious for adventure, always looking the part of the rich young man. But then a series of events started to make me think, and I began to sense that God was moving me to repair his house, which was in ruin. When I began to carry this out, my father became very angry with me and I began to fight with him.

"He was so totally dedicated to making money and building up the business. I hated his love of wealth, his status-seeking and his seeming indifference to anything else."

"Did you try to communicate with him. Francis?"

"Yes, Luke, I often tried to make him see that I simply had no interest in the business. I argued with him, but I always felt he wasn't really listening to me. Over and over he would say to me, 'You'll change your mind. You're just young and foolish.'"

Luke took out some food they had just begged from a farmer. He offered a chicken leg to Francis as they walked along the dusty road on the way to visit Sister Clare. Luke had been with Francis through thick and thin. He marveled at how well Francis still looked. His beard was flowing and he was brown as a nut. Francis preferred to walk barefoot. The soles of his feet had become as thick as sandals.

"What was it like, Francis, when you had the final showdown?"

"Most people thought I had lost my mind. I can't say that I blame them. It all took place at the bishop's house. My father had me summoned there to 'bring me to my senses.'

"We exchanged some very harsh words, and then my father proposed to beat me—right in the presence of the bishop. Happily, the bishop stood between us and tried to calm Father. I had reached the point where I knew words were useless. That's when the idea struck me."

"Is this the story of the stripping, Francis?"

"Luke, it wasn't as easy as it now seems in legend and story. I was convinced that I had to dramatize how I felt about the exaggerated devotion to wealth I'd seen in my own family and elsewhere in Umbria. With all the impetuosity of youth, I took off my clothes in the presence of the bishop and everyone.

"They were pretty stunned. Standing there, naked, I publicly renounced any and all inheritance that was mine by birthright."

"What did they do then, Francis?"

"At first they scarcely moved. Finally, the bishop took a cloak and put it around me. He advised my father and the other people to leave and let no more be said for the moment."

At that Luke and Francis had arrived at Clare's convent.

"Hello, Clare. Luke and I have been talking over old times."

"I'm glad to see you, Francis. Luke, I can see you're taking good care of my brother."

"He's just been telling me the story of the day he publicly embraced poverty—or, as poets have since put it, the day he married Lady Poverty."

"It still seems unbelievable," said Clare, "even after all these years. You and the brothers have done so much to touch the consciences of people who clutch their money and land and possessions."

"I wish," said Francis, "that all people could know the freedom I experience. Jesus told his apostles to travel light. Perhaps I cannot expect everyone to do this, but at least I want my friars to be an example of this in the community."

FOR FURTHER READING

Bodo, Murray, O.F.M., and Susan Saint Sing. *A Retreat With Francis and Clare of Assisi.* Cincinnati: St. Anthony Messenger Press, 1996.

Chesterton, G. K. *St. Francis of Assisi.* New York: Doubleday Image Books, 1957.

_____. *St. Thomas Aquinas.* Kansas City, Mo.: Sheed and Ward, 1933.

Monshau, Michael. *Praying With Dominic.* Winona, Minn.: St. Mary's Press, 1993.

VIDEO

Brother Felix and the Virgin Saint. Films for the Humanities (75 minutes).

Castle. Unicorn Products (60 minutes).

The Sleep of Reason. Films for the Humanities (53 minutes).

▼ ▬▬▬▬▬▬▬▬▬▬

FOR BACKGROUND

Shortly after its founding in 1209 the Franciscan Order was divided over how closely Francis' guidelines concerning poverty should be followed. This eventually led to the formation of three separate Franciscan bodies.

Observants (O.F.M.). In the early fourteenth century, decline in religious life and observance led many friars to call for a return to a stricter observance of the rule. Due to associations with the heretical Franciscan Spiritualist movement, however, these aspirations were suppressed. But the reform would not die, and at the Council of Constance in 1414 they were granted Church recognition and the right to pick their own vicar-general. Efforts for reunion with the Conventuals failed and in 1517 they separated to carry out a ministry that tended to be itinerant in nature.

Conventuals (O.F.M. Conv.). Due to the rapid growth of the order, with its pressing needs for houses of study and other necessities for the exercise of ministry, one group of friars petitioned Rome for a declaration concerning the obligation of poverty. In 1230, Pope Gregory IX declared the right of the friars to possess property in common under the ownership of the Holy See. Shortly thereafter the churches under their guidance were identified as conventual churches (hence the name) in contrast to collegiate and parish churches. After Trent, the Conventuals were allowed to own property in the name of the order as distinct from the Holy See. They officially broke with the Observants in 1517 by decision of Leo X and were seen as living out a more moderate expression of Francis' ideals.

Clare replied, "As you know, Francis, there is already a movement among the friars away from your ideal. They admire your ideal, but they say it is now impractical."

"Society itself," said Luke, "does not seem as willing to support you as it did in the early days. I've heard people argue that they could put up with a dozen people like you, Francis. But a thousand of you is a different matter. How will we all survive by only begging for the day?"

This topic always visibly annoyed Francis. Losing his usual calm, he paced angrily back and forth on the brick pavement. He saw change coming and he didn't like it.

Only the day before he had fought with Cardinal Ugolino, the official protector of his order, over the prelate's solution to the problem. Great sums of money were beginning to pour into the friars' treasury. Ugolino said the Church would assume the ownership of the money. The friars would have the custody of it.

This meant the end of the life of simplicity that Francis insisted should be the ideal. But the Ugolino proposal did win the day, thus changing the vision that Francis wanted to keep alive in the Church.

"You have no idea," said Francis to his friends, "how critical evangelical poverty is for curbing greed in the people and in the Church. An economic investment leads to an emotional investment. Then one mixes with the other until nothing can be clearly seen. I still say with my Lord and Master, 'Travel light!'"

Clare was in perfect sympathy with Francis. Knowing how disappointing the Ugolino decision was to Francis, she tried to cheer him up by directing the conversation to another aspect of poverty.

"Francis," she said, "you have found the way of poverty to be a source of great happiness to yourself, but I notice you have no dislike of the world."

"For me, Clare, that's the proper way to feel about poverty. Those who followed the Cynic philosophy practiced poverty, but in such a tight way. They decided not to own anything, so that they could never feel bad if what they possessed were taken away."

"That's playing games. That's based on a suspicion about other people. It says in advance that people can't be trusted. I wasn't interested in a peace of mind produced by that kind of poverty."

"But then there is the special kind of poverty practiced by the early Christians," said Luke, "in which they toughened themselves up for martyrdom. Had that any appeal to you. Francis? Did you think of the discipline of poverty as a means to fight off evil temptations?"

"No, Luke, that never entered my mind. Ever since I was a boy, I've passionately loved this world and all its people. Inside me, I knew my love affair with the world would flower when I was freed from any clutching after it. I could exult in the birds of the air, the sun in the heavens, the lilies of the field and the people of the land only when I could lay no special claim to any of them."

Luke went on to say, "Francis, do you believe that everyone could follow your ideal?"

"I wouldn't be human, Luke, if I didn't want everyone to embrace evangelical poverty, because I want everybody to have the happiness and peace it has brought me.

"This has caused conflict for me. First with my father and now with the brotherhood. I have been reconciled to my father. I must learn to accept the path the friars wish to walk. Obviously not everyone can espouse Lady Poverty. For those who can, something beautiful is gained both for themselves and for the world."

"I see the poetry in your message," said Clare, "but I sense you also have a very practical reason in mind."

"The immensely practical result," said Francis, "is that the Church will not forget its mission to the poor. If the Church should become wrapped up in economic investments, it would have little time for the poor and be blind to their needs.

"The very money it collects would be used to perpetuate the Church instead of being used to raise all to their human dignity. I want Franciscan poverty to keep the social conscience of the Church alive."

With an amen to these words of Francis, Clare bade good night. Each went to sleep that evening pondering the message of Francis—wondering indeed how well the Christian people would be able to sustain his vision.

Capuchins (O.F.M. Cap.). This reform movement began in Italy in 1525 when the Observant friar Matteo da Bascio received permission from Pope Clement VII to follow the rule "to the letter." They were allowed to wear beards and adopted a habit with the long, pointed hood. They became so identified with this particular hood that they were called *capuccino* by the children in the streets; hence their name, Capuchin. Though esteemed for their work in social welfare and charity, they tended to emphasize a contemplative way of life.

Thomas: At the University of Paris
(c. 1292)

"Pardon me, sir," said Eric, a touring merchant from Norway, "but could you direct me to the university?"

"Yes," replied Reginald, secretary to Professor Thomas Aquinas. "I happen to be going that way myself. Are you a stranger in town?"

"I'm from Norway, and am here on business. I've always been fascinated by stories about the universities, and now I'd like a firsthand look."

"In that case," said Reginald, "I'd be happy to answer any of your questions and give you a short tour of the campus."

"I understand," said Eric, "that relations between town and gown have improved since the student riots a year ago."

"We can thank Pope Gregory the Ninth for that," replied Reginald. "For almost a decade, the students were griping about the high cost of food and board. They rightly complained about garbage in the streets and the low quality of wine in the taverns. On the other hand, the citizens of

FOR BACKGROUND

One of the greatest events in the course of Christian history was Thomas' writing of the *Summa Theologica*. This theological work, used now by Catholic and Protestant scholars alike, continues to be influential even seven hundred years after its publication. The *Summa* was never fully completed, however. Three months before his death, Thomas had a mystical experience after which he said, "All that I have hitherto written seems to me nothing but straw compared to what has been revealed to me." Thomas wrote no more before his death in 1274.

We must love them both, those whose opinions we share and those whose opinions we reject. For both have labored in the search for truth, and both have helped us in finding it.

—Thomas Aquinas

Paris resented the proud and scornful airs of the professors and students."

"What was the riot like?" asked Eric.

"It went pretty far," said Reginald, "with both sides using swords, clubs, boiling water, bows and arrows, and pails of slop thrown from the windows. Several students were killed. This so shocked the teachers that they appealed to the papal legate for help. At first nothing happened, so the students and professors left town. It was the equivalent of their going on strike."

"That must have been when the pope stepped in," said Eric.

"The pope did intervene at that point," said Reginald, "by issuing a charter to the university that gave it the right to manage its own affairs, to determine rents and to suspend classes whenever the town harassed them."

"As a businessman I can appreciate that," said Eric, "for in leaving the city, the students deprive the storekeepers of lots of revenue."

The two of them were now at the campus, which was a series of Gothic-like quadrangles. The atmosphere was full of lively and youthful expectancy.

"Tell me what an average day is like for the students," said Eric.

"They get up at five in the morning for Mass," said Reginald. "Classes begin about six and last until ten, when they have breakfast. Classes resume again until five, when they pause for supper. Then they review their notes until about nine, when they go for a walk, after which they go to bed."

"What is the teaching like?" asked Eric.

"It's changed a good deal since I was a student," said Reginald. "In my day, we studied the 'authorities' such as the Church Fathers. Our teachers handed on the traditional information. We never presumed to question or contradict the material."

"Who brought about a change?" inquired Eric.

"The man mostly responsible," said Reginald, "was the celebrated teacher, Abelard. He wrote a book called *Yes and No* in which he presented one hunded fifty-eight questions about religion and gave conflicting answers from the Bible and the Fathers."

"I've read about Abelard," said Eric. "I believe he said, 'The first key to wisdom is frequent questioning. By doubting we come to inquiry, and by inquiry to the truth.'"

"That wasn't too popular an idea at first," said Reginald. "Eventually he got into trouble, but his ideas about learning lived on and developed into the method of disputation that is used now."

"So now the students learn by debating the text readings through the question and answer approach," said Eric. "This must produce wars of logic."

"The disputation is like a tournament," said Reginald. "The students take sides with their favorite debaters and cheer and stomp and whistle. All agree, however, that it is training these young people to think."

"My goodness, that's an odd-looking professor," said Eric.

"That's Roger Bacon," replied Reginald. "He's our scientist. His most recent invention is a pair of glasses for reading. At first people wouldn't use them because they thought it was a devil's trick. They didn't want something between themselves and reality."

"Who is that very old professor lecturing in the Great Hall?" asked Eric.

"You are looking at the eighty-four-year-old German Dominican, Albert the Great," said Reginald. "He came here from Cologne to defend the teachings of his former student—and my master—Professor Thomas Aquinas."

"Someone told me," said Eric, "that Aquinas is the most radical professor this university has ever known."

"He's a mild man for such a title," replied Reginald, "but it's very true. I know the Bishop of Paris and the Archbishop of Canterbury believe that Thomas is a heretic. It's easy to see why when you hear him going against the eight-century-old tradition set by Saint Augustine. Augustine said that all necessary knowledge comes by revelation from God and that purity of heart is more important than clearness of mind. Still, in spite of the disagreement, Thomas owes a great deal to Augustine and acknowledges him a master."

"But that doesn't leave much room for the work of reason," said Eric. "If God gave us a mind, doesn't he expect us to use it? I know it's important to be a virtuous man, but I tend to beware of the unthinking man."

"Just what Thomas would say," replied Reginald. "Thomas took the logic of Aristotle and applied it to morality, dogma, politics and psychology. People fail yet to see that Thomas is not denying that important truths are in revelation, but he asks us to have an equally healthy respect for human intelligence and its workings. Furthermore, he is not opposed to the life of virtue. I think he is the holiest man in Christendom."

Reginald led Eric into a broad-ceilinged room where Thomas Aquinas was conducting a lively exchange between himself and his students.

"Master Aquinas, what is the cause of love?"

"There are many causes, my friend, but I believe they can be reduced to these three—knowledge, goodness and likeness. A blind man cannot enjoy the beauty of spring flowers for he can't see them. A deaf person fails to appreciate the melodies of great music for he can't hear them. It is the same with love. You must know a person in order really to love.

"Goodness, too, is important. This is another way of talking about the magnetic attraction lovers have for each other. The lover is drawn to the beloved by the powerful goodness and beauty that is sensed.

"Lastly, likeness produces love. Lovers must have something in common. Birds of a feather flock together. Knights and stonecutters join different guilds since they

FOR DISCUSSION/REFLECTION

A brilliant tenured professor at a midwestern Catholic college is teaching that the opinions of theologians are to be considered equal in weight to the teachings of the pope and bishops. A group of rich donors have warned the president to stop the professor: Silence him or remove him somehow. If not, they will withdraw pledges of several million dollars to the capital fund campaign. Should the professor be allowed his freedom of expression? Should the board try to silence or fire him? Is the intervention of rich donors a form of blackmail?

The editors of a student newspaper at a northeastern Catholic college have taken an extreme right-wing position on political and moral issues. They have angered a number of people not only with their positions, but also because they have made pointed personal attacks on certain faculty members and other students. Are they acting within the bounds of academic freedom and freedom of the press? If you disagreed with their approach, what would you do about it? What moral principle(s) would you invoke in this case?

FOR BACKGROUND

On August 4, 1879, Pope Leo XIII issued the encyclical *Aeterni Patris*, which sought to "restore scholastic philosophy in general and that of Saint Thomas Aquinas in particular." Using Saint Thomas Aquinas as its guide, the encyclical said: "Those therefore are the best philosophers who combine the pursuit of philosophy with dutiful obedience to the Catholic faith, for the splendor of the divine truths irradiating the soul is a help to the intelligence; it does not deprive it of the least degree of its dignity, but even brings it an increase of nobility, acuteness and strength." Thomas' harmony of faith and reason as presented in his *Summa Theologica* was now a model for seminaries throughout the Church. Thus a man who at one time had been accused of heresy now became the model theologian-philosopher for the Church to imitate.

The Catholic Church sponsored the growth of medieval universities such as those at Paris, Oxford, Cambridge and Padua. From the very beginning, as in the case of Thomas Aquinas, academic freedom produced tensions. How much dissent can be allowed in a Catholic institution of higher learning? Here are some case studies to help you reflect on this matter:

have different interests. Lovers find each other through a common interest."

"What, then, is the result of such love?"

"As every true lover knows, ecstasy is the greatest effect. Those who really love can know the greatest happiness that is possible here on earth."

"Why do lovers talk so much?"

"That is because they want to live in each other's minds. Hence, hand in hand they walk under the chestnut trees, pouring out the secrets of their hearts to each other."

"Aren't lovers too possessive?"

"Those really in love naturally want to possess each other's hearts. God says in the Bible, 'My son, give me your whole heart.' That is why the girl may say to her boy, 'Tell me how much you love me! Tell me again a thousand times!'"

"Does this explain why they want to be with each other so much?"

"Of course. Love demands presence. Even when they are parted for one reason or another, the lovers remain bound to each other in affection and thought."

Eric and Reginald withdrew at this point and went toward The Lion and the Arrow for lunch.

"So that is your master," said Eric. "He speaks with such warmth, intelligence and gentleness that I wonder why anyone would oppose him."

"It's like everything else in life," said Reginald. "So much prejudice and misunderstanding is based, even as Thomas said, on not knowing the person. Those who really know Thomas as I do can't fail to love him."

With that they ordered strawberries and wine to eat and drink in honor of the great Christian University of Paris and its most honored professor, Thomas Aquinas.

Friars—Looking Back

Saint Francis of Assisi

1181 Giovanni Francesco Bernardone was born at Assisi. His father was a wealthy textile merchant and his mother was a member of a distinguished French family. He was called Francis ("the Frenchman") because of his love of French clothing and life-style. Francis' youth was marked by a general spirit of worldliness; his wealth and love of life made him a leader among the youth of Assisi.

1202-1203 Francis participated in the inter-city feud between Assisi and Perugia and was imprisoned for a time. He became gravely ill and subjected himself for the first time to serious self-analysis.

1205-1206 Francis renounced his worldly possessions to embrace a life of poverty. Although a layman, he began to preach to the townspeople; after this, his first followers joined him. Francis composed his first rule, which made the gospel his way of life.

1209 When Francis and his followers numbered twelve, they went to Rome and obtained the approval of Pope Innocent III for the rule.

1212 Francis reactivated the missionary activity of the Church and undertook a missionary journey to Syria.

1221 The rule of Francis' order, which had developed without much direction, was revised and promulgated. Francis devoted himself to the spiritual growth of his order. He preached throughout the countryside, but repeatedly interrupted his activity to retreat to a solitary hermitage.

1224 Francis received the stigmata on September 14.

1226 Francis died at Assisi.

The early rule of Saint Francis, which has not survived, set as its aim "to follow the teachings of Our Lord Jesus Christ and to walk in his footsteps." Probably no one in history set himself so seriously as Francis did to imitate the life of Christ and to carry out so literally Christ's work in Christ's own way. This is the key to the character and spirit of Francis. He was a lover of nature, a social worker, an itinerant preacher, a lover of poverty. Perhaps Francis is most widely recognized, however, for the deep sense of brotherhood he felt with all of God's creatures.

The Medieval University

The medieval university was a special creation of the Christians of the Middle Ages. Ancient Greece had a respect for education and founded academies for learning, but these were never as ambitious as the university turned out to be. The word *university* originally applied to any official grouping of people in medieval times. Eventually, it was applied directly to the educational enterprise itself.

Items stressed in the episode:

1) Student unrest was common. Records of battles between "town and gown" are a recurrent theme throughout history.

2) A papal charter was the medieval method of gaining academic freedom for the university. Generally, it was the city fathers who wanted to coerce and suppress freedom at the university. It was the Church who threw a protective mantle over the campus.

3) Educational methods changed. In the early stage the main emphasis was on quoting authorities to explain a point. Hence, one would teach the meaning of the Incarnation by showing how great Church authorities talked about it, quoting from Augustine, Ambrose, Chrysostom, Origen

FOR DISCUSSION/REFLECTION

When approaching Francis, how can we get beyond the legendary and romantic, almost tame person and truly discover his radicalism? Where does Francis challenge us, the Church, and society today?

Thinking that scholarship and learning would tempt one to substitute knowledge about God for knowing God, Francis discouraged his friars from such pursuits. Would you consider this a valuable warning or a display of anti-intellectualism?

Francis lived a life of absolute poverty and said that when his friars went into the world they were "to carry nothing for the journey, neither sack, nor scrip, nor bread; neither money, nor staff." Is this way of life possible or must compromise be made today? Where does Francis' love of poverty and simplicity fit into our consumer-oriented technological society?

It has been said that no one in history has imitated the life of Christ more closely than Francis. Do you agree? Why or why not?

and similar people. To a great extent, the feeling was that these authorities had pretty much said all there was to say on the topic. Hence, it was the job of the student to master the thought of the authorities, organize it in his own mind, present it in turn to the rest of the class.

But with the rise of the scholastics, especially Abelard, Bonaventure, Thomas Aquinas and Duns Scotus, the method changed from lecture and authority-quoting to disputation. This was somewhat like a debate, calling for maximum student involvement and the rigorous use of logic and careful research. The authorities were still quoted, not slavishly, but in a critical sense to make sure they were understood in a contemporary light. Other elements were also brought into play, such as the philosophy of Aristotle, the scientific style of Albert the Great and the special cultural elements of medieval times.

In terms of modern educational theory, it was a shift in emphasis from the lecture system to participational learning. This doesn't mean that lectures were ruled out, but they were no longer the sole basis for learning.

4) Aquinas was a radical, and was believed to be a heretic. This is all the more ironic when we observe that he is the favored theologian of today's conservatives.

5) Aquinas taught that reason was friendly to revelation and that common sense was as important as virtue.

The parallels between thirteenth- and twentieth-century universities are evident: Young people in universities have been perennially rebellious. Universities enjoy their academic freedom today as much as they did in medieval times. We are still moving from "authorities" to "disputation."

Francis was known to practice a common devotional exercise of the Middle Ages: meditating on a skull. The purpose was to bring people concretely and vividly to the realization of mortality as well as to remind them of the death of Christ at Golgotha, "Place of the Skull." In correspondence with others Francis was even known to embellish letters with drawings of skulls.

Reverence the Environment, Serve and Love the Poor—Connecting to Our Times

Saint Francis of Assisi celebrated nature, ministered to the poor and probed the depths of the prayer of simplicity. For those who were migrating to the new medieval cities, he reminded them to stay in touch with the beauty of creation. For rich merchants who built fine homes behind city walls, he urged them to reach out and help the naked and the starving marooned outside those fortresses. For all busy Christians he modeled the need for meditative prayer and inspired them with poetry such as "The Canticle of Brother Sun."

The Lord has called me into the way of simplicity and humility, and he has indeed made this known through me and through all who choose to believe me and follow me. So I prefer you not to talk to me about any other Rule, whether St. Benedict's or St. Augustine's or St. Bernard's, nor recommend any other ideal or manner of life than that which the Lord in his mercy has revealed and given to me. He told me I am to be a new kind of fool in this world.
—Francis of Assisi

14. Crusades

Holy War: A Sad History
(1096-1270)

Holy wars are the most frightful of all wars. A holy war means that the people think God desires it; hence they bring all the ferocity of religious conviction to the fight. War is hell enough as it is, but when religious fervor is added, it is super-hell.

There had always been plenty of ordinary war between Christians. And the medieval Church attempted to reduce the brutality of these "unholy" wars by enforcing the Truce of God and the Peace of God. The Truce of God allowed no fighting to take place from Wednesday evening to Monday morning—or on holy days. Since there were so many holy days, combat would be at best an occasional sport. The Peace of God limited the extent of combat by forbidding attacks on merchants, farmers, nuns, pilgrims, priests, or on the animals and properties belonging to these people.

Knights and princes were urged to come forward and vow to keep these rules. They piously took the vows—and just as religiously broke them. The bishops raised armies to punish the princes for breaking their vows. Then the kings raised armies to stop the bishops.

The Council of Clermont in 1095 brought a stop to this "unholy feuding" and enlisted the efforts of all sides against a new enemy in a "holy" war. A plea for help had come from the Emperor Alexius at Constantinople. For almost a century, the East had been fighting off Asiatic invaders whom the Byzantines called *Sarakenos*, "Easterners." (The word *Saracen* came to mean any barbaric and fanatical fighters.) The latest invasion of the "Easterners-Sarakenos" was that of the Seljuk Turks, who occupied a good deal of Asia Minor and were threatening Constantinople itself.

'God Wills It'

Pope Urban II used the Council of Clermont as the setting for a speech that would bring about the first Crusade. The scene was decked out with the full forces of Church pageantry—cardinals, bishops and noblemen with all the trappings of early medieval color and pomp. A vast crowd of people awaited the pope's talk. We have no accurate record of what the pope said that day, but whatever it was, he so excited the people that they cried out: *"Deus vult! Deus vult!"*—God wills it! And the holy wars began.

For the duration of the Crusades, Christians ignored Augustine's idea of a just war. Augustine had said that wars may be fought for the cause of justice, but now war was

FOR BACKGROUND

Knights Hospitalers (Knights of St. John): Founded in 1113 for the care of sick pilgrims in the Holy Land, they originally engaged in actual nursing. In 1118 they added defense of the "holy places" to their duties and thereafter became primarily a military order.

Order of Knights Templar: Founded in 1118 to protect pilgrims coming from Europe and to defend the Christian conquests in the East, these soldier-monks had few applicants until Bernard made them known and admired throughout Europe by writing a rule for them at the request of the Council of Troyes. For the remainder of the Crusades, their ever-increasing number, power and wealth were the mainstay of the holy war. Because these characteristics aroused so much political and ecclesiastical opposition, Pope Clement V ordered their dissolution at the Council of Vienna in 1311.

FOR DISCUSSION/REFLECTION

Some historians argue that the Crusades were justified by medieval people on three grounds: The infidel Muslims should be driven out of Christian lands such as Spain; Christians, not Muslims, should be in charge of the holy places in Palestine; new land needed for a growing population was being acquired through conquest of lands held by the infidels.

How could Christians have drifted so far from Christ's teachings on peace and love, doing good to enemies, not living by the sword, loving one another?

Did the crusaders act as Pope Urban II and others instructed them to? Was the object to loot cities and try to gain personal power? Were the intentions of the crusaders good or evil?

In today's world would such an undertaking be possible? Are people more or less zealous than in the Middle Ages?

We are impressed and engaged to fight/To chase those pagans in those holy fields/Over whose acres walked those blessed feet/Which fourteen hundred years ago were nailed/For our advantage on the bitter cross.
—Shakespeare, Henry IV

being fought for the cause of faith. Augustine also said that the state should manage wars; but now the Church was sharing this responsibility. Ordinarily, the soldier is obedient to his prince, but now he marched in obedience to the cross.

The just war code insisted that we trust the good faith of the enemy and show special care for the civilian population. The Crusaders decided that these norms did not apply to the infidel. They found justification for their theory of holy war in the biblical account of Joshua's conquest of Canaan.

The immediate advantage of the Crusades was that they brought to an end the bickering among Christians and focused their hostility on a common enemy outside themselves. Further, it brought about the widespread sense of unity, fervor and idealism that would be captured by the word *Christendom*.

The Crusades began in 1096 with an unofficial phase known as the "People's Crusade." Fired up by the hypnotic, bearded, wild-eyed Peter the Hermit, nearly fifty thousand peasants surged out of Western Europe toward the East. It was a reckless and tragic venture.

Along the way these "crusaders" massacred communities of Jews and ravaged the rich farms of people they considered heathens in the Balkans. Those attacked fought back by slaying the peasants at night as they slept by their campfires and by poisoning the wells ahead of the crusaders with dead sheep.

Not many of the original fifty thousand were left by the time they arrived at Constantinople. The Emperor Alexius saw the ragged survivors as a potential threat. He shipped them over to the Turks, who promptly slaughtered them all.

The official "Crusade of the Princes," however, was a resounding success. The backbone of their expeditionary forces were the Normans, who still had the courage and cunning of their Viking forebears in their blood; and they were fresh from victories over England and Sicily.

Within two years the Crusaders captured Asia Minor and the important cities of Edessa, Antioch, Tripoli and— best of all—Jerusalem. Covered with blood, they sang in jubilation as they entered the Holy City and knelt in ecstasy before the tomb of Christ.

What was the result? The Crusaders set up four Christian states collectively known as Outremer—the land "beyond the seas." The four states centered around Edessa, Antioch, Tripoli and Jerusalem. Basically, Outremer was a string of fortresses that stretched along the Mediterranean coastline.

Outremer lasted for two hundred years and maintained the Christian presence in the Mideast. Italian ports such as Genoa kept the supplies coming. Two new religious orders, the Knights Templar and the Knights Hospitaler, defended the forts.

Seven more Crusades were to follow this first one, but none could quite match it. Romantic literature has dwelt on the Third Crusade (1189-92), when Frederick Barbarossa, Philip Augustus and Richard the Lion-hearted set out to fight the great Saladin. It was a massive confrontation, but the Crusaders failed. Frederick drowned, Philip went home and Richard signed a treaty that reduced Christian holdings to a strip of coastland.

The two children's Crusades were the saddest. Twelve-year-old Stephen of Cloyes, claiming he had a vision from Christ to free the Holy Land, persuaded thirty thousand French children to follow him. They marched to Marseilles, expecting the Mediterranean to open for them as the Red Sea did for Moses. Instead, slave traders took them and sold them to the Muslims. Germany produced its own version with twenty thousand children who marched to Italy. It also ended in failure.

The Results

Culturally, the Crusades proved an enrichment for the West. Persian carpets, real mirrors, glassmaking techniques, silks, sugar and spices were among the numerous benefits of contact with the East.

In religious terms, the Crusades accelerated the worsening relations between the Eastern and Western Church. The emperor Alexius and the Crusaders quarreled over control of the reconquered city of Antioch. The Crusaders made the awful error of expelling the Greek Patriarch in Antioch and putting a Latin one in his place.

FOR DISCUSSION/REFLECTION

All recent popes have denounced any intention to wage nuclear war. The American bishops have echoed this teaching and called for arms reduction and a freeze on nuclear buildups. Is it right to have a nuclear deterrent so as to deal from strength in arms limitation talks? Is it right to possess nuclear arms so long as we have no intention to use them even if nuclear attack is launched against our country?

Is forcing conversion on people a reasonable way to salvation? Do you think it would be justifiable to baptize people who do not really understand Christianity? In the same sense, were the crusades a "moral failure"?

Do we suffer from a cultural arrogance in this country? Because we feel our way of life is superior to others, do we have the right to force our way of life on others? Should we be respectful of the cultures of other countries?

Is war or any type of violence the answer to problems or does it cause problems of its own? Are nuclear weapons necessary? Should our tax money be used elsewhere? Are there any clear-cut answers?

The sack of Constantinople in 1204 by a Crusader army was the worst affront of all. The soldiers tore down the tapestries in St. Sophia cathedral, ripped apart the silver iconostasis (altar screen) and divided it as booty. They placed a prostitute on the patriarch's throne and toasted her with altar wine in stolen chalices. They installed a Latin patriarch and emperor. Cordial relations were virtually impossible after such a desecration.

Historically, the Crusades mark a bloody page in the story of a violent time. They remind us that holy war is a perversion of God's will and a disgrace to Christian moral behavior. The Crusades should teach us that holy wars have no place in Christianity; they are anti-Christian in theory, practice and outcome.

THE RISE OF ISLAM

The Crusades were to free the Holy Land from the grip of the Muslims, the so-called infidels. Islam had its origins in the early seventh century with the Prophet Mohammed (570-632) and the revelation of the *Quran*, the sacred scripture of Islam, from the angel Gabriel. Mohammed saw it as his mission to restore monotheism to the peoples of Arabia. From about 610 forward, Mohammed proclaimed the message of Islam (Arabic for "submission to the will of God").

Finding little success in Mecca, Mohammed took refuge in Medina, founding the first Moslem city where religious and civil life were combined according to the principles of Islam. Shortly after this he and his followers set out on a military and political campaign through which they gained Mecca. By the time of Mohammed's death in 632, a major part of Arabia was in the control of Muslims. In steady succession the ancient centers of Eastern Christianity fell: Damascus (635), Jerusalem (638), Alexandria (642) and Carthage (695). Many people, having lived through so much intra-Christian hostility, saw the Muslims not as oppressors but as liberators and converted to this new faith. Muslim advance in Spain was halted only in 732, when Charles Martel defeated them at the battle of Tours. Constantinople was constantly under attack, yet withstood the pressure until its fall in 1453.

Thus, from the seventh century on Europe was effectively cut off from the East. The Mediterranean was a Muslim sea. For the next five hundred years Europe and Christianity would be threatened by the Muslims.

Crusades—Looking Back

In our own time we have known the horrors of ideological war, as in the case of the Nazis. Ideological war is a secular version of holy war. The Bible described holy war in the Book of Joshua, where the Israelites were instructed by God to wipe out the enemy completely, letting no man, woman, child, animal or piece of treasure survive the biblical equivalent of an atomic holocaust. Some of us may shudder at the prospect of holy war, but it has an uncanny way of surviving.

The Crusades were holy wars in the unabashed raw. Popes, bishops, mystics and saints gave wholehearted support to the enterprise and fired up thousands of people to embark on war against the infidels.

The material in this section has been presented in historical narrative form rather than as a fictionalized account. It raises again the question of the Church and war, and highlights the paradoxes of Church behavior. The Abbey of Cluny had attempted to lower the temperature of wars between Christians by vigorously promoting and supporting the Truce of God and the Peace of God, which had been initiated by regional councils of bishops and nobles. Yet at Clermont, the Church unleashed a war machine that was as cruel and heartbreaking as ever known.

It is difficult—perhaps impossible—to render an adequate judgment on the Crusades. There is much that we can lament and condemn, especially the exploitation of children, the massacres of the Jews and the brutalities toward both Eastern Christians and the Muslims. Centuries later, we wonder how religion could have gotten mixed up in all of this.

Yet, even in our own time, campaigns against the enemy sometimes assume a religious quality and thus become a kind of holy war. At the same time, every modern pope has strenuously spoken out against war and for peace.

Even though this account of the Crusades definitely

deglamorizes expeditionary forces or crusading armies, it is not meant to take either a dove or a hawk position on war. Christ had a friendly relationship with army men: He cured a soldier's boy; a soldier was apparently the first one to call Jesus "Son of God" at the crucifixion; the Church uses a soldier's prayer, "Lord, I am not worthy," for the Communion service. The main purpose here is to urge the review of issues of war and peace in a thoughtful way.

Peace Movement During the Crusades

Toward the end of the thirteenth century, a new attitude toward the Crusades appeared in war-weary Europe. Ramon Lull (1235—1315), Spanish preacher, prolific writer, mystic and practical politician, raised his voice throughout Europe and strongly urged that peaceful rather than warlike methods be used to achieve the goals of the Crusades. Educated preachers, he emphasized, would be more successful than armies in winning over Muslims. Although the constant, indefatigable efforts of Lull along these lines achieved little in his own day, he does represent a realization of the greater value of peaceful methods.

The Just War Theory in the Contemporary World

The theory of just war, beginning with Augustine and later developed by Catholic theologians such as Thomas Aquinas and Francis Suarez, required that certain conditions be met: The war must be declared only as a last resort, by a lawful authority, for a just cause, using just means and with reasonable expectation of success. The military action cannot produce a greater evil than it seeks to correct.

In applying an evolving just war theory to the contemporary world, persons sincerely trying to form their conscience must judge whether or not the end achieved by a particular war is proportionate to the devastation wrought by that war. On the basis of the judgment, they could justify either participation or abstention from war.

Some conclude that just war in the modern world is not possible, citing Pope John's statement in *Pacem in Terris*: "Therefore, in this age of ours which prides itself on its atomic power, it is irrational to believe that war is still an apt means of securing human rights."

Among those who accompanied Christian armies on the Fifth Crusade to Egypt in 1219 was Francis of Assisi. During the siege of Damietta he crossed enemy lines to preach to the Muslim sultan, Malik-al Kamil. Despite his great admiration for the Christian holy man, the sultan did not convert, but did allow Francis safe passage back to the crusaders' camp.

'Lord, Make Me a Channel of Your Peace'—Connecting to Our Times

Jesus said there will always be wars and rumors of war. But Jesus also urged us always to practice reconciliation and work for peace. Unhappily, the Church of the Middle Ages became embroiled in holy wars with many tragic consequences. On the positive side, Church leaders today advocate an unremitting search for peace. Human experience shows that it is harder to

I say it to those who are present. I command that it be said to those who are absent. Christ commands it. All who go thither and lose their lives, be it on the road or on the sea, or in the fight against the pagans, will be granted immediate forgiveness for their sins. This I grant to all who march, by virtue of the great gift which God has given me.
— **Pope Urban II**

FOR FURTHER READING

U.S. Bishops. *The Challenge of Peace: God's Promise and Our Response.* Washington, D.C.: United States Catholic Conference, 1983.

VIDEO

The Crusaders: Saints and Sinners. Brown-ROA (28 minutes).

make peace and relatively easy to make war. Too many people enjoy a fight.

Negotiation is better. President Kennedy got it right when he said, "We must never negotiate out of fear, but we must never fear to negotiate." The passions of anger, revenge and pride have driven the world of the twentieth century into the two greatest wars in history. President Reagan said, "We seek peace through strength." He meant military power. The popes teach that we should quest for peace through justice for all and the development of inner moral strength.

The wars on the battlefields and in the skies begin at home. The quarrels that rack families are breeding grounds for the arguments that tear nations apart. Too many people get used to fighting as a way to solve problems. They practice the love of power and not the power of love.

Jesus lifted no hand against his enemies. He told Peter to put his sword back in the scabbard. Jesus taught us to love our enemies and proceeded to practice what he taught. He told Pilate he could enlist "legions of angels" to protect him from the force of the state, but he declined to do so. He taught and practiced that witnessing truth and love are better ways to resolve human problems.

War is always terrible, whether it is fought with spears or with missiles. Mothers lose sons and daughters. Wives lose husbands and husbands lose wives. The killing fields are not pleasant places for strolls. They only look that way when the heat of battle is gone and the grass has regrown.

Yes, there will be wars and rumors of wars, but we should not resign ourselves to this condition. We should make peace in our families and nations a constant goal. Love is better than hate. Reconciliation is better than murderous anger. Peace is better than revenge.

15. The Great Schism

'Let Them Be Anathema'
(July 16, 1054)

On July 16, 1054, Michael Cerularius, Patriarch of Constantinople, stood before a bonfire with his assembled bishops. Into the fire he cast a parchment scroll. Solemnly he pronounced the excommunication of the papal legate who had deposited it in his cathedral the day before, along with "all who had helped in drawing it up, whether by their advice or even by their prayers." In that dramatic moment the final rupture between the Eastern and Western Churches occurred.

The quarrel which precipitated the rupture was the result of six hundred years of developing strain. When Cerularius became patriarch, he reminded his clergy of the issues which had long divided the East and the West—clerical celibacy, the use of unleavened bread for Eucharist, the wording of the Creed—and forbade his priests to follow the Latin Rite on pain of excommunication. In 1053 he closed all the churches in Constantinople which persisted in following Rome's directives.

Pope Leo IX immediately responded to that action with a strongly worded letter demanding that all patriarchs recognize papal supremacy and branding any congregation which refused such acknowledgment as "an assembly of heretics, a conventicle of schismatics, a synagogue of Satan." His ire vented, the pope then sent a delegation under the leadership of Cardinal Humbert to discuss the differences between the two Churches.

Humbert's approach was less than conciliatory. His legacy had not come, he insisted, "to listen and discuss, but to instruct the Greeks." The patriarch countered by challenging their competency to deal with the issues. In the midst of the stalemate Pope Leo died, and his successor would not be elected for a year. Three months after Leo's death, the frustrated and embittered Humbert decided to take matters into his own hands. The cardinal composed a bull excommunicating Cerularius and hurled it upon the altar of Hagia Sophia, the great sixth-century basilica in Constantinople. The scene was set for the patriarch's angry response—and for the division of Christendom.

FOR BACKGROUND

Besides the political and cultural differences that divided the Latin and Greek Churches, religious differences also added to the tensions which eventually broke in 1054. The most obvious concerned the Holy Spirit. Led by Photius, the patriarch of Constantinople, the Greeks severely criticized the Latins for tampering with the formula of faith as found in the Nicene Creed by adding *filioque*. The old Creed read that the Holy Spirit proceeds "from the Father" to which the Latins added "and from the Son."

This addition brought with it a subtle theological nuance in the understanding of the role of the Holy Spirit—one that the Greeks were unwilling to accept. The Latins were so familiar with the phrase they went so far as to accuse the Greeks of having cut the expression out.

Being unable to bear these unprecedented injuries and these outrages directed against the chief apostolic see...we sign against Michael and his supporters the anathema that our most reverend pope has pronounced against them if they do not return to their senses....
— **From the sentence of excommunication by Cardinal Humbert against Michael Cerularius**

In John Paul II's encyclical on ecumenism, *That They May Be One*, Catholics are reminded that they can look to other Christian bodies as sources of truth about the mystery of Christ and the Church. With this in mind, what can the Eastern and Protestant Churches teach the Roman Catholic Church? What have you learned from other Christian traditions besides your own?

One of the major pushes for Church union in the twentieth century began because of missionary experiences. In Africa and Asia efforts to gain converts were hampered because of competition and disputes between the various Christian groups. The scandal of Church disunity became very apparent. What might be some of the advantages (or disadvantages) if Christians coordinated their missionary efforts?

The *Decree on Ecumenism* states that "in order to restore communion and unity or preserve them, one must 'impose no burden beyond what is indispensable' (Acts 15:28)." How can Christian union allow for diversity without division? In this process, can the various identities of each Church be preserved or will one expression predominate?

The Great Schism—Looking Back

To some extent the division between the Eastern and Western Churches goes back to the directions each took after the fall of the Roman Empire in 476. The bishops of the Western Church filled the power vacuum (see Chapter 8) and provided the stability and continuity needed during the chaos of the barbarian invasions. The bishops acquired a good deal of political and economic power as a result. This led to the papal theocracies of the Middle Ages wherein popes exercised vast temporal as well as spiritual power.

In the East, where the government remained relatively stable for many centuries, the Church did not acquire political eminence as in the West. The Eastern Church, however, did develop a sophisticated liturgy, theology and spirituality. The Eastern Church's supremacy in these areas lasted for many centuries and fostered a sense of superiority in regard to the Western brothers and sisters. Not until the high Middle Ages, when universities like Paris and Oxford flourished, did Western theologians reach a competitive level. But by then the two Churches had drifted alarmingly apart and the Crusades had eroded whatever common ground one might have hoped for.

The major split between Eastern and Western Christianity described in this chapter's episode took place just before the Crusades began. But strains had developed over the centuries ever since Constantine had moved the capital of the empire to Constantinople in 330. Rome had retained its place as mother Church and primary seat of Christianity, but Eastern Christians found it increasingly difficult to submit to Roman rule in spiritual matters. Several times throughout these centuries the Church in Constantinople had tried to make itself independent of Rome. As political instability afflicted Europe and infected even the papacy in the early eleventh century, relations between East and West deteriorated even more. When Michael Cerularius became Patriarch of Constantinople the stage was already set for a break.

The two sides disagreed about questions of liturgy, theology and Church discipline; each felt the other held a foreign brand of Christianity. The patriarch's persecution of Constantinople's Latin Churches and the pope's angry response added fuel to the argument. The clash between the stubborn Cerularius and the hotheaded Humbert provided the final spark—and the name-calling in each writ of excommunication leaves no doubt that these two men were an incendiary combination.

Although the cardinal was later censured for his hasty action, Cerularius considered it sufficient excuse for the break from Rome his Church had long wanted. At first Rome ignored the Eastern Schism, dismissing it as a personal quarrel between patriarch and papal legate; only years later did the pope acknowledge that a split had indeed taken place and appoint a bishop for the Latin Churches in Constantinople.

Hopes of reconciliation between East and West plummeted in the thirteenth century when Crusaders plundered shrines and churches in Constantinople. The result of the Crusades was to confirm the separation in bitterness and hostility. Although attempts at reunion were made at the general councils of Lyons in 1274 and Florence in 1438, their success was short-lived. The Eastern Church remained separate, adopting the name *Orthodox* ("holding the correct faith").

Zealous missionary efforts achieved reconciliation between a few groups and Rome. These groups, called Uniate Christians, were for the most part allowed to keep their traditional rites and customs. Over four hundred years, six such groups expressed their allegiance to Rome: the Chaldean, Syrian, Maronite, Coptic, Armenian and Byzantine Rites. The vast majority of the East, however, remained within the Orthodox tradition.

The most dramatic step toward reconciliation since the schism occurred in our own century. In 1964 Pope Paul VI and Orthodox Patriarch Athenagoras met in the Holy Land and publicly embraced each other. In December of that year, they issued a solemn declaration expressing regret for the "offensive words...and reprehensible gestures" which marked the events of 1054 and removed the sentences of excommunication pronounced by Cerularius and Humbert as a first step in reopening the dialogue between East and West.

FOR FURTHER READING

Decree on Oriental Catholic Churches and *Decree on Ecumenism*, in *The Documents of Vatican II*, ed. Walter J. Abbott, S.J. New York: Herder and Herder, 1966.

VIDEO

Byzantium: From Splendor to Ruin. Films for the Humanities (52 minutes).

The Greek Orthodox Church. Films for the Humanities (30 minutes).

Orient/Occident. Films for the Humanities (30 minutes).

FOR DISCUSSION/REFLECTION

Vatican II's *Degree on Ecumenism* refers to the division of Christianity as a rending which has "damaged the seamless robe of Christ" (#13). It affirms the richness of Eastern liturgy and spiritual traditions, and acknowledges the debt owed by the West for theological insights first formulated in the East.

Does the division of Christianity worry you at all? What do you think it does to the effective preaching of the gospel in today's world? What skills or insights were lost to each side in the schism?

The practice of celibacy differs between the Churches of the East and West. In the Eastern Churches bishops are required to be celibate and are usually drawn from the ranks of monks. Their priests may marry once, and must do so before ordination. In the Western Church, celibacy is mandated for bishops and priests. Vatican II teaches: "There are many ways in which celibacy is in harmony with the priesthood. For the whole mission of the priest is dedicated to the service of the new humanity which Christ raises up through the Spirit" (*Life of Priests*, #16).

Uniate Christians maintain Eastern traditions in liturgy and discipline while acknowledging the primacy of the pope. How much room is there in the Church for such diversity?

Learning More About the Eastern Church— Connecting to Our Times

Pope John Paul II has frequently said, "The Church must breathe with two lungs, the East and the West." He is referring to the two main segments of the Catholic Church, the Latin Church of the West and the various communities of the Eastern Church, such as that of the Byzantine Rite. In a special way he is thinking of the Orthodox Churches, with whom he feels a special empathy. He hopes and prays for reunion with them.

With the end of the Cold War it was hoped that significant progress might be made toward reunion with the Orthodox Churches. Since the majority of their membership—except for Greek Orthodox—is in former Iron Curtain countries such as Russia, Ukraine, Rumania and Bulgaria, their energies have been directed more to recovering after years of tyranny than to ecumenical endeavors.

The Russian Orthodox Church, in particular, feels besieged and threatened both by fundamentalist Protestant missionaries and the rebuilding of Latin Rite Catholic life in that country. In Ukraine there is tension between the Orthodox and the Uniate Catholics (Eastern Rite Catholics in union with Rome). The Catholics want returned the thousands of churches taken from them by Stalin and given to the Orthodox. These problems will not be settled quickly or easily. Still, the faith-filled quest for unity must continue.

In the United States there are many Catholic Uniate as well as Orthodox parishes. We should vigorously pursue ecumenical dialogue with the Orthodox. We should also become familiar with the liturgy and approach to doctrine of the Uniate Churches. Their approach to worship stresses the divine and transcendent mystery of God. We have much to learn from them, for they can enrich our own approach to liturgy and catechesis. We must also pray to the Holy Spirit, who is living and active in Uniate, Latin Catholic and Orthodox Churches, that a loving unity may be achieved.

16. Heretics

The Church has always been active, not only in expressing religious truth but also in protecting against error in religious matters. The regulations below from the Synod of Toulouse show how tragically caught up the Church has been, in certain times and places, in the fear of heresy. But the adaptation of the Vatican II statement on religious freedom that follows shows the balanced view the modern Church takes with regard to persons' rights to believe as they see fit.

Regulations of the Synod of Toulouse
(1299)

Whoever allows a heretic to stay on his property either for money or any other cause, if he confesses or is convicted, loses his property forever and his body is handed over to the civil authority for punishment.

He is also subject to legal punishment whose property, without his knowledge but by negligence, has become the abode of heretics.

The house where a heretic is found must be torn down and the property must be confiscated.

The sheriff who lives in a suspicious place and is not diligent in searching for heretics loses his job—and is not permitted to be employed either there or in any other place.

If anyone who is tainted with heresy freely gives up the heresy, he is not allowed to live in the house where he formerly lived in case the house is under suspicion of heresy. He must move to a Catholic house which is free from suspicion. Besides he must wear two crosses on his coat, one on the right and the other on the left, and of a different color from his coat. Such persons cannot hold public office or be admitted to legal actions unless they are fully reinstalled after due penance by the pope or his legate.

Males and females who have attained the use of reason must confess their sins to a priest three times a year or, with their priest's permission, to another priest. They must perform the imposed penances humbly and according to their strength. They must receive the Eucharist three times a year. *Whoever does not do this is under suspicion of being a heretic.*

Laypeople are not permitted to possess the books of the Old and New Testament. But they can possess the Psalter,

FOR DISCUSSION/REFLECTION

Holy wars were one dark moment in our Church history; the torture and persecution of heretics is another blotch on our past. Inquisitors, or heretic hunters, were quite willing to torment their victims. They burnt their feet, snapped their muscles with tight ropes and choked them with force-fed water. Like an early form of the KGB, inquisitors created vigilante committees of informers who terrorized their neighbors with fear of being named a heretic. Heretics and their families were denied civil and human rights.

Heretics have often been called the "pioneers" of the faith in that they attempt to explain the truths of Christianity in new ways. Would you see them as having a positive benefit for the Church?

Today we live in a world of plurality where individual rights and liberties are cherished. Unable to use the coercive methods of the past (which in the end were ineffective), how can the Church preserve right belief or orthodoxy and yet respect the freedom of its members? How would you deal with those who deviate from Christian teachings?

In our world today, can the word *heretic* even be used? Is it an effective way of calling attention to those individuals, groups or practices which are at odds with traditional Christian teachings?

Given that heresies so often reappear in new forms, what role might religious education provide in combatting them?

the breviary and the little office of the Blessed Virgin—but not in the vernacular.

Women who own castles and fortresses are not permitted to marry enemies of the faith and peace.

Pastors must explain these regulations to their parishioners *four* times a year. (Emphases added.)

FOR BACKGROUND

One of the great heresies of the Middle Ages was Albigensianism. Known in the beginning as Cathars, or "pure ones," this heretical sect spread through much of western Europe, gaining a foothold in northern Italy and southern France. They were especially strong in the town of Albi, France, from whence their name comes.

Like the earlier Manichees, the Cathars believed in two gods. The good god created an invisible spiritual realm, whereas the bad god, identified with the God of the Hebrew Scriptures, created the visible, material world. The body, the creation of the bad god, was evil. Following the example of Christ, the believer was to free the spirit from the body and attain salvation. Their anti-matter dualism led them to reject central Christian doctrines including the incarnation, the sacraments and the resurrection.

Much of the Cathars' popularity and success was due to their austere and ascetic life, which contrasted sharply with the lives of the clergy. Thus, following the Cathars can be construed as a form of protest against the Church's corruption. In response to the Cathars' continued presence and growth, Pope Innocent III launched a crusade against them in 1208. The establishment of the Inquisition followed and eventually rooted out the heresy.

Vatican II's General Principle of Religious Freedom
(1965)

This Vatican Synod declares that the human person has a right to religious freedom. This freedom means that no one should be forced by any person or group to act in a manner contrary to his or her own beliefs. Nor, within due limits, is anyone to be stopped from acting in accordance with those beliefs.

The Synod further declares that the right to religious freedom has its foundation in the very dignity of the human person, as this dignity is known through the revealed word of God and by reason itself. This right of the human person to religious freedom is to be respected by the laws of all governments. It is to be a civil right of every citizen.

It is in accordance with the individual's dignity as a person—that is, a being who has reason and free will and, therefore, personal responsibility—always to seek out the truth, especially religious truth, follow it once it is known, and live all of life in accordance with it.

However, one cannot freely do so unless free from all types of pressure or force, whether physical or psychological, which impel a certain manner of acting. The right to religious freedom has its foundation in the nature of humanity itself. Consequently, each person, no matter who, has this right and can exercise it, provided that the just requirements of public order are observed.

(*Declaration on Religious Freedom*, #2)

Heretics—Looking Back

There are differing arguments about the repression of heretics in an earlier time. The Church argued for preserving the purity of the gospel and the faith of the people. The state argued that this approach sustained the public order. Critics today argue that this was a cruel repression of human freedom. They abhor the witch-hunting mentality that occurred as an offense against simple decency and a dishonor to the human person.

What are we to think? Certainly the Church has the right to preserve the purity of the gospel and the faith of the people. Assuredly, the state has the right to insure the public order. Without a doubt, human freedom—not license—deserves to exist immune from harm. But how do you resolve conflicts that arise when gospel purity, human freedom and public order appear to clash? The medieval world turned to such solutions as those found in the "Regulations of the Synod of Toulouse." Today's world addresses the issues with a position such as that of Vatican II's document on religious freedom.

Pluralistic democracies do not experience the tight repressiveness of the Church in a medieval society. Yet we do see such behavior in totalitarian regimes of the left in China and Russia, and in the right-wing totalitarian governments of Latin America and Korea.

Medieval religion appears to have acquired the characteristics of an ideological state. We know how China and Guatemala handle dissent. They repress it because they apparently fear any permissiveness would lead to the dissolution of their societies. Those in power in the medieval period—Church authorities and politicians alike—also feared deviant behavior. Hence their fierce repression of the Cathari and the Poor Men of Lyons in the south of France and their hot reaction to other pockets of resistance to orthodoxy that arose persistently despite all efforts to eradicate heresy.

We will see this dynamic again in the Church's struggles with Protestantism and with the rise of secular liberalism.

Roman Catholic participation in interdenominational services or events was not allowed, except with the Holy See's permission, right up until Vatican II. This was especially distressing in America, a country where there were multiple Christian confessions. Because of the Vatican's stance against interdenominational cooperation, in 1947 Congressman John F. Kennedy was forced to cancel a scheduled appearance at a Philadelphia fundraiser for a chapel to be built in honor of four chaplains—Catholic, Protestant and Jewish—killed during World War II.

Chronology of the Formal Treatment of Heretics

1139 Canon of the General Council of 1139 called on the civil power to repress the Albigensians.

1163 Decree of the Council of Tours demanded that heretics be tracked down and their property confiscated. In England, at the same time, it was decreed also to destroy their houses.

1179 A general council renewed the exhortation of Tours to Christian princes.

1184 The decree *Ad abolendam*, the outcome of a meeting between Frederick Barbarossa and Pope Lucius III at Verone, was passed.

1215 The Fourth Lateran Council adopted *Ad abolendam* and formed the law which Pope Gregory IX applied when he began the Inquisition in 1231. The Lateran Council set extremely severe regulations, but their enactment depended on the energy of local bishops. Pope Gregory found it impossible to police all the bishops, so he appointed inquisitors who had supreme power as papal representatives.

1231 Torture appeared in heresy trials, restored to use by Frederick II.

1233 Pope Gregory appointed the Dominicans as inquisitors in Languedoc, France. They were unwilling to be identified with the project, however, and the pope, therefore ordered the Franciscans to help them.

1252 Pope Innocent IV prescribed the use of the rack for those suspected of heresy.

1478 Pope Sixtus IV reorganized the Inquisition (see Chapter 21) at the request of Ferdinand and Isabella of Spain. An important change, however, was that he allowed the king and the queen to choose the inquisitors.

1479 The Spanish Inquisition began and for years was motivated mainly by political rather than religious reasons.

FOR DISCUSSION/REFLECTION

Vatican II has taken a positive stand on religious freedom. John XXIII said that error has no rights, but people do. Is it ever all right to punish people for their religious belief? If someone disagrees with your beliefs, does that make the person a heretic? Exactly what is religious freedom and dignity?

Are there places in the world where people are being persecuted for religious beliefs? Discuss the following locations:
—Rwanda
—Sudan
—Bosnia
—Northern Ireland

FOR FURTHER READING

Chapter One of the *Declaration on Religious Freedom* in *The Documents of Vatican II*, ed. Walter Abbott, S.J. New York: Herder and Herder, 1966.

Miller, Arthur. *The Crucible.* New York: Viking, 1957.

Do You Demonize Those Who Disagree With You?—Connecting to Our Times

It is a common human tendency to "demonize" those who do not agree with us in belief, attitude and practice. In the Middle Ages this took a deadly form when Church members branded dissenters from Catholic truth as heretics and used this as a chance to oppress and persecute them. In the Reformation of the sixteenth century and for many years thereafter, Catholics and Protestants considered each other heretics and practiced many forms of oppression on one another.

Today, thanks to the graces of the Holy Spirit, the ecumenical movement has considerably reduced and often eliminated this mutual demonizing of one another on religious matters. We do still disagree, frequently on substantial issues, but we do so in a charitable manner and engage in dialogues and mutual humanitarian endeavors which benefit society.

Within the Catholic Church today, however, there are divisions between conservatives and liberals that sometimes become acrimonious. One side tends to invoke authority on doctrinal and moral issues while the other inclines to a political advocacy especially on social issues, but also on debates concerning married clergy, inclusive language and gender equity. A centrist group tries to hold the community together through persuasion and flexibility where possible.

Society itself is torn by political correctness and single-issue politics. The advice of Rudyard Kipling is pertinent, "Keep your head when all about you are losing theirs." Both in the Church and society we will encounter these stresses. When we do, we should learn from history not to demonize those with whom we disagree, and certainly not seek to persecute them.

The New Testament Church had many divisions of its own. Paul urged the medicine of kindness. "Let no evil talk come out of your mouths, but only what is useful for building up, as there is need, so that your words may give grace to those who hear....and be kind to one another, tender-hearted, forgiving one another, as God in Christ has forgiven you" (Ephesians 4:29-32).

17. Black Death

The Black Death has been called one of humanity's "epochal scourges." Jews of the time not only suffered the plague but also became scapegoats. Rumors circulated from town to town that Jews had poisoned wells by putting death-dealing drugs in them. Despite the efforts of Pope Clement VI (1342-52) and other rulers to maintain order, for three years (1348-50) Jewish communities throughout Europe were uprooted and destroyed. In some towns whole populations of Jews were burned; in others they were expelled and their property confiscated. It has been estimated that over two hundred Jewish communities, large and small, were destroyed.

The Ezekiel Reaction: Changing Concepts of God
(c. 1390)

The characters:
    Conrad, a German merchant
    Lorenzo, an Italian cardinal
    Elizabeth, an English duchess

The scene: A pavilion at Lake Como, where wealthy survivors of the fifty-year Black Plague are on vacation. Their conversation touches on some of the facts and feelings of that terrible time (roughly 1347 to 1400).

Elizabeth: It looks as though we are getting some relief from the plague. I wish it were over for good, but I suspect it will return.

Lorenzo: I think your feelings are justified. At Rome the reports from our various embassies are far from optimistic.

Elizabeth: It's been a sorry time for us all. Tell me, how did the plague actually start?

Lorenzo: It came from Asia, where it had caused terrible trouble in China and Turkistan. During a battle in the Crimea the Asiatic enemy catapulted plague-infected corpses into the camp of our Genoese troops. They brought the plague back on the ships on their return.

Elizabeth: Couldn't anything have been done to stop it?

Lorenzo: The doctors tried everything but to no avail. The Church urged fasting and prayer with no success. Some religious fanatics started penance processions in which the people whipped themselves bloody. And that certainly didn't help.

Conrad: What's even worse, my sister-in-law's family is Jewish and she tells me there were mass burnings of Jews. The Christians claimed the Jews caused the plague by poisoning wells.

Lorenzo: That shows what panic mixed with prejudice can do.

Conrad: The plague touched both the mighty and the lowly.

Elizabeth: How well I know. My home is Canterbury. The plague struck down two of our archbishops. And what was really sad—King Edward III's daughter Joan died on the way to her own wedding.

Lorenzo: And think of the great writer in our country, Petrarch, losing his beloved Laura, the inspiration of so many of his poems.

Conrad: A century ago Europe had nearly four million people. It's lucky to have two million today. I know of no war or plague that's ever struck us so badly.

Elizabeth: As a merchant, Conrad, you are probably in a position to know what it has done to our economy.

Conrad: It's had a terrible effect on food production, ruining the landowning classes. It's caused an excessive rise in wages. The expanding economy of such cities as Siena has come to a standstill. The citizens there have abandoned plans for enlarging their cathedral. Catalonia depended a great deal on a rising birth rate for its economic growth. So, of course, the plague has had a devastating effect on its economy.

Elizabeth: Cardinal Lorenzo, I believe the plague has had a profound impact on the spiritual life of our people.

Lorenzo: Of course it has. We are getting what I would call an "Ezekiel reaction."

Elizabeth: What's that?

Lorenzo: Do you recall that in the Old Testament Ezekiel was the prophet of the Jewish exile?

Conrad: You mean the time they were brought to Babylon and made slaves?

Lorenzo: That's right. Once upon a time all had been prosperity for them. God had seemed to be their friend. Now all is unutterable disaster. They are helpless. In a sense it's their Black Death.

Elizabeth: Then what is the Ezekiel reaction?

Lorenzo: Ezekiel composes for the people a picture of God that is awesome, almost frightening. He tells them their present misery is due to the fact that they have angered God. He is particularly hard on the priests: "Its priests have done violence to my teaching and have profaned my holy things; they have made no distinction between the holy and the common, neither have they taught the difference between the unclean and the clean, and they have disregarded my sabbaths, so that I am profaned among them" (Ezekiel 22:26).

Conrad: I see what you are getting at, Cardinal Lorenzo. There is a feeling that the Black Plague is really the result of the sins of people who have angered God.

Elizabeth: Is that what accounts for many of the scary sermons we've been hearing?

Lorenzo: I hope you haven't been hearing too many, Lady Elizabeth. But you're right. Some of our preachers are getting morbid, almost fanatical.

Elizabeth: Wouldn't you say this is an unhealthy approach to God?

Lorenzo: If it becomes exaggerated, it's a bad idea. No extreme is good. I believe this approach has value when it helps people toward moral responsibility. That's what Ezekiel had in mind for the people of his day.

Conrad: So he wasn't out so much to frighten people with an angry God as to draw them to holiness and spiritual backbone?

Lorenzo: Exactly. The Ezekiel reaction, when properly handled, begets a basic wisdom in thoughtless people.

FOR DISCUSSION/REFLECTION

The Black Death reached Europe by means of an early form of bacterial warfare: Asian soldiers catapulted plague corpses into Italian camps. Contagion spread through infected fleas who rode with the rodents aboard naval vessels headed for Italy. From 1350 to 1400 the plague occurred again and again, killing close to a third of Europe's population. The impact on economy, culture and religion was devastating.

Thousands of teachers, scholars and spiritual leaders suddenly died. What happens to a Church when the continuity and stability of its intellectual and spiritual tradition is abruptly broken?

During the fourteenth century, as a result of the Black Death, Europe was a death-oriented society. This orientation found reflection in the art, literature and theology of the time. Could one say that we too live in a death-oriented society?

In the face of great suffering, what is the role of the Church? What purpose do you see it serving? What would you look for it to provide?

FOR DISCUSSION/REFLECTION

To many people the Black Death seemed like the end of the world. It was like the opening of the "sixth seal" in the Book of Revelation: "[T]he stars of the sky fell to the earth as the fig tree drops its winter fruit when shaken by a gale.... Then the kings of the earth...the rich and the powerful, and everyone, slave and free, hid in the caves and among the rocks of the mountains...for the great day of their wrath has come, and who is able to stand?" (Revelation 6:13, 15, 17)

Are there signs in our times portending the end of the world?

What is the genuine Christian attitude about the end of the world?

Conrad: I guess it is only natural that with so much doom in the air these last fifty years, its mood would filter into religious thinking.

Elizabeth: All the more then must we work to balance this with the spirit of love and hope.

Lorenzo: You find the same in the gospel, Lady Elizabeth. Jesus gives his Last Judgment sermon the same week that he delivers his marvelous Last Supper discourse on love. If we had the balance and wisdom of our Master, we would never go overboard.

Conrad: I'm so glad we had a chance to talk about this. I was privately sharing Lady Elizabeth's concern.

Elizabeth: I'm grateful too. I hope we can get together again before we all leave.

Lorenzo: I'm sure we can. It's been a pleasure being with you both.

Black Death—Looking Back

The Black Death is the name given to the great plague which raged during the reign of Pope Clement VI between 1347 and 1350, the same period in which the Hundred Years' War between England and France was beginning. It struck every country in Europe, killing one-third to one-half of the population. No one has yet worked out a definitive analysis of its immediate effects.

Chronology of the Plague

In early 1347 the disease first appeared at Genoa, carried by a ship from the Genoese colony of Kaffa in the Crimea. It spread rapidly to Venice where a hundred thousand died. It then traveled down central Italy to Florence where another hundred thousand died. It reached Siena where about eighty thousand (four-fifths of the population) died. Sicily was struck very hard. In Marseilles fifty-seven thousand died in one month (two-thirds of the population) along with the bishop and nearly all of his clergy. Narbonne, Arles, Montpellier were all struck. Avignon lost over half of its people in seven months. Later in the year, northern France fell to the disease. In Paris eighty thousand died. In July the plague reached England and spread over it for eighteen months. No part of northern and western Europe escaped. It ravaged Spain in 1349. The plague crossed the Alps from Italy swept through Switzerland, struck the Rhine Valley and then Germany and the Low Countries. It continued by way of Denmark to Sweden and Norway.

The plague's traveling speed and the fact that so few who contracted it seemed to recover caused panic and despair everywhere. Wild outbreaks of lawlessness and debauchery took place.

At Avignon, Pope Clement VI organized medical and

sanitation aid. He also intervened to protect the Jews (especially those from cities in the Rhineland); when they were accused of causing the plague Clement offered them sanctuary in his state.

Through the winter months of 1349-1350, this first onslaught of the plague wore itself out. But there were many recurrences from 1361 to 1400. In 1361 the plague struck England and France almost as severely as it had in 1348.

Results of the Plague

In many ways medieval life was never the same again. The European population did not climb back to its former density. The spirit of earlier centuries was totally lost. In religion, negative attitudes of fear and guilt became acute. The Church suffered enormous losses in personnel; very few abbeys were ever filled again. Because the abbeys needed large staffs to operate effectively, the entire monastic system began to weaken. Steps should have been taken to institute stopgap measures. The existing houses should have been amalgamated but they were not. Much of Benedict XII's monastic reform was thus aborted.

Why Worry About the End of the World?— Connecting to Our Times

Some people wonder how the world began. Others worry about how the world will end. The creation story in the Book of Genesis gives us a sense of the origin of the world and its creatures. The apostles pondered the end of time and asked Jesus when it would happen. Jesus told them that no one will know the day nor the hour except the Father. New Testament Christians believed the world would end in their lifetime. When it did not happen, they realized that the timing of the end is a mystery and that in the meantime, we should get on with Christian living.

In our own day there are Christian sects who claim they know an exact date when the end will come. Their followers gather on a mountain or in some remote space and fruitlessly await an end that does not happen. This does not seem to bother them. They simply believe they left some detail out of their calculations and proceed to search for a new date.

The year 2000, the beginning of the third millennium, appears to some to be the signal for the end. If there happens to be a gathering of worldwide catastrophes such as plague or the emergence of a "hot zone" caused by a death-dealing germ or a series of earthquakes and volcanic eruptions along with the threat of a nuclear war, it will convince end-of-world-seekers that this is evidence enough on their behalf.

All of this should be taken with a grain of salt. We

DIES IRAE

This brooding, doom-laden hymn caught the mood of a world facing the Black Death and what seemed to be the end of the world. It remained part of the funeral liturgy until after Vatican II.

Day of wrath! O day of mourning.
See fulfilled the prophet's warning.
Heaven and earth in ashes burning.
Oh, what fear man's bosom rends
When from heaven the Judge descends
On whose sentence all depends!
Death is struck, and nature quaking.
All creation is awaking,
To its Judge an answer making
Lo, the book exactly worded
Wherein all has been recorded.
Thence shall judgment be awarded.
When the Judge his seat attains
And each hidden deed arraigns
Nothing unavenged remains.
Ah! that day of tears and mourning!
From the dust of earth returning
Man for judgment must prepare him.
Spare, O God, in mercy spare him!

should live every day as though it were our last, filling it with love and service and prayer, whether there is a worldwide crisis or not. It does little good to increase panic when there is enough already to alarm people. Fear tends to paralyze people and impair their judgment. "Today's trouble is enough for today" (Matthew 6:34). The precious minutes we have are more valuable than the imagined ones that have not come.

FOR FURTHER READING

Gonfried, Robert S. *The Black Death: Natural and Human Disaster in Medieval Europe.* New York: Free Press, 1983.

Tuchman, Barbara. *A Distant Mirror: The Calamitous 14th Century.* New York: Alfred A. Knopf, 1978.

Ziegler, Phillip. *The Black Death.* New York: John Day Co., 1969.

18. Medieval Women Who Made a Difference

The Black Plague was one of three catastrophes to burden the people of the fourteenth century. The other two calamities were the Hundred Years' War and the Avignon papacy. Two women arose in the midst of this chaos to change the course of history. Joan of Arc galvanized her people to drive out their oppressors and terminate the Hundred Years' War. The Church canonized her and France chose her as patron saint. Catherine of Siena changed the mind of a pope and closed the door on the Avignon papacy. Chosen by Italy as patroness, she was named first a saint and then a Doctor of the Church. In this chapter we first review the life of Joan and then meet Catherine in conversation.

Joan of Arc: A Meteor Who Burned Out at the Stake
(1412-1431)

On the feast of the Epiphany in 1412, the English appeared to have subdued France once and for all. They installed a colonial governor in Paris and made a puppet prince out of the Duke of Burgundy, who had betrayed his people. England planned to drain France of its money and resources. France's crown prince, the Dauphin, was a weak and defeated young man who doubted his blood legitimacy as heir to the throne. He and his forces controlled some sections of the south of France, but fear and doubt prevented him from claiming his deceased father's crown.

All France was dark on that feast of Epiphany, 1412—except Domremy, where Joan was born that day. Joan would light up the lives of her people and decisively unlock the forces that would drive the oppressors out and terminate the Hundred Years' War. In her early teens, Joan heard the voices of Saints Michael, Catherine and Margaret urging her to political action on behalf of her people. Joan did not act hastily. She listened for three years before she finally decided to embark on her public career at the age of sixteen.

She targeted the French commander at Valcoeurs as the man she must convince about her visions and her goal. The commander did not take her seriously at first. He made fun of her, suggested that she was sexually ripe for his soldiers

THE HUNDRED YEARS' WAR

The dominant political and military event in the fourteenth and fifteenth centuries was the Hundred Years' War (1337-1453), an event to which Joan of Arc is inseparably linked. This conflict between England and France was due in large measure to the rising sentiment of nationalism taking place throughout Europe. People were becoming more conscious of their own language and traditions with rivalries developing as a result.

There were many reasons for the war, a semi-continuous series of military campaigns: chiefly England's continued possession of lands in southwestern Fance and claims to other French provinces, and a dispute concerning the succession to the French throne complicated by English intrigue. Armed with a new weapon, the longbow, the English won impressive victories in 1346 but were unable to remain in France due to lack of funds. In 1380 Charles VII came to the French throne, but soon gave signs of madness and was replaced by a regent; civil war followed.

It appeared that the English would secure victory in France, but in 1422 Charles VI died and his son the Dauphin, besieged in Orleans, declared himself King Charles VII. The tide began to turn when Joan of Arc entered the scene. She rallied the French people to the Dauphin's cause and eventually broke the siege. She then accompanied the Dauphin to Reims Cathedral where he was crowned.

Joan wished to return home, but was pressed into service and eventually captured in battle. This led to her trial by the English for heresy and witchcraft, for which she was burned at the stake in 1431. At the time of her death, Charles VII had ended the civil war and by 1453 secured most of France, thereby concluding the Hundred Years' War.

and kept her cooling her heels for weeks. Joan persisted, pleaded and argued with him. No rebuff deterred her from her determination to make him see her point of view. She wore him down until he gave in. He took her to see the Dauphin.

The Dauphin Charles disguised himself and melted into the crowd of courtiers in his audience room when Joan entered. Joan identified him immediately and approached him with these words: "I am Joan of Domremy. The King of Heaven sends me to you with the message that you shall be anointed and crowned in the city of Rheims. You shall be the lieutenant of the King of Heaven, who is the King of France."

Having stripped his external mask, she probed further and bypassed his internal defenses. She read his mind about his belief that he was not a legitimate son of his father. Clairvoyantly, she told him she knew of a prayer he had made last All Saints' Day, asking to know if he was the real king of France. Joan dispelled his doubts and convinced him he was the true royal heir.

Charles put her to one more test. He dispatched her to Poitiers where he ordered a team of theologians to examine her and discern whether she was genuine or a mystic charlatan or a witch. Joan survived their scrutiny quite well. Charles then sent her to the army that was attempting to lift the siege of Orleans.

Dressed in man's armor, Joan rode to the front carrying a banner showing the world supported by angels and displaying an image of Christ flanked by the words Jesus and Mary. Joan perceived her role as a moral leader and source of inspiration to the troops. She made the soldiers go to confession and practice sexual abstinence. She banished the prostitutes. She did not plan any battle or kill anyone.

The English had surrounded the city on three sides. Joan rode into the city on the unguarded flank. She insisted that diplomatic means be used to lift the siege. A four-day truce was called while these negotiations proceeded. The talks failed and the fighting began. On May 8, 1429, the fighting lasted for twelve hours. The French forces were exhausted and decided to stop.

Joan urged them to continue. She rode through their ranks, giving them spirited courage. Then Joan was wounded by an arrow. Once her wound was treated and bandaged, she returned to the battle. The sight of her gave the soldiers a shot of adrenalin that spurred them to do the impossible. They won the battle and lifted the siege.

Bells rang. People sang and danced. They praised the Lord and every saint they could name. Above all they surged around Joan with an outpouring of affection and dubbed her with a still-enduring title: the Maid of Orleans. Strategically, the victory was small; psychologically, it marked the turning point of the war. Joan had created in the French the will to win and terminate one of the worst wars in history.

Within a year, however, Joan was to face tragedy. The

newly crowned Charles lacked the inner drive to push ahead. The generals disliked the fact that a young woman had upstaged them. Joan urged the king to keep up the momentum of battle while the generals told him to ignore her. Never deviating from her goal, Joan pressed the king to capture Compiegne. The enemy captured Joan in that campaign and turned her over to a Church court chaired by the French Bishop Cauchon. They charged her with heresy and sought to prove that her visions were spurious.

Joan, the illiterate peasant girl of nineteen, faced an imposing court: one cardinal, six bishops, thirty-two theologians, seven medical doctors and one hundred three hangers-on.

They asked Joan to swear to tell the truth on the Book of the Gospels. She replied, "I don't know if I should. Perhaps you will ask me things that I will not tell you."

"Are you in the state of grace?" they asked.

"If I am, may God keep me there. If I am not, may God put me there." (As subtle an answer as any theologian could give, and delivered by a girl unlettered in theological disputations!) She stood alone before the court. The wretched Charles abandoned her. The generals were secretly glad she was out of their way. The court pompously said to her. "We are the Church!"

Eying them as though they were a bunch of roosters clad in red and preening, Joan simply said, "Where the Church is there is Christ. I have no reason to fear the Church."

They tortured her to make her say the words they wanted her to utter. When she recovered and saw her forced confession, she repudiated it immediately and swore that no further torment would ever shake her again.

They burned her at the stake on May 30, 1431.

Twenty-five years later a Church court reversed that decision and declared her innocent. The Church declared her a saint in 1920 and named her patroness of France.

Her star had shone over France for three years, from her seventeenth to her twentieth year. Her meteor literally burnt out at the stake.

She was a young woman of paradox: She loathed killing, but she rode with an army and goaded them to fight. A girl of peasant faith, she set a cast of theologians on their heels. Thoroughly feminine, she wore a man's armor. In a negative world, she resolutely maintained a positive mental attitude.

She won a kingdom on earth. She captured a greater one in heaven.

FOR DISCUSSION/REFLECTION

Joan of Arc was a young woman called by God in visions to crown the French king and to lead the French Army. Why did the Church become involved in all of this? Why was she burned at the stake? Why is she a saint today?

People who claim to have visions are scoffed at today. What made Joan of Arc different? Is this kind of message possible today?

FOR FURTHER READING

Gies, Frances. *Joan of Arc: The Legend and the Reality*. New York: Harper & Row, 1981.

Seward, Desmond. *The Hundred Years' War*. New York: Atheneum, 1978.

Williams, Marty and Anne Nichols. *Women in the Medieval Ages: Between Pit and Pedestal*. Princeton, N.J.: Markus Wiener Publishers, 1994.

Catherine of Siena: Reflections on a Colorful Life

(1347-1380)

It is your duty to love your neighbor as your own self (Mark 12:33). In love you ought to help them spiritually with prayer and counsel, and assist them spiritually and materially in their need—at least with your goodwill if you have nothing else. If you do not love me [God], you do not love your neighbors, nor will you help those you do not love.... Every help you give them ought to come from the affection you bear them for love of me....

—Catherine of Siena

In a small apartment in Siena, Catherine the mystic is approaching her death. She and her lifelong spiritual director, Dominican Father Raymond of Capua, are reviewing the events of her colorful life.

Raymond: How did you manage to develop your interest in prayer at so early an age?

Catherine: It wasn't easy. I was the twenty-third child of my mother. We had a crowded and noisy Italian household—lots of love and affection to be sure! My father was a dyer and made good money. I was very young, four or five, when I felt an intense attraction to prayer. I shocked my parents on my seventh birthday when I declared that I was never going to get married. I had already betrothed myself to Christ. They were somewhat amused by that. But when I demanded my own private room for prayer, they were not amused.

Raymond: I'm not surprised. Even for spiritual reasons that sounds a bit selfish, given the shortage of space in so large a family.

Catherine: I was strong-willed early on. They would just have to find a way. My mother was against my proposal. It was my father who gave in and built a small addition to the house just for me.

Raymond: Were you firm in your intention to pray and pursue the inner attraction you felt?

Catherine: In some ways it was not a matter of being firm. I loved praying. I could do it as easily as my brothers who loved fighting played knights and Turks. By the time I was sixteen I would regularly drift into trances and ecstasies after Communion at my parish church.

Raymond: What was your goal in prayer?

Catherine: I was very fond of Bernard's commentaries on the Canticle of Canticles. He spoke of attaining a fixed state of union with Christ. That was my goal. I yearned for it. I learned to read when I was twenty. I wanted to be able to read Bernard's writings and the Canticles.

Raymond: Did you ever think that you were reaching for an impossible dream?

Catherine: Never! I never doubted Jesus would fix me in faith and make me his messenger of salvation. I believe I was twenty-one when it happened. Jesus took me for his bride in a ceremony performed by his holy mother. Saint John, Saint Paul and Saint Dominic were there. David played music on his harp.

Raymond: Why didn't you join the Dominican Sisters?

Catherine: I applied for the order. They refused me. I did not did find out why.

Raymond: Is that why you joined their Third Order?

Catherine: Yes. I planned to be an active single woman in the world. And you know that people frown on that. Unless I had the protection of the Dominican Order, I would either have to be a recluse at home or find some convent to join. As a tertiary I could have an active, public life.

Raymond: So you did more than pass time in contemplation in your private room?

Catherine: I have always had a thirst for action as well as a hunger for prayer. I spent hundreds of hours at the hospital working with the poorest of the poor. One of my favorite ministries was death row at the local prison. I made it a point to be with those prisoners about to be hanged or beheaded. I prayed with them, urged them to repent. I brought them home-cooked meals and tried to cheer them up. I stood by them at the scaffold and the chopping block, encouraging them in faith to the end.

Raymond: When did you begin your spiritual support groups?

Catherine: My trances and ecstasies at the local church marked me as a spiritual oddity at first. A small town does not take easily to nonconformity and peculiar behavior. My activism at the hospital and the jail also drew hostile comment. But when people saw my persistence and the evident good work, they changed their attitudes. People began coming to me for spiritual guidance. I guess I was about twenty-three or so. I held weekly prayer meetings and told people about my visions of Christ and what he wanted me to tell the world.

Raymond: That was about ten years ago. I met you soon after that. I recall being among the secretaries who took down the record of your visions.

Catherine: I remember you well, especially how you would fall asleep in trying to keep up with my endless outpourings. I understand people now call the record of my visions *The Dialogues of Catherine of Siena.*

Raymond: You were not content in dictating your visions. You also dictated dozens of letters to the Christian kings and princes of Europe, telling them how to run their governments. You fancied yourself an adviser in foreign affairs.

Catherine: Amazing, wasn't it? The gall of it! Yet it was the strength and wisdom of the Lord that moved me. I felt a calling to offer my service to Christian rulers in the administration of their people.

Raymond: Doubtless that is a major reason why the city-state of Florence engaged your services in settling the war between them and the papacy.

Catherine: Think of it! I had no experience in diplomacy. I was a woman in a strictly man's world. Yet they entrusted me with a major diplomatic mission.

Raymond: Still, your foreign correspondence was often with women.

Catherine: I was not above appealing to feminine influence. It was not Bernardo Visconti I wrote to, but to his strong-minded wife. I discovered I could not work with the King

AUDIO

Joan of Arc (Ignatius Press), 100 minutes.

VIDEO

Julian. Paulist Press. 60-minute video with study guide.

FOR DISCUSSION/REFLECTION

Catherine of Siena was a mystic, a charity activist and a social reformer—a rare combination. Why do some people enjoy prayer but feel no need to get involved in social action? Why do others love social action but have no time for prayer?

Why do some love social action but grow impatient with one-to-one acts of charity and mercy? Why do others again prefer one-to-one charity and have no inclination to social action?

FOR BACKGROUND

Catherine of Siena belongs to an elite group: the Doctors of the Church. This is a title conferred by a pope or general council to designate someone as a source of sound teaching and doctrine for the whole Church. The norms for being a Doctor of the Church, set by Pope Benedict XIV, include the following: orthodoxy, personal holiness, eminent learning and explicit commendation by the highest Church authority. Teresa of Avila is the only other woman to hold the title.

of Hungary so I relied on his dominant mother, Elizabeth of Poland, to score my points.

Raymond: You went to Avignon with an alternative goal besides making peace between Florence and the papacy, didn't you?

Catherine: I knew my greater achievement would be to persuade the pope to leave Avignon and bring the papacy back to Rome. I was convinced that keeping the papacy in Avignon would only prolong the corruption of the Church at its very center. The Church was in financial bondage to the French. The pope was like a political slave to the French king. Worse yet, papal taxes from all the parishes of Europe were being used to finance the hedonism of the papal court.

Raymond: And the parish clergy were angered and frustrated by that.

Catherine: An understatement. I know of cases in Germany where papal tax collectors were mutilated, imprisoned and strangled. Many clergy resigned the priesthood in disgust, leaving numerous villages with no resident priests, no Communion, no sacraments. Many churches were left to rot or become barns. The Swedish ex-queen Brigitta, then living in Rome, wrote to me. "Our Church has thrown away fear of God. A bottomless bag of money has taken its place. All the Ten Commandments have been reduced to one: Bring in the money."

Raymond: Where did you live in Avignon?

Catherine: I took an apartment across the Rhone River from the papal palace. "Babylon on the Rhone," people called it. Every day for four months I went over there. If I could not see the pope personally on a given day, then I left a note expressing my thoughts on the progress of negotiations about both peace and the move to Rome.

Raymond: I hear you were not intimidated by the pope or by the awesomeness of the papal palace.

Catherine: Why should I be? I thought the place stank of sin. And those women courtiers! Do you know what they did? Whenever I lapsed into a trance after Communion in the papal chapel, they would pinch me and stick needles into my feet to test my ecstasy. I felt nothing when they did that. But when I woke up and felt the pain from the bruises and the needles I was furious. I told them, "You wash your bodies with the aromas of Arabia. To me you smell like garbage. Your souls are rotting."

Raymond: I am amazed that you hectored Pope Gregory XI the way you did.

Catherine: No question. I did come on strong. Maybe it was a good thing I was not trained in diplomatic niceties. Some days in my frustration I would shout at him, "Be a man, Holy Father! Get up. Reform your priests. Get out of this sink of sin. Put down the sword of war and take up the cross of peace."

Raymond: And you were loud enough for everybody to hear.

Catherine: Few of the audiences were private. I had my say in front of everyone in the great audience hall. But when I thought I had been too severe, I would change my tempo. I knelt gently before Gregory and called him *dolce babbo mio*, my sweet daddy, and tried to cajole him to my point of view.

Raymond: What finally convinced him?

Catherine: A combination of things: My incessant hammering away at the themes of peace and leaving for Rome. The fact that Gregory was not totally without a conscience. The clincher came when I had a vision that revealed to me he had made a promise while still a cardinal that if he became pope, he would bring the papacy to Rome. You should have seen his face when I told him that! It was a secret he had kept to himself. And I knew!

Raymond: So then he finally agreed to close down the Avignon papacy. The news must have alarmed many people.

Catherine: Devastated is more to the point. The French king totally opposed the move. Said he, "Rome is wherever the pope happens to be." And he insisted the pope's departure would slow down the negotiations to stop the Hundred Years' War between France and England. Gregory withstood plenty of dissent. He was a Frenchman too, and it was hard to leave the land of his birth. To add to the anxiety, a thunderstorm had damaged some of the ships of the papal entourage. Was this a warning sign he was making the wrong decision?

Raymond: His father's behavior didn't help.

Catherine: Who would believe it? His father threw himself on the ground in front of the gangplank crying. "Don't leave, my son!" Gregory was forced to walk over his father's body to get on the boat. Someone claimed they heard Gregory speak a line from the Psalms—something about "trampling on the adder and treading down the basilisk." I stood nearby watching this and hearing some bishops say, "O God, if only the mountains would come and block our way."

Raymond: Thanks be to God you succeeded. You have given a tremendous gift to the Church. Now you are an international celebrity.

Catherine: It's been awful. Three years ago I took the overland route back to Siena. Crowds mobbed me in every town. I like people, but I have no taste for popular acclaim. I am so glad I have had these few quiet years to complete my "dialogues."

Raymond: You have been a good *mamma* to your spiritual support group.

Catherine: You have all been like *bambini* to me. My children. My only regret is that I do not believe I have loved Jesus enough.

Raymond: Have no fears. You have loved Jesus more than you know.

Catherine died in her thirty-third year, secure in the knowledge that the papacy had been reinstated in Rome and that reform was underway in the Church.

FOR DISCUSSION/REFLECTION

Three of the outstanding Catholics of the late Middle Ages were women. Joan of Arc established the conditions that led to the end of the Hundred Years' War. Brigitta of Sweden resided in Rome and undertook a ministry to the leadership, persuading them to join in the needed reform of the Church. Catherine of Siena changed the mind of Gregory XI and moved him to take the papacy back to Rome, thus creating a situation where Church reform was more possible.

For many, Catherine of Siena is a woman of contradiction: a defender of the Crusades and an opposer of the Avignon papacy. How do you see her—as a woman of contradiction or a woman of her time?

From what you have read, do you feel that women in the medieval period had more or fewer opportunities to serve the Church than women today? Why or why not?

What lesson might both female and male Christians take from the lives of Catherine and Joan?

A contemporary of Catherine of Siena, overshadowed but not diminished by her, was Bridget of Sweden. Like Catherine, Bridget was unafraid to call for reform and even reproach a pope (Gregory XI) for his continued papal exile in Avignon: "In thy curia arrogant pride rules, insatiable cupidity and execrable luxury."

Today a statue of Catherine stands on the Via Della Conciliazione, the Roman avenue that leads up to St. Peter's Square. Her head is tilted in such a way that her face is toward the Vatican and her eyes are still on the pope.

FOR FURTHER READING

Baldwin, Anne B. *Catherine of Siena: Biography*. Huntington, Ind.: Our Sunday Visitor: 1987.

Brigitta of Sweden: Life and Selected Writings, ed. Marguerite Harris. Mahwah, N.J.: Paulist Press, 1989.

Catherine of Siena: The Dialogue, Classics of Western Spirituality Series, trans. Suzanne Noflke, P.O. Mahwah, N.J.: Paulist Press, 1980.

Freze, Michael, S.F.O. *They Bore the Wounds of Christ: The Mystery of the Sacred Stigmata*. Huntington, Ind.: Our Sunday Visitor: 1989.

McBride, Alfred. *Saints Are People*. Dubuque, Ia.: W.C. Brown, 1980.

Undset, Sigrid. *Catherine of Siena*. Kansas City, Mo.: Sheed and Ward, 1954.

Vinje, Patricia. *Praying With Catherine of Siena*. Winona, Minn.: St. Mary's Press, 1990.

The Middle Ages—Looking Back

The Church's historical experience is a combination of responding to and of shaping the world in which it finds itself. The monks found a way to answer the need for contemplation; the friars responded to the need for an active evangelical ministry. In founding the universities the Church undertook to participate in and shape the intellectual community.

In the Crusades the Church moved into the area of holy war. Simultaneously, it sustained the just war theory, urged humane treatment of prisoners of war, and instituted structures such as the Peace of God and the Truce of God to lessen—even to suppress—war.

In the world of art, the Church became the source of the Gothic explosion that has been an enduring source of aesthetic and religious inspiration to this day.

In handling heretics, the Church participated in forms of repression which today are incomprehensible to the modern mind, in the sense that a Christian community would be a party to them. We see plenty of repression in our own century, but now it usually originates from secular sources, often dictators, ruthless businessmen and a variety of tyrants.

Faced with the Black Death, the Church moved toward more somber liturgy and theology, not so much to approve the experience of doom, as to find meaning and hope in the midst of it all.

Women in Today's Church—Connecting to Our Times

The roster of medieval women whose leadership in the Church was extraordinary boasts of a Joan of Arc who set in motion the conclusion of the Hundred Years' War and a Catherine of Siena who redirected the course of the papacy. We should also remember Dame Julian of Norwich, an anchorite who has been a light of spirituality from her own time to the present.

Early on Dame Julian received a series of "showings" or personal revelations from God. At first she wrote out a short account of these showings. Some years later she expanded on them and their meaning. Britain honors her as the first woman to write a book in the English language. Her powerful observations that flowed from her showings serve as inspiring prayer starters for us today.

In the early part of this century women religious (sisters) exercised a most beneficial ministry on behalf of the Church in parochial schools, CCD, Catholic publishing and Catholic hospitals. At the same time the traditional contemplative life has drawn large numbers of women to the cloisters where their prayer draws abundant graces upon the Church.

Now thousands of laywomen have taken over the administrative and staff duties of our schools, hospitals and religious education programs. Women have assumed leadership in Catholic publishing houses, the writing ministry and television. Countless others are involved in some form of pastoral ministry and diocesan administration, such as becoming chancellors. At the same time, women are seeking further involvement in the Church's ministry. At this writing, what that will involve remains unclear. Nonetheless, we should be grateful for the incalculable service of women to the Church throughout Christian history and stand with them supportively as new opportunities for service arise.

AUDIO

Dialogue of St. Catherine of Siena. Distributed by Ignatius Press.

The Life of Saint Catherine of Siena, by Raymond of Capua. Distributed by Ignatius Press.

VIDEO

Joan of Arc: Portrait of a Legend. America (100 minutes).

Joan of Arc. Educational Video Network (36 minutes).

Julian. Paulist Press (60-minute video with study guide).

No longer resist the will of God, for the starving sheep wait for you to return to the see of St. Peter. You are the Vicar of Jesus; you must resume your proper seat.... Come as a bold man without fear; but above all, for the love of life, do not come with a military escort, but come with the cross in your hand like a gentle lamb.

—Catherine of Siena

Part Three
Reformation

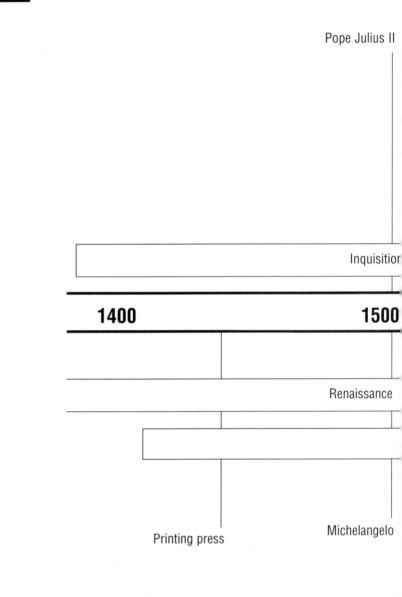

EVENTS IN THE CHURCH

Pope Julius II

Inquisition

| 1400 | 1500 |

Renaissance

Printing press

Michelangelo

EVENTS IN SOCIETY

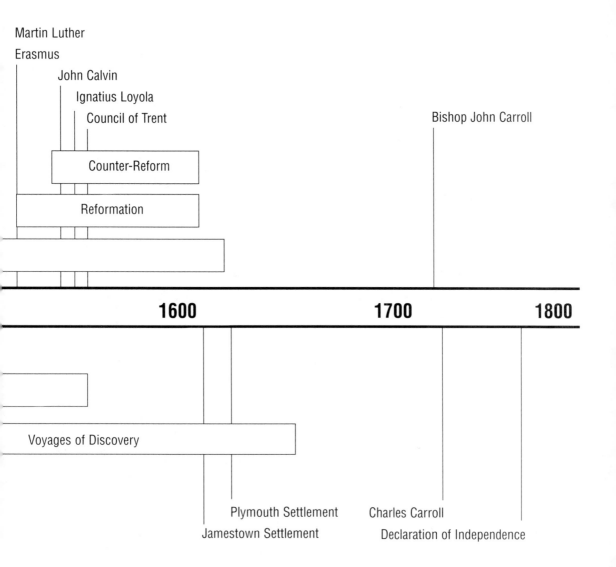

Martin Luther
Erasmus
John Calvin
Ignatius Loyola
Council of Trent

Bishop John Carroll

Counter-Reform

Reformation

1600   **1700**   **1800**

Voyages of Discovery

Plymouth Settlement
Jamestown Settlement
Charles Carroll
Declaration of Independence

19. Reformers: Luther and Erasmus

It is empty talk when the Romanists boast of possessing an authority such as cannot be properly contested. No one in Christendom has authority to do evil, or to forbid evil from being resisted. The Church has no authority except to promote the greater good. Hence, if the pope should exercise his authority to prevent a free council, and so hinder the reform of the Church, we ought to pay no regard to him or his authority.

—**Martin Luther**

As the sixteenth century opened, the Church could count some real blessings. The great problems of the late Middle Ages had passed. The attempt of late medieval Church councils to replace the pope had failed. Spain, which had wavered between the Church and Islam, cast its lot with Rome. The fierceness of the Inquisition, with its brutal treatment of heretics, had let up.

Still, new problems arose for the Church to solve.

The Black Death thinned the ranks of the clergy. It killed off so many teachers that educational systems broke down. It undermined morale in some places to the extent that clerics began to lead immoral lives.

The growing practice of selling Church offices for enormous sums of money angered the faithful, since they paid the bill in the long run. In fact, this was an immediate cause of the Reformation. A man named Albert purchased the office of the Archbishop of Mainz with a loan from the banking house of Fuggers. The Holy See allowed Albert to institute a sale of indulgences so that he could pay off his loan. (Whatever was left would go to Rome to help build St. Peter's Basilica.) One of the priests under the new Archbishop's authority was an Augustinian monk named Martin Luther.

Worst of all was the chaotic state of parish life. Many pastors were illiterate and untrained men. Since most of the money from parish collections went to support the princely ways of bishop and pope, a pastor then had to be given several parishes in order to have enough money to live on. But the pastor had too many people to work with. Hence the majority of his parishioners were neglected.

Reform was underway. Holland initiated education of the clergy. Spain brought order and discipline into the clerical ranks and attempted to explain in clear language what the people were to believe about faith and morals. The move to education and discipline was a healthy start. Regrettably, it was too little and too late.

The man who began the Reformation, Martin Luther, was born on November 10, 1483, in the village of Eisleben in Saxony, Germany. His father was a copper miner. Luther studied at the University of Erfurt, earning a master's degree.

Soon after his graduation, he was caught in a thunderstorm so frightful that he thought he was going to die. He vowed that, should he survive, he would become a monk. Several weeks later he fulfilled his vow by entering the Augustinian monastery at Erfurt. He was twenty-one.

The following is an interview with the man who set in motion the forces that gave birth to the Protestant Churches.

In the second half of this chapter we will meet Erasmus, Luther's contemporary, who approached reform from a very different perspective.

An Interview With Martin Luther
(c. 1523)

Interviewer: Dr. Luther, by all accounts, the first real crisis between your conscience and the Church was caused by the sale of indulgences in your diocese. Would you comment on this?

Dr. Luther: The Dominican friar, John Tetzel, was appointed to preach the special sale of indulgences. I can still hear the jingle he used: "As soon as the coin in the coffer rings, the soul from purgatory springs."

Interviewer: Was this what led you to post the ninety-five theses on the door of Wittenberg Castle Church?

Dr. Luther: Yes. I was so angered by this abuse, along with so many others, that I felt someone had to speak up. As you well know, the best way to get a hearing is to post your views in a public place and call for a debate.

Interviewer: What were some of the questions you raised in the theses?

Dr. Luther: I wanted to correct a wrong impression that was being created by the sale of indulgences. I think when people sin they ought to do personal penance and thereby gain an indulgence, which is an elimination of punishment for sin. Buying off the punishment is hardly the same as a personal atonement. I strongly disagreed with the practice and said that it was a corruption of biblical teaching.

Interviewer: What did Tetzel think of that?

Dr. Luther: He was out for my skin. After he read my theses, he said, "Within three weeks, I shall have that heretic thrown into the fire."

Interviewer: Why didn't he?

Dr. Luther: Mainly because the pope was not too concerned. He spoke of it as a "monkish squabble."

Interviewer: But he changed his mind.

Dr. Luther: I can thank the invention of the printing press for that. I began turning out a series of pamphlets and became a best-selling author. The authorities couldn't ignore me.

Interviewer: Were you summoned to Rome?

Dr. Luther: Yes, the summons came. Thanks to my friend Prince Frederick, the pope allowed the hearing to take place on German soil. It took place at Augsburg and was conducted by the pope's representative, Cardinal Cajetan.

Interviewer: How did that hearing go?

Dr. Luther: Cajetan read me the papal teaching on indulgences, namely, that there is a spiritual treasury of merits gained

FOR BACKGROUND:
The Peasants' Revolt

For decades prior to the Reformation, economic conditions had been worsening for German peasantry. Uprisings took place in 1476, 1491, 1498, 1503 and 1513. None of these were to be as widespread or as devastating, however, as the rebellion of 1525. The peasants, believing that Luther's religious teachings supported their new economic demands, took their proposals to the German lords in the form of the "Twelve Articles." They went so far as to say that if any of their demands contradicted Scripture it would be withdrawn. Upon reading the "Twelve Articles," Luther was sensitized to the plight of the peasants and counseled the German princes to respond to the depressed conditions reported by them. The demands, however, fell on deaf ears and armed rebellion broke out under the leadership of Thomas Munzer. Luther attempted to resolve the conflict peacefully, but finally called on the princes to suppress the movement. Though he urged mercy, nearly a hundred thousand peasants were killed. Consequently, many peasants either returned to Catholicism or joined the rising Anabaptist tide.

FOR BACKGROUND

The imaginary interview in this episode hinges on several pieces of historical data about Luther, though they are not all explicitly stated in the episode:

1. His trip to Rome as a young priest
2. The ninety-five theses
3. Three confrontations:
   a. The hearing at Augsburg
   b. The debate with Eck at Leipzig
   c. The final break at the Diet of Worms
4. Two of his major documents
   a. *Address to the Christian Nobility of the German Nation*
   b. *Babylonian Captivity of the Church*

FOR DISCUSSION/REFLECTION

If Luther were alive today what would he protest against?

Looking back, do you think that the Councils of Trent and Vatican II satisfied all of Luther's demands? Do any of Luther's concerns yet need to be addressed by the Catholic Church?

Luther was a man of the *sola*: Scripture alone, faith alone, grace alone. How are these statements balanced by the Catholic Church?

by the saints. The pope claims the power to draw on that treasury and issue indulgences. I refused to accept that doctrine. I quoted from the Epistle to the Romans which says that people are saved by faith—hence, not by buying indulgences.

Interviewer: Did Cajetan see any merit in your argument?

Dr. Luther: Not at all. He demanded I accept the pope's position. I flatly refused. Negotiations broke down at that point.

Interviewer: Wasn't it soon after that that you had your debate with the theologian Johann Eck at the University of Leipzig?

Dr. Luther: Yes, and you should have seen the audience that day! Dr. Eck is quite a speaker and a powerful defender of the traditional faith. He didn't bother with the indulgence questions. Rather he dwelt on papal authority, saying that from the beginning it has been taught that the authority of the pope comes from God.

Interviewer: And you replied with the position of Jan Hus, a Bohemian scholar who was burned at the stake a century ago?

Dr. Luther: Right. I replied that the papacy as we know it is probably only four hundred years old. I denied that God founded the papacy and stated that it was a human creation. If I wanted authority I would look to the Bible, not to the pope.

Interviewer: That must have stunned the assembly.

Dr. Luther: Understandably enough. By appealing to the authority of the Bible and denying authority to the pope, I was undermining him.

Interviewer: What was the pope's reaction?

Dr. Luther: He wrote a document against my position. It began with these words, "Arise, O Lord, and judge your cause. A wild boar has invaded your vineyard." I was supposed to reply in sixty days, but I didn't even get the document until three months after he sent it. It was just as well, because I was deeply involved in writing at the time.

Interviewer: When did your final break with Rome occur?

Dr. Luther: At the Diet of Worms in 1521. I went there expecting a trial in the ordinary sense of the word. Emperor Charles was in charge. Prince Frederick promoted my cause among the bishops. The Dutch scholar Erasmus sought support for me among the professors of the university. The pope sent two legates as observers.

Interviewer: What was the mood of the city?

Dr. Luther: You should have seen it! Shop windows were filled with my books. Wall posters and signs flowered everywhere on my behalf. On all sides were shouts of "Luther!" and "Down with Rome!"

Interviewer: You mentioned it didn't turn out to be a trial.

Dr. Luther: That's right. I was shown a stack of twenty books, placed as prime exhibits. They asked me to recant the heresies contained therein. That was the critical moment for me. I said, "Unless I can be proved wrong from the Bible or from reason, I neither can nor will recant anything. Here I stand. I can do no other. God help me. Amen."

Martin Luther was excommunicated a month later. His stand paved the way for the breaking up of the unity of Christendom. He lived to see his behavior result in the appearance of other Protestant Churches, such as the Presbyterian tradition begun by John Knox.

Luther—Looking Back

The historical and critical literature about Luther is large enough to fill a library. During the time when Catholics and Lutherans were actively hostile to each other, a good deal of the literature was embarrassingly prejudiced from both sides. In these ecumenical days, both groups have become less shrill and more cordial, and the literature more objective.

Luther pointed out a need for reform in the Church. Tragically, when reform did take place it resulted in a revolt, splitting the unity of the Church. We are now past the time for laying blame except to acknowledge humbly that there was fault on both sides. Beyond this we need to heal the divisions we have inherited in a humane and intelligent fashion. Above all, we must pray that the one God will abundantly pour forth the Spirit of unity upon us.

The Lutheran experience led the Catholic Church to undertake a radical and fruitful reform of its discipline and a clarification of its doctrine, especially the teaching on the sacraments and the role of good works in religion.

This episode teaches many lessons: A living Church must always be ready for reform and renewal. Christian doctrine always needs a fresh expression for its timeless message. Divided Churches must heed Christ's insistent call "that they may all be one."

Profile

1501 Luther entered the University of Erfurt as a lay student.

1505 Caught in a thunderstorm, Luther promised he would become a monk if he were spared. He was, and he entered the Augustinian monastery at Erfurt, thus disappointing his father, who wanted him to become a lawyer.

1507 He was ordained a priest.

1508-1517 Three events conspired to turn Luther into a radical reformer:

1) *The fit in the choir.* Luther had a convulsion caused by the realization of his own sinfulness and the purity of God.

2) *The revelation in the tower.* While meditating on Romans 1:17, he was overwhelmed by the teaching of Paul that we are justified by faith. Luther thought of himself as a sinner, but he felt the mercy and grace of God was greater. No human deed could move him toward God, but the grace-filled call of God could make it possible.

FOR DISCUSSION/REFLECTION

Luther gave the Christian world a profound insight into the glory of God's love, manifested in the saving grace of Christ. He illumined the essential need for a living faith. It was the issue of selling indulgences—without proper emphasis on the interior need for penance and prayer—that sparked the Reformation. Extremist statements were made by both sides. Luther said, "Christians should be taught that if the pope knew the demands of the indulgence preachers, he would rather the Basilica of St. Peter's be burned to ashes than built up with the skin, flesh and bones of his sheep" (Thesis #50, nailed to door of Castle at Wittenberg, October 31, 1517). Pope Leo X's private theologian Prierias wrote the document summoning Luther to Rome on charges of heresy. He was also unrestrained, as these words show: "Luther is a leper and loathsome fellow...a dog and the son of a bitch, born to bite and snap at the sky with his doggish mouth, having a brain of brass and a nose of iron" (see *Martin Luther*, by J. Todd).

Why can religious issues stir up such passion in people? Why do people lose all civility when quarreling about religion? Was there some wisdom in the old saying not to talk about religion or politics at a party?

When people debate religious differences instead of dialoguing, what is the inevitable result?

What rules for dialogue about religious differences would you lay down today?

FOR BACKGROUND

Much of Luther's impact was due to circumstances he neither created nor controlled. The movable type printing press pioneered by Johann Gutenberg, gave the reformers an audience that would not have otherwise had. Growing German nationalism fed by Luther's German translation of the New Testament, offered valuable support. While disagreeing with some of Luther's positions, many thought he deserved a hearing. Such political considerations as Charles V's preoccupation with the Muslims made it inopportune to intervene against Luther and possibly anger Lutheran princes. Thus, elements that lay behind the Reformation also assured its success.

FOR FURTHER READING

Chadwick, Owen. *The Reformation.* New York: Penguin Books, 1972.

Grave, Leif. *The Augsburg Confession,* trans. John Rasmussen. Minneapolis: Augsburg, 1987.

Haile, H.G. *Luther: An Experiment in Biography.* New York: Doubleday, 1980.

Hughes, John Jay. *Pontiffs: Popes Who Shaped History.* Huntington, Ind.: Our Sunday Visitor, 1994.

For further development of the psychology of Luther, see Erik Erikson's *Young Man Luther* (New York: W.W. Norton & Company, Inc., 1958).

3) *Tetzel's indulgence preaching.* Given Luther's conversion and new insight, it's easy to see how the Tetzel experience set him on the path of radical reform.

1517 Luther nailed his ninety-five theses to the door of Wittenburg Castle Church.

1517-1521 Luther's productive mind plus the newly invented printing press made his teaching exceptionally available to the people of the time. He translated the Bible into German, wrote a catechism, composed hymns, created liturgies and issued a long series of spirited theological tracts. Various judicial hearings made attempts to reconcile Luther to the Church; all failed. As the interview indicates, the Diet of Worms issued the final blow and Luther left the Church.

1524 Luther broke with his former friend and defender, Erasmus.

1546 Luther died after a nine-year illness.

The Humanists

Luther was not the only one interested in reform in the sixteenth century. Popular preachers had long sought reform by calling the people to prayer, fasting and self-discipline. If they could improve the spiritual life of the common people, they believed, Christendom could be saved.

Others, such as Paris professor Jean Gerson and curial Cardinal Nicholas of Cusa, maintained that reform must take place in Church organization. This group argued for regular ecumenical councils to improve Church organization. They argued that the organization often speaks louder than sermons. Therefore, no matter how eloquent the preacher, the people were not likely to change unless the organization obviously witnessed the gospel.

The third reform-minded group were the humanists, including Thomas More, John Fisher and John Colet. They were called humanists because they devoted their energies to things that would develop the humanity of people. Hence they showed keen interest in education, poetry, art and ideals that would persuade people toward self-improvement.

The humanists put great faith in education and felt that good schooling would be the best instrument of Church reform. They were grieved by the ignorance of the majority of people. Even with education, however, they saw little point in drawing the people into quarrels and arguments over religious doctrines, which tended to tear people apart and ruin the unity of the Church.

Erasmus of Rotterdam was a member of this third group and the greatest humanist of them all. Born in 1466, he grew to be the most brilliant man in Europe. Popes and kings, reformers and scholars turned to him for advice.

The interviewer who spoke with Luther now interviews Erasmus to get a broader view.

An Interview With Erasmus

(c. 1536)

Interviewer: What do you think of Martin Luther?

Erasmus: I believe he is a good man who saw evils and spoke out against them. Saint Augustine and Saint Bernard also wrote against such evils. I believe a good deal of what he says and I have defended his right to speak out.

Interviewer: If you agree with Luther, why have you gradually withdrawn your support from him?

Erasmus: I knew reform was needed and thought Luther would be just the man to spur it on. But then he became more and more headstrong, abusive and sometimes crude in his criticisms. He called the pope the anti-Christ, the bishops seducers and Rome an abomination before God. That was a bit much.

Interviewer: You have a reputation for being advanced in your own ideas. How do you compare your own position with Luther's?

Erasmus: When I read his pamphlet on the Holy Eucharist, I knew the Church would never accept his ideas. I didn't disagree with the ideas themselves, but I did disagree with their consequences. I knew that he would be excommunicated and that much of Germany would follow him. Germany had been itching for a long time to get out from under Rome's thumb.

Interviewer: What is your reaction to this realization?

Erasmus: I fear it will cause much ruin. The reformers are growing rigid. They accused Rome of intolerance; now they are just as intolerant. They denounced Rome for having a party line; now they have a party line of their own.

Interviewer: Then you are not sympathetic to the revolution that is underway?

Erasmus: Not at all. I admit I have the head of a rebel, but not the behavior of one. I think the chaos of revolution is worse than the cruelty of tyrants.

Interviewer: Have you suffered for your moderate position?

Erasmus: Well, I've been exiled from my native Holland. But more painful to me was the death of my dear friend, Thomas More, who was beheaded in Protestant England. And comrades of mine have been burned at the stake in Catholic Paris. I hate to say it, but I think I am living in the worst century since Christ.

Interviewer: Would you be willing to give us a statement of your beliefs?

Erasmus: I would be pleased to do so. This is my creed:

> I believe that we should pay more attention to our interior lives than to devotions and ceremonies. How foolish it is for people to revere the bone of the apostle Paul encased in glass and not to feel the glow of his spirit enshrined in his Epistles. How is it that the slipper of Thomas Becket, Archbishop of Canterbury, per-

NOTE

For the purposes of this book, treatment of the Renaissance is delayed until Chapter 22. The spirit that shaped the reformers in this chapter and the next, however, cannot be understood without appreciating the interplay between Renaissance and Reformation. The humanism of Erasmus was the northern expression of the same movement which produced Michelangelo in Italy.

FOR BACKGROUND

Erasmus wrote no concise summary of his beliefs. The "Credo" in this interview pulls the consistent threads from a lifetime of writings.

Erasmus

VIDEO

A Man for All Seasons. United Artists (120 minutes).

Rome in the Footsteps of Peter and Paul. Part Three. Brown-ROA (20 minutes).

The Reformation. Encyclopedia Brittanica (42 minutes).

Where Luther Walked, by Roland Bainton. Vision Video (30 minutes).

I detest dissension, because it goes both against the teachings of Christ and against a secret inclination of nature. I doubt that either side in the dispute can be suppressed without grave loss. It is clear that many of the reforms for which Luther calls are urgently needed. My only wish is that now that I am old I be allowed to enjoy the results of my efforts. But both sides reproach me and seek to coerce me. Some claim that since I do not attack Luther I agree with him, while the Lutherans declare that I am a coward who has forsaken the gospel.

—Erasmus

forms miracles now—which it could not do when he was alive?

I believe we should avoid quarrels about religious doctrine. Better to use our energies in piety and love.

I believe that nationalism is wrong: I can't understand why Frenchmen, Englishmen and Spaniards suddenly consider themselves natural enemies, when they have been born as brothers in Christ.

I believe in the reforming power of education. The enlightenment that comes through learning can do much to reduce the prejudices, superstitions and magic mentality that are currently the result of ignorance. I look for the day when every farm boy can whistle the Psalms as he furrows the soil.

I believe that the chaos of revolution is worse than the yoke of tyrants.

I believe that reason is to be preferred to angry deeds.

Erasmus—Looking Back

Erasmus (1466-1536) was the son of a priest. He was raised and educated at an Augustinian monastery and showed intellectual promise from the start. His guardians planned that he should be a monk, but Erasmus had no taste for the life, though he appreciated the education he received. He accepted ordination to the priesthood, but soon left the monastery to work for the bishop of Paris.

He continued his education both at Paris and later at Turin, where he took a doctorate in theology. His horizons were further widened by visits with the major members of the European intellectual community, including Thomas More in England. His intellectual tastes moved him away from the tradition of the medieval scholastics back to primary theological sources such as the Bible and the writings of the Fathers of the Church. His careful translation of the New Testament into a new Greek edition became the basis of subsequent vernacular translations.

Erasmus lived during a time of great papal corruption. For example, the Medici Pope Leo X, after ascending the papal throne in 1513, said: "Now that we have attained the papacy, let us enjoy it!"

In his book, *Dagger of the Christian Soldier*, Erasmus emerged as a liberal academic calling for reform in the Church and society. His writing technique was satire—not biting or sarcastic, but a gentle prodding of the high and mighty. He questioned the militarism of Pope Julius II and spoke for peace. He mastered the art of being a critic of the great while, at the same time, serving as their counselor.

He was a gentleman in Newman's sense of the word—that is, one who will never deliberately harm another. He could not bring himself to enter or approve violent controversy either at the level of conversation or the more brutal level of war. He placed great faith in the power of reason and education to solve problems. In short, he was the prince and father of humanists, putting great trust in the power of learning to liberate people from strife and pettiness.

In his relationship with Luther, he was at first sympathetic, but later withdrew his support. He liked Luther's biblical and patristic theology, but he could not support Luther's political ties and revolt against the Church. It was one thing to explore new ways to preach the gospel and improve Christian behavior, but it was quite another to destroy the unity of Christendom.

He lived to see Luther's strategy prevail and to hear Rome cite humanism as one of the elements which aided the rise of heresy and the split in the Church. In spite of his challenging ideas, Erasmus never lived under any threat of excommunication or of trial for heresy. In fact, in his old age he was offered a cardinal's hat. He graciously declined.

He saw no contradiction between humanism and faith. The tumult of the times obscured his quiet wisdom, but today we look at him again and are more prepared to see the direction in which he would have led the Church.

FOR DISCUSSION/REFLECTION

Erasmus was a Christian humanist. He believed there was no fundamental contradiction between a scholarly life—research and learning—and living the Christian faith. Is this always true? Should scientific researchers have refused to invent the atomic bomb? Ought they avoid any further research on genetic engineering? Does the fact that so many of today's artists, poets, historians and writers are professedly nonreligious prove that Erasmus was naive about the presumed compatibility of humanism and religion? What examples demonstrate that Erasmus was right?

The Holy Spirit Is the Soul of Ecumenism— Connecting to Our Times

"Grow or die" is a principle of business. Conversion and renewal are watchwords of the religious and moral life. The Catholic Church of the sixteenth century needed to grow out of its medieval cocoon and embrace reform and renewal. Because it was slow to do this, the conditions for the Protestant Reformation occurred. In our own day the Church did not wait for a similar crisis to arise, but embarked on a process of self-renewal at the Second Vatican Council.

One of the productive outcomes of the Council was the ecumenical movement. Four hundred years ago we and the Protestants locked horns with each other. We practiced "no prisoners theology," fighting each other as though we were secular states at war. By the grace of God and the movement of the Holy Spirit we have been liberated from that contentious attitude and today strive to achieve spiritual unity—and possibly one day an institutional union.

For many years now there have been dialogues between the Catholic Church and such major denominations as the Anglicans, Lutherans, Methodists and Presbyterians. At the theological level, many misunderstandings have been cleared away. At the pastoral level, covenants have often been made between Catholic and Protestant parishes. At the human level, people of all Christian faiths have formed a common bond in humanitarian endeavors and projects for

It wasn't until 1524 that Erasmus and Luther, both of whom attacked Church corruption, parted ways over the issue of freedom of the will. Though grateful to his one-time defender, in the end Luther would see Erasmus as a faint-hearted reformer unwilling to take his ideas about Church reform to their final conclusion. As a result Luther said that Erasmus "would die ultimately in the wilderness without entering the promised land."

the good of society in general.

It is clearer now that the goal of unity of Christian Churches will be a long-range project. It is more evident that all Christian communions must be humbler and more open to the divine power of the Holy Spirit, for this worthy goal is in essence dependent upon the action of grace. We must continue to work for Christian unity at all levels, while being even more fervent in imploring the Spirit—the principle of unity—to bring us together in the bond of love and the blessedness of peace.

FOR DISCUSSION/REFLECTION

Erasmus believed it was better to study the Bible in a scholarly way than to concentrate on theology, which he felt caused too many quarrels. Catholics, however, have tended to concentrate on tradition and theology, while Protestants have tended to concentrate on the Bible. Which is the better way? What is the value of studying both Bible and theology?

It has been said that Erasmus was "a moderate man in the most immoderate times." In light of his own response to the corruption of the Church during his day, how can we be critical of some of the Church's practices while, at the same time, remaining faithful to it? In this process of questioning and change what situations need to exist to ensure that tolerance and moderation triumph over extremism?

It has long been said that Erasmus, given his travels, studies and intellect, read the signs of the times and foresaw the need for Church reform. Reading the signs of the times in our own day, what, if any, Church reforms would you suggest? Do you think they could be implemented without causing division?

20. The Rise of Protestantism

Although the sixteenth-century protest against the Church began with Luther in Germany, it soon spread to other countries. In Switzerland two distinct types of Protestantism developed: Anabaptism and Calvinism. The first was founded in Zurich by a Swiss priest named Ulrich Zwingli. The second was begun in Geneva by the French lawyer John Calvin. These two leaders disagreed strongly with one another.

In Scotland John Knox led the revolt. Since he had lived for a time in Geneva and had been greatly impressed with Calvinism, Knox included many of its basic beliefs in the development of Presbyterianism.

For the most part the Protestant revolt was led by such differing personalities and views that all attempts at agreement failed. The movement on the whole brought about a splintering of the Christian Church.

The following playlet will give some insight into the ideas of these Protestant leaders.

Blue Laws and Clean Streets
(c. 1545)

The characters:
Margaret, cousin of John Knox
Karl, an original disciple of Zwingli
Kristin, secretary to Calvin
Frederick, a Lutheran clergyman

The scene: A hotel dining room in Geneva where four people have met at lunch to discuss developments in the Reformation.

Frederick: I'm amazed at how quickly Switzerland picked up the fire of the Reformation. Luther, however, sometimes regrets the direction it has taken here. He blames your hero Zwingli for that.

Karl: I was with Zwingli when he had his summit meeting with Luther. Zwingli argued that the Church should be stripped of all pageantry. That was why he took the crucifixes, chalices, vestments, censers and even the organs out of the churches. He loved music and used to play the flute in class to quiet rowdy boys. But in church he wanted no interference between humanity and God.

FOR DISCUSSION/REFLECTION

Discuss your reactions to the following:
— Work makes one holy and closer to God.
— Religion means no fun anymore.
— If you have fun, you can't be close to God.
— God will reward you with money and good fortune if you work hard.
— Faith is the only thing necessary for salvation.
— Should churches ban drinking, smoking and gambling?
— With freedom comes responsibility.
— Are the rich obligated to care for those less fortunate?
— Protestantism fits in best in the middle class.
— What was the difference between the Pilgrims and the Puritans?
— What is a "work ethic"?
— Shops should not open on Sunday, because it is the Lord's Day.
— Is the emphasis today more on money or the family?
— God rested on the seventh day; shouldn't we?

FOR BACKGROUND

While the Reformation was raging in continental Europe, the papacy had one of its ablest defenders in Henry VIII, King of England. In 1521 he wrote a book against Luther for which Pope Leo X conferred on him the title "Defender of the Faith." Henry, however, was soon to join the ranks of the Reformers.

Unable to produce a male heir with his wife, Catherine of Aragon, Henry sought an annulment from Rome. Since she was the aunt of Charles V, the Holy Roman Emperor, Pope Clement VII stalled, not wanting to alienate a needed ally. At this point Henry consulted the major universities, which declared that his marriage with Catherine was invalid.

Events culminated in 1534 in the Act of Supremacy, when Parliament declared Henry head of the Church of England. It also forbade the payment of taxes and other contributions to Rome, ruled that Henry's marriage to Catherine was not true, and that their child Mary was not an heir to the throne. Thus the reformation in England was based not on doctrinal issues but political ones. Henry sought to restore the rights of the crown against undue papal intervention. This would lead to the beheading of Thomas More who, as chancellor of England, refused to recognize Henry as head of the Church.

Kristin: At least he had the good sense not to encourage his followers to smash the stained glass.

Frederick: Luther would say amen to that, but he was unhappy about Zwingli's other teachings.

Kristin: Didn't they have quite an argument over how to tell whether God liked you?

Karl: Yes, and you have to admit it's an important issue. I mean, after all, if you believe that some people are destined to go to heaven and others to hell and it all depends upon whether or not God likes you, then it's rather important to know if you can tell where you stand with God. Luther said no, you can't tell; only God knows whom God likes. But Zwingli said you could tell—those who publicly profess their faith and join in the Lord's Supper are God's friends.

Frederick: From what I gather they were not able to come to an agreement.

Karl: They came to the end of the meeting in total disagreement. Zwingli offered to shake hands with Luther, but Luther refused.

Frederick: That's too bad. That must be the reason for the statement I heard Luther make later when he said of Zwingli, "I will not let the devil teach me anything in my Church."

Margaret: As a Scot, something that has interested me about the Swiss Church is its apparently democratic style.

Karl: The smallness and mountain seclusion of Switzerland gave us a kind of democratic opening. Each of our thirteen cantons, or states, has a lawmaking body for both domestic and foreign affairs. In one canton every man is in the legislature. Even in the Catholic days, the legislature supervised discipline and taxation in churches and cloisters.

Kristin: We Swiss have always been a freedom-loving people. We like to determine things for ourselves. Our new Church in Geneva reflects this spirit. We want to participate in the running of the Church.

Margaret: You know my cousin, John Knox, owes a great deal to your John Calvin. Tell me a little about him.

Kristin: Originally, Calvin was a French Catholic student of theology. It was when he studied law under the humanists at Orleans that he became a Protestant.

Karl: His law training served him well when he came to write *Institutes of the Christian Religion.*

Kristin: That has become a standard textbook for the Reform. In it Calvin spoke movingly of the majesty of God. Like Zwingli, he held there were visible proofs that God liked you: Belief in the true faith, leading a good life, going to the Lord's Supper regularly.

Margaret: Does this have something to do with the "holy commonwealth" here at Geneva that I've heard so much about?

Kristin: Yes, Calvin has transformed Geneva into a holy commonwealth. All its members attempt to live up to the three ideals of faith, behavior and worship.

Margaret: I've noticed the people are quite loyal to these ideals. I've also been astonished by their energy. They must be the hardest working people on earth. Does this have something to do with their religion?

Kristin: In some ways, yes. The people do seem to derive great strength and a sense of purpose from their faith. They see their prosperity as a blessing of God and a sign that God loves them.

Frederick: As an observer, may I mention something I don't like about your holy commonwealth?

Kristin: What is that?

Frederick: Like Margaret, I do admire the religious zeal and the devotion to hard work among your people. But as a German and a lover of the excitement of taverns, I dislike Calvin's "blue laws." They take all the fun out of tavern life.

Karl: Which ones do you mean?

Frederick: Well, if anybody so much as says "By the body's blood" or "zounds," he'll be punished. And you know how beer loosens the tongue. It's likely that a few off-color words will slip out after a few beers.

Kristin: I imagine you don't like the ban on gambling, dancing and indecent songs.

Frederick: How could I? It makes the place like a graveyard. I'm of peasant stock like Luther and we never saw anything particularly wrong in these matters. You're too solemn here. Imagine stopping at an inn and not being able to stay up after nine o'clock at night. Why, it's like a monastery!

Kristin: In many ways it is. All the Catholics, dissenters and heretics have left town. We have nothing but Calvinists here. By the way, we do allow informers to stay up after nine.

Frederick: Then you're like a police state.

Kristin: A holy one, indeed.

Margaret: It certainly is the cleanest town I've ever seen.

More Reformers—Looking Back

Ulrich Zwingli (1484-1531)

Ulrich Zwingli received a humanist education before being ordained a Roman Catholic priest. He was respected and esteemed in his ministry in Zurich, Switzerland. As his own thoughts veered away from orthodoxy, he continued to teach and preach traditional doctrine. It was not until 1516 that Zwingli openly manifested his beliefs. In many instances these resembled Luther's, since Zwingli also acknowledged the supreme authority of Scripture. He felt only laws that agreed with Scripture were binding. Marriage was therefore lawful to all, clergy and laity alike.

He differed from Luther irreconcilably in his belief that human flesh, rather than humanity in general, was corrupt. Zwingli's view of the sacraments was negative. He considered the Mass a sacrilege, denied the real presence and for-

The Puritans

Similar to European Calvinists were the English, and later American, Puritans. Intent on abolishing any remnant of Catholicism, the Puritans even banned Christmas. In the words of the famous American Puritan, Cotton Mather: "Can you in your conscience think, that our Holy Saviour is honored by mad Mirth, by long Eating, by hard Drinking, by lewd Gaming, by rude Revelling; by a Mass fit for none but a Saturn or a Bacchus or the Night of a Mahometan Ramadan?"

Ulrich Zwingli

Those who teach the word of God, yet not to the honor of God, but for themselves and their head, the pope, for protection of their fabricated high station, are harmful wolves, coming in sheep's clothing.

—**Ulrich Zwingli**

FOR FURTHER READING

Barr, Gladys. *The Master of Geneva*. New York: Holt, Rinehart and Winston, 1961.

Brown, Robert McAfee. *The Ecumenical Revolution*. New York: Doubleday, 1967.

John Calvin

Testifying to the character and influence of John Calvin, Pius IV, the pope at the time of Calvin's death, is reputed to have said: "The strength of that heretic consisted in this, that money never had the slightest charm for him. If I had such servants my dominion would extend from sea to sea."

bade the use of art and music to uplift the spirit in acts of worship. Zwingli's major effort was to rethink all Christian doctrine in essentially biblical terms.

Soon Switzerland became a state divided over religious belief and, in 1531, Zwingli was killed in battle during a religious war.

John Calvin (1509-1564)

Calvin, born in 1509 to a bourgeois family and destined by his father for a career in the Church, left home at fourteen for theological studies in Paris. At the college of Montaigu, he excelled in his studies. His ability won recognition from students and teachers alike, and by nineteen he had his master's degree in theology. His father then ordered him to transfer his studies toward a law career. In obedience, he journeyed to the University of Orleans, where he eventually took his doctorate in law.

In Paris, Calvin became aware of the tension between humanism and scholasticism. The connection between Lutheranism and humanism tended to make Catholic states wary of the "new learning." Calvin soon became friendly with a group that was translating Scripture into the vernacular in secret because of the Church's ban on such projects. His connection with the group was evident and he became recognized generally as a gifted young Christian humanist, but his ties to the Church were still strong. Transferring support from the authority structure of the Church to a position of public protest against that authority was a gradual and painful move for Calvin. In 1534, when he was twenty-five, Calvin made the final step by renouncing his benefices and his ties with his local diocese and speaking openly on the side of the Protestants. Two years later he published the summary of his already matured thoughts, *Institutes of the Christian Religion*.

On one of his journeys, Calvin was detoured to the city of Geneva. There the leader of the evangelical reform movement appealed to him to stay and use his God-given talents to organize and solidify the advances already begun. It was not Calvin's wish, but he considered the request a divine call and decided to undertake it.

In Geneva, Calvin suffered from indigestion, sleeplessness, headaches and loneliness. His cold, reserved personality coupled with characteristic severity toward himself and others kept him alienated and aloof from the people. Yet he excelled as teacher, writer and organizer and was able to make Geneva the center of Protestantism. It became a theocracy, with the Church in the driver's seat in state affairs. Leadership within the religious community fell to those who were "moved by the Spirit," thus threatening a professional ministry. This principle became the basis of all Protestant theocracies.

Calvin insisted upon his spiritual authority to teach, preach and censor. Often the people or the city council resisted him. Two years after he arrived in Geneva, with characteristic brashness, Calvin excommunicated the entire city on Easter, 1538. The next day he was banished from the city. For three years, Geneva lived in political and religious chaos.

Finally, in 1541, Calvin was officially invited back. He came determined to carry out the full reform which he envisioned. The "Ecclesiastical Ordinances" which he adopted were greatly influential in Europe and the British Isles. For twenty-two years, until his death in 1564, Calvin inculcated his theories and Church policy into Geneva. It became a classical type for many attempts at reform.

John Calvin's brand of reform—with its emphasis on thrift, business, cleanliness and its Old Testament style of observing the sabbath day—came to American shores with the Puritans. Zwingli had already introduced the idea of a church building shorn of all decoration in statuary and stained glass.

Probably the Swiss style of democratic government eventually led to the adopting of the "people's church" or congregational mode as it appeared in our country. Rome centered authority in the pope, Germany in bishops and Geneva in the leaders (presbyters).

Calvin's stern views about God carried over into the Puritan religion of early American Protestantism. It was a mood that affected all the Churches with a "fire and brimstone" attitude toward sin.

Many have noted the link between this form of Protestantism and the rise of capitalism. The richer and cleaner people were, the more it seemed God had blessed them. Since no money could be spent on personal adornment or "foolish pleasure," everything was put back into the business. It was inevitable that the Calvinists and their posterity should become prosperous people.

Like Luther, Calvin did not believe that he was starting a new religion. He was reforming Christianity by returning it to a pristine state of existence. His theological theories were, like Luther's, based on the basic human inability to reach God. He believed that, for some mysterious reason, God redeems us even though we are unworthy or incapable of earning merit on our own. The Holy Spirit confers the grace of redemption, and the righteousness bestowed is manifested in personal life. The mystery of divine choice selects some and passes over others.

John Knox (1514-1572)

Knox was born in Scotland about 1514 and did not go beyond a bachelor's degree before ordination. He had a thoughtful, argumentative cast and initially became the tutor of nobles' sons. While thus engaged he came into contact with the reformed faith and was converted to it sometime before 1545. Soon his abilities were recognized and he became the spokesman and protagonist for Scottish Protestantism. During the period of religious persecutions and war which followed, he became a fugitive and, for a period of nineteen months, even lived as a galley slave. Freed through the intervention of the English government, Knox

VIDEO

Zwingli and Calvin. Vision Video (28 minutes).

John Knox

Once, while in conversation with John Knox, Mary Queen of Scots pleaded with him to help protect Catholic priests, against whom Protestants were taking up the sword. In response, Knox replied: "The sword of justice is God's, and if princes and rulers fail to use it, others may."

FOR BACKGROUND

One of the most divisive issues of the Reformation (and one that disallowed any union among the Reformers) was the understanding of the Eucharist. Luther believed in Christ's real presence in the Eucharist. He spoke of the bread and wine "coexisting" with the Body and Blood of Christ, which he termed *transubstantiation*. Furthermore, Luther said that the Mass was not a sacrifice because he could find no verification for it in Scripture. He saw the Mass as a "work" which went against his notion of "faith alone."

In 1530 the Marburg Colloquy was called by a German prince to reach doctrinal agreement and to present a united front against Rome. There, in the presence of Luther, Zwingli stated that the Eucharist was a symbolic sign of Christ's presence, not a real one. He preferred to emphasize the importance of faith in the recipient.

Between Luther and Zwingli was Calvin. He stressed the spiritual nature of the communion with Christ in the Eucharist. Calvin said that in the Eucharist grace flows from Christ, who "is in heaven and not here."

Confronting the Reformers, the Council of Trent declared that in the Eucharist the bread and wine are substantially changed into the Body and Blood of Christ. This was termed *transubstantiation*.

was made a licensed preacher in England. There he left a lasting effect on the Church of England by helping to shape its *Articles* and its *Book of Common Prayer* and by encouraging the country to accept Puritanism.

When Mary Tudor came to the throne in 1553, Knox went into his second period of exile, spending his happiest years in Geneva until his return to Scotland in 1559. He then participated in the armed advance of the "true religion" and became its dominant spirit. A combination of circumstances brought victory to this group and Knox became the principal figure in drawing up the constitution, liturgy and doctrines of the Reformed Church. The question of financing the Church then became a stumbling block and a divisive factor between Knox and the nobles.

At this juncture Mary Queen of Scots arrived in Scotland and a grim war over religion ensued. The Reformed Church was in real danger until Mary's abdication in 1567. When peace finally seemed to be in view, news of her execution threw Scotland into turmoil. Succeeding events literally taxed the life out of Knox, and he died in Edinburgh in 1572. Although a controversial figure, he had a strong effect on both the Church of England and the Church of Scotland.

Celebrate a Positive Work Ethic— Connecting to Our Times

One of the enduring themes of the Protestant Reformation that endures to this day is the "Protestant work ethic." We trace this mostly to Calvin and Zwingli. The idea grew out of their teaching of predestination. God has predestined those who are to be saved. But how is one to know? Is it enough to be a good person, or should there be a sign—such as prosperity? If this is a reasonable indicator, then should not one work hard, be thrifty and save so that one has in hand the symbol of predestination?

Now this is an oversimplification. Doubtless Calvin and Zwingli would have thrown up their hands in despair at such a cheapening of their spiritual insights. They struggled with the doctrine of predestination and should be commended for trying to understand how it applies in a world of freedom. But by the time their theology reached a popular level, it often resulted in the Protestant work ethic and its tenuous connection of economic prosperity and divine salvation. In its most absurd form it would mean that only the rich and energetic are saved, while the poor and listless are doomed.

Regardless of how the idea of a work ethic originated, there is no question it has been a constant attitude in American life. Today it has been diluted and secularized in workaholism, greed and fast-track pursuit of money. This is prosperity divorced from faith. At the same time, we should heed its sensible teaching that hard work, thrift and perseverance are better for us than welfare dependency, living on the "edge of the plastic credit card," too much reliance on luck and a tendency to give up when the going gets tough.

Whatever its theological shortcomings, the Protestant work ethic made practical sense—and still does. It generated a tremendous middle class in our culture, a social group that provided stability and continuity for society. Of course, it is arrogant when it patronizes the poor and helpless and fails to reach out a helping hand. But, granting its deficiencies, the work ethic still has a significant role to play for us.

FOR DISCUSSION/REFLECTION

Record your answers to the following opinion poll and then discuss with others:

Reformation Protestants stressed salvation by faith. Yet they became best known for the Protestant "work ethic."
Yes___ No___ Not sure___

Of the two great reformers, Calvin had more influence on American Protestantism than Luther.
Yes___ No___ Not sure___

It is easier to become rich when you do not waste your money on wine, women and song.
Yes___ No___ Not sure___

The rise of capitalism coincided with the rise of the Protestant work ethic. Protestantism caused capitalism.
Yes___ No___ Not sure___

Historically, Catholic monasteries demonstrated the adage, "Diligence begets abundance." Is this a "Catholic work ethic"?
Yes___ No___ Not sure___

Prohibition of alcohol in America was an outgrowth of Protestant blue laws.
Yes___ No___ Not sure___

Our world would be better off if we had no drinking, smoking, gambling or dancing.
Yes___ No___ Not sure___

If all poor people practiced the Protestant work ethic, they would become prosperous.
Yes___ No___ Not sure___

American Catholics have become prosperous because they practiced the Protestant work ethic.
Yes___ No___ Not sure___

21. Counter-Reform

After Luther and Calvin, it seemed as though Protestantism would claim the whole of Europe. But the Church of Rome responded vigorously in a stunning comeback known as the Counter-Reformation. One center of this movement was in Spain.

In the Middle Ages Spain had been a fairly tolerant country. Catholics, Jews and Muslims lived side by side. By the mid-fifteenth century the scene changed. The Spanish monarchy moved to eliminate all non-Catholics from Spain. Ferdinand and Isabella requested the Church reestablish the Inquisition—an organization set up to find and punish heretics. In effect, this meant torture, prison and exile for Jews, Muslims and any Catholic who differed with the Church's teachings. The Inquisition was a time of cruelty and intolerance.

Eventually, a positive movement developed in Spain. The man most responsible for the movement to bring about Church reform in Spain was Cardinal Jimenez. As archbishop of Toledo, Jimenez, a man spiritually as tough as an oak tree, set out to discipline all of Catholic Spain. He purified the monasteries of corruption, eliminated moral laxity in the clergy and thus gave the Church a foundation of steel.

Jimenez lived what he preached. Underneath his cardinal's robes he wore a hair shirt. In his palace he lived with the simplicity of a monk. He had a strong belief in the power of education and founded the University of Alcala, which very soon became an outstanding center of learning. He managed to reform the Church in Spain and still keep it in union with Rome. The followers of Luther and Calvin made no headway there. Instead, Spain became prominent as one of the centers of the Counter-Reform.

Out of this world of reform and discipline came Ignatius of Loyola, the founder of the Jesuits.

Ignatius Loyola

Teach us good Lord, to serve thee as thou deservest; to give and not to count the cost; to fight and not to heed the wounds; to toil and not to ask for rest; to labour and not to ask for any reward save knowing that we do thy will. Through Jesus Christ our Lord.

—Ignatius of Loyola

Ignatius Loyola and the Company of Jesus

(1491-1556)

Ignatius' early career did not suggest the future he was to live. He liked pleasure and the diversions of an army man's life. He enjoyed reading tales about knights and the art of courtly love. His ambition was to be an adventurous soldier. His hopes evaporated when a cannon ball blasted one leg, crippling him for life.

While the wound was healing, he passed his time reading the lives of the saints and the story of Christ. The idealism that once moved him toward the army now encouraged him to be a soldier for Christ. He spent a year in prayer, meditation and self-examination. The experience led him to write the *Spiritual Exercises,* a short book on how to develop self-control so that the will, the emotions and the body could be put at the service of the spirit.

Now he felt a strong need for education. He was in his mid-thirties, but was not embarrassed to go back to our equivalent of high school and learn Latin. He spent ten years at various universities in Spain and Paris.

It was at the end of this education period that Ignatius founded the order which would become known as the Jesuits. In 1534 in the small chapel of St. Denis in Paris, he gathered a group of men who promised to live a life of poverty and celibacy. They called themselves the "Company of Jesus."

They went to Rome to see Pope Paul III and to offer him their services. They said they were ready to do anything he asked of them; the pope could count on full obedience from the Company of Jesus. The pope accepted their offer, officially approved their order and made Ignatius the Father General. Ignatius and his successors have worked so closely with the popes that the general of the order has frequently been called "The Black Pope," a title derived from the black robe adopted as the official Jesuit garb.

In a short time the order expanded and met with enormous success. The Jesuits were particularly effective in two areas: the missions and education.

In the person of Francis Xavier, they dramatized the missionary enterprise. Francis, one of the original members of the Company of Jesus, went to the Orient. There he preached simple sermons and exerted a personal, evangelical charm and faith that converted thousands in India, Japan and the East Indies.

But it was in education that the Jesuits emerged as international leaders. Ignatius founded many schools for the training of his seminarians. In time the Jesuits established and staffed many of the universities of Catholic Europe. The task required so many of their men that the majority of them

FOR FURTHER READING

Bergan, Jacqueline Syrup and Marie Schwan. *Praying with Ignatius of Loyola.* Winona, Minn.: St. Mary's Press, 1991.

Hollis, Christopher. *The Jesuits: A History.* New York: Macmillan, 1968.

VIDEO

The Company: Inigo and His Jesuits, produced and directed by Joseph D. Fenton, S.M. Credence Cassettes (52 minutes).

were occupied in some form of education. Many feel that the secret of the Jesuits' success lay mainly in their firm discipline and stress on obedience. Ignatius had not forgotten his military days. He saw no harm in borrowing traits from military life and applying them to life in his order. But, equally important, he insisted that his men should have a good education. He did not want untrained men in the classroom. Hence, they received years of training before they themselves stood at the teacher's podium.

Ignatius shaped an army of men for the service of the Church in the Counter-Reformation. He trained them to help people recover confidence in the Church and remain loyal to it. Many other groups within the Church helped spur the Counter-Reform, but few matched the energy and zeal of the Company of Jesus.

The reform of the Spanish Church and the founding of the Jesuits were but two among many efforts to stem the tide of the Protestant advance. It was in the Council of Trent that these and other movements found fulfillment as the Church pulled itself together and began a new life.

THE FOURTH VOW

Like other religious orders of the day, the Jesuits took vows of chastity, poverty and obedience. What set them apart, however, and at times led to suspicion, was their fourth vow: "special obedience to the sovereign pontiff regarding the missions." Ignatius referred to it as "our beginning and the principal foundation of the Society." In contrast to the vow of stability made by monks, this is one of mobility, a commitment to travel anywhere in the world for the help of souls. Jesuits rely on the pope's vision of the Church's role in the world to show where they are most needed.

Counter-Reform—Looking Back

It was almost inevitable that the most powerful movement of the Counter-Reform should come from Spain. As the above commentary points out, Cardinal Jimenez had already brought to Spain a sense of order and reform that was so thorough that, had it been followed in Germany, Luther would have had no complaints.

The work of Ignatius fell into three areas. First, he provided the Church with spiritual exercises that brought new and needed vitality to spiritual life. Second, he established an ideal of discipline and education that left a healthy imprint on the intellectual life of the Church. Third, his fostering of the missions helped bring the Catholic message to the far-flung borders opened up by the exploration that followed the discoveries of Columbus and those who penetrated the Far East.

Today it is probably the intellectual competence of the Jesuits that is best known, since they still run so many educational institutions. Their missionary explorations have become part of the exciting literature of mission history. The method of prayer called the "Ignatian method," which was formulated by Ignatius, has long been an outline for meditations used in convents and monasteries throughout the Western Church.

Teresa of Avila—Connecting to Our Times

We rightly remember the Jesuits as the quintessential embodiment of the Church's response to the Protestant Reformation. The Order of Saint Ignatius of Loyola inaugurated a worldwide system of schools and colleges and mission stations that should impress the multinational corporations of today. The Ignatian method of prayer remains a powerful and practical source of spirituality for the busy modern.

We should also remember Saint Teresa of Avila for her reform of the Carmelite Order, especially her order of cloistered Carmelite nuns whose great houses of prayer encircle the globe today. The Jesuits and other active orders have an intensely public presence in our Church, hence we tend to notice them and admire the great work they do. But Teresa's cloisters are like our own souls—there, but not so evident amid the rush of modern life.

Just as our hearts beat silently thousands of times a day, sending our lifeblood to every corner of our bodies, so the women of these great cloisters are the heartbeat of the Church, acting as channels of grace for every corner of the Mystical Body. These are not frail, frightened women running from the world. They are strong, purposeful women who have responded to God's call to a life of liturgical and contemplative prayer. They are missionaries of the Spirit. They know that just as no flesh lives without a soul, so the Mystical Body will not flourish without the life-breath of prayer.

Teresa's silent cloisters were born in the noisy turmoil of the Counter-Reformation. Four centuries have neither dimmed their vitality nor rendered their vocation irrelevant. Their cloisters dot our secular landscape like stars in the night and remind us all that there is a daylight of hope despite the pressures of contemporary madness. Thank God for their graces. Praise the Lord for their generous and joyful spiritual gifts to all of us.

FOR DISCUSSION/REFLECTION

Traditionally the Jesuits have gone to some of the world's toughest mission fields. If you were the pope, where would you send them today? What do you think are some of the worldwide mission needs of the Church today?

One of the great Jesuit missionaries was Matteo Ricci. He worked in China and spent his life adapting the gospel to Chinese traditions and culture. This brought with it the question of how far Christianity can go in accommodating to a new culture and still remain faithful to the teachings of Christ and the Church. As the Church continues to expand in Africa and Asia, how do you see this issue being settled? How much of Christianity lends itself to accommodation? What does not?

For many people the hallmark of the Jesuits is education, not only of their own members, but also through their establishment of institutions. Is education in the faith as strongly needed today as it was in Ignatius' time?

22. Renaissance

FOR BACKGROUND

The birthplace of the Renaissance and humanism was Italy. It produced men and women devoted to developing their skills to the full. These humanists sought to be the pioneers of a new culture. One of the greatest was the Italian poet Petrarch, who emulated the Latin style of Cicero and brought about a revival of Platonism. Though a master of the Italian language, Petrarch felt his Latin writings were the more important. Due to his prestige and influence, they led to the growth of classical studies and increasing enthusiasm toward the Latin language.

VIDEO

Michelangelo: Artist and Man. A & E Biography (50 minutes).

Return to Glory: Michelangelo Revealed. Ignatius Press (52 minutes).

Amid all the fire and smoke of the Reform and Counter-Reform, the Church played a key role in fostering the dazzling outburst of the art and architecture of the Renaissance. The humanists had recovered for Europe a taste for the wisdom and art forms of classical Greece and Rome. Mix this interest with an economic boom and you create an enormous demand for talented people.

The roll call of artistic giants in that period includes Raphael, memorable for his paintings of Mary; Michelangelo, creator of the dome of Saint Peter's, the ceiling of the Sistine Chapel and the statue of David, to mention but a few of his works; and Leonardo da Vinci, a genius who foresaw such inventions as the helicopter, the machine gun and the automobile. Leonardo's "Last Supper" is perhaps the best known representation of that event.

The merchant princes of Florence and the popes of Rome were the major patrons of these artistic geniuses. The works of art that resulted are now the delight of the tourist, the art expert and all people who love beauty.

The Church did not insist that the artists restrict their work to the sacred. Popes and cardinals were equally willing to see the images of classical pagan myths produced alongside the traditional representations of the Bible, the saints and the history of the Church.

Irving Stone's novel *The Agony and the Ecstasy* captures the mood of those dynamic days in presenting the life of Michelangelo Buonarroti. The excerpt that follows describes the scene in which Pope Julius II commissions Michelangelo to paint the ceiling of the Sistine Chapel.

Michelangelo doesn't want to do it, for he considers himself a sculptor rather than a painter. He finally gives in. He realizes that his job is not merely to decorate a ceiling. He is to cover the ugliness of a building that had originally been designed as a fortress. His achievement has become one of the masterpieces of the world.

'Decorate the Sistine Chapel, Michelangelo!'

(c. 1508)

His eyes bulged when he saw the marbles dumped like a cord of firewood, discolored by rain and dust. Giuliano da Sangallo gripped his arm. "The Holy Father is waiting for you."

They passed through the smaller of the throne rooms of the papal palace, filled with a variety of supplicants hoping for an audience. Once in the large throne room, he advanced toward the throne, bowing to Cardinal Giovanni de Medici, nodding formally to Cardinal Riario. Pope Julius caught sight of him, suspended a conversation with his nephew Francesco, Prefect of Rome, and Paris de Grassis. Julius was dressed in a white linen cassock, his pleated knee-length tunic had tight sleeves, while the elbow-length scarlet velvet cape was trimmed in ermine, as was the scarlet velvet skull-cap.

"Ah, Buonarroti, you have returned to us. You are pleased with the statue in Bologna, are you not?"

"It will bring honor on us."

"You see," cried Julius triumphantly, throwing out his arms energetically to include the entire room. "You had no confidence in yourself. When I made this splendid opportunity available to you, you cried out, 'It is not my trade!'" The pope's mimicking of Michelangelo's slightly hoarse voice brought appreciative laughter from the court. "Now you see how you have made it your trade, by creating a fine bronze."

"You are generous, Holy Father," murmured Michelangelo with a twinge of impatience, his mind occupied with the pile of stained marbles lying just a few hundred yards away.

"I intend to continue being generous," cried the pope heartily. "I am going to favor you above all the painting masters of Italy."

"'...painting' masters?"

"Yes. I have decided that you are the best artist to complete the work begun by your countrymen Botticelli, Ghirlandaio, Rosselli, whom I myself hired to paint the frieze in the Sistine Chapel. I am commissioning you to complete my uncle Sixtus' chapel by painting the ceiling."

There was a light patter of applause. Michelangelo was stunned. Nausea gripped him. He had asked Sangallo to make it clear to the pope that he would return to Rome only to begin carving on the sculptures for the tomb. He cried passionately:

"I am a sculptor, not a painter!"

Julius shook his head in despair.

"I had less trouble conquering Perugia and Bologna than I have in subduing you!"

PROFILE: Renaissance Popes

Giuliano della Rovere took the name Julius II as pope, indicating that his model would not be a Christian saint, but rather Julius Caesar. So feared in battle he gained the nickname "the Terrible," through his military and diplomatic exploits Julius was able to reorganize the Papal States, which reorganization had been opposed by France and Germany.

Perhaps the most corrupt of the Renaissance popes was Alexander VI. People of his day were heard to say: "Alexander is ready to sell the keys, the altars and even Christ himself. He is within his rights, since he bought them."

FOR BACKGROUND

In the early 1990's the ceiling of the Sistine Chapel was cleaned and restored after many years. Keep in mind that for four centuries the chapel was lit by candles. They produce quite a bit of soot, which had collected on the ceiling. The restoration took over three years; now the colors on the ceiling are vivid. One can see the figures much better. It was a "renaissance" for Michelangelo's famous painting on the ceiling of the Sistine chapel.

FOR FURTHER READING

Stone, Irving. *The Agony and the Ecstasy.* New York: Doubleday, 1961.

"I am not a Papal State, Holy Father. Why should you waste your precious time subduing me?"

The room went silent. The pope glared at him, thrust out his bearded chin, demanded icily, "Where did you have your religious training, that you dare to question your pontiff's judgment?"

"As your prelate said in Bologna, Holiness, I am but an ignorant artist, without good manners."

"Then you can carve your masterpiece in a cell of Sant' Angelo."

All Julius had to do was wave a hand at a guard, and he could rot in a dungeon for years. He gritted his teeth.

"That would bring you little honor. Marble is my profession. Let me carve the Moses, victors, captives. Many would come to see the statues, offering thanks to Your Holiness for making them possible."

"In short," snapped Julius, "I need your sculptures to assure my place in history."

"They could help, Holy Father."

There was an audible gasp from those around the throne. The Pope turned to his cardinals and courtiers.

"Do you hear that, gentlemen? I, Julius II, who recovered the long lost Papal States for the Church and brought stability to Italy, who have cleaned out the scandals of the Borgias, published a constitution abolishing simony and elevated the decorum of the Sacred College, achieved a modern architecture for Rome.... I need Michelangelo Buonarroti to establish my historical position."

Sangallo had gone deathly pale. Cardinal Giovanni stared out a window as though he were not there. The pope loosened the collar of his cape against his own warmth, took a deep breath and started again.

"Buonarroti, my informants in Florence describe your panel for the Signoria as 'the school of the world'...."

"Holiness," interrupted Michelangelo, cursing himself for his envy of Leonardo that had led him into this trap, "it was an accident, something that could never be repeated. The Great Hall needed an accompanying fresco for the other half of the wall.... It was a diversion."

"*Bene.* Make such a diversion for the Sistine. Are we to understand that you will paint a wall for a Florentine hall, but not a ceiling for a papal chapel?"

The silence in the room was crushing. An armed courtier, standing by the pope's side, said, "Your Holiness, give me the word and we will hang this presumptuous Florentine from the Torre di Nona."

The pope glowered at Michelangelo, who stood before him defiant but speechless. Their eyes met, held in an exchange of immovability. Then a wisp of a smile drifted across the pontiff's face, was reflected in the tiny amber sparkle of Michelangelo's eyes, the barest twitching of his lips.

"This presumptuous Florentine, as you call him," said the pope, "was described ten years ago by Jacopo Galli as the best sculpture master in Italy. So he is. If I wanted him fed to the ravens I would have done so long ago."

He turned back to Michelangelo, said in the tone of an exasperated but fond father:

"Buonarroti, you will paint the Twelve Apostles on the ceiling of the Sistine, and decorate the vault with customary designs. For this we will pay you three thousand large gold ducats. We shall also be pleased to pay the expenses and wages of any five assistants you may choose. When the Sistine vault is completed, you have your pontiff's promise that you shall return to the carving of the marbles. My son, you are dismissed."

What further word could he say? He had been proclaimed supreme among his country's artists, made a promise that he would resume work on the tomb. Where could he flee? To Florence? To have Gonfaloniere Soderini cry out, "We cannot go to war with the Vatican because of you." To Spain, Portugal, Germany, England...? The pope's power reached everywhere. The pope demanded much, but a lesser pontiff might well have excommunicated him. And if he had refused to come back to Rome? He had tried that too, for a barren seven months in Florence. There was nothing to do but submit.

He kneeled, kissed the pope's ring.

"It shall be as the Holy Father desires."

Later, he stood by the front entrance of the Sistine Chapel, his mind aswirl with revulsion and self-incrimination. Sangallo was just behind him, his face haggard, looking as though he had been whipped.

"I did this to you. I persuaded the pope to build himself a triumphal tomb, and to call you here to sculpture it. All you have had is grief...."

Sangallo wept. Michelangelo shepherded him inside the protective doorway of the chapel, put an arm about the trembling shoulders.

"*Pazienza, caro*, patience. We will work our way out of this predicament."

"You are young, Michelangelo, you have time. I am old. Nor have you heard the crowning indignity. I volunteered to erect the scaffolding for you, since I renovated the chapel and know it well. But even this I was denied. Julius had already arranged with Bramante to build it.... All I want now is to return to my home in Florence, enjoy a little peace before I die."

"Do not speak of dying. Let us speak instead of how we can tackle this architectural monstrosity." He threw both arms up in a despairing gesture that embraced the Sistine. "Explain this...edifice...to me. Why was it built this way?"

FOR DISCUSSION/REFLECTION

Medieval culture and education emphasized the divine and the supernatural. The Renaissance period looked more at the human and the natural. Which approach do you prefer? What are some advantages and disadvantages of each approach? Are you more inspired by St. Peter's in Rome or Notre Dame Cathedral in Paris?

Renaissance humanists thought that education was an instrument of moral improvement and growth in piety. To some extent this did not happen. Why not? Today's public schools are not allowed to promote acts of piety or any express moral training. Is this a good idea?

The Duomo, Florence

VIDEO

The Agony and the Ecstasy. UA/MGM (120 minutes).

On This Rock: A Look Inside the Vatican, produced by Daniel White. Cineco-Centrill Media Productions (30 minutes).

When painting the picture of hell and the souls of the damned in the Sistine Chapel, Michelangelo drew one of the souls so like a cardinal who was an enemy of his that protests were immediately voiced to Pope Clement VII to have it altered. To this Clement responded: "You know that I have power to deliver a soul out of purgatory, but not out of hell!"

Renaissance—Looking Back

Michelangelo belonged to a period of history known as the Renaissance. The Renaissance marked a new outburst in the fields of learning, the arts and architecture. Michelangelo lived in a time when men like Da Vinci, Raphael, Bramante and Donatello painted, sculpted, frescoed and built masterpieces that are works of genius. In the north of Europe, intellectual humanists like Erasmus, Thomas More, John Fisher and Colet revolutionized approaches to learning and education.

What were the principal characteristics of this Renaissance?

Three elements dominated the genius of those days: (1) a return to the classical cultural ideals of Greece and Rome; (2) a new interest in the human and the natural; (3) a belief that education was the best means of helping people be moral and pious.

Ancient literary classics and classical art existed all along. The monks copied the masterpieces of Greek and Latin learning. But at that time no one thought such "pagan" writing had much to say to the development of a Christian person. A major exception to this rule had been the rebirth of interest in Aristotle in the medieval period. Thomas Aquinas and the other medieval schoolmen adapted Aristotle's thinking to their explanations of Christian teachings. Aristotle's orderly synthesis suited the medieval thinker's structured world. His works were a philosophical form of a Gothic cathedral.

Renaissance humanists looked rather to Plato as their mentor and took his Socratic dialogues as a model for education. Rather than mount the orderly steps of an Aristotelian proposition to their peak, they wove their way according to the circular thinking of a Plato. Plato was more human, less confined to mental abstraction—round, poetic, idealistic. Thus the artists portrayed humans more realistically, though in their ideal and glorious form. Round domes on symmetrical churches, like the Duomo in Florence, gathered people as a human community in contrast to the medieval naves that drew one's eyes to the beyond.

Medieval artists had painted Mary as a stiff-looking woman, flat, holding her child forward on her knee like a stern little king. Renaissance artists painted a Madonna, a rolling cushion of a woman hugging her baby in the fold of maternal warmth.

Medieval artists had used pagan figures as ornaments on their canvases, set pieces like a Cicero or a Virgil or an Ovid robed in medieval clothes and standing like servants before the Christian Lord. They had no life or meaning of their own. How differently Michelangelo portrayed them! Bursting with anatomical energy, they stand out on their own, seemingly uttering their pagan wisdom alongside apostles and saints—and robed in classical folds, if indeed clothed at all.

The flat, perspectiveless figures of medieval paintings

are always fully clothed, with the occasional exception of the infant Christ. The full-bodied, perspectived figures of the Renaissance are often nude, with an occasional classical drapery—a conscious imitation of the Greek and Roman way of sculpting and painting.

Michelangelo secretly dissected dead bodies (it was against the law) to learn how the muscles underneath the skin worked to produce their visual effect. Thus his David, Moses and the figures on the ceiling and walls of the Sistine Chapel pulsate with physical as well as spiritual vitality. No longer was the human figure hidden from view by neck-to-toe garments so that we might keep our mind on heavenly beings; now the glory of the human body was opened to view that we might celebrate the human form and rejoice in God's creation of natural order.

It was thus believed that the wisdom of the classical authors and the artistic models of the classical period, far from distracting us from God and good behavior, would in fact make us more moral and draw us closer to the Lord. The intellectual humanists promoted the study of Latin, Greek and Hebrew, not only that the classical authors might be studied, but also that the Bible be better understood and that the Church Fathers be approached once again.

It was a heady time, intellectually and artistically. The humanists set in motion an educational ideal that ultimately led to the birth of the scientific mind and the value of mass education. But the dream that education would produce piety never materialized. Once people learned to read, they just as easily read a potboiler novel as a Tolstoy masterpiece. Nonetheless, literacy did produce positive results. The concentration on the natural universe produced Newton, Descartes, Adam Smith and a host of inventors who made the industrial revolution and scientific advancement possible.

The revolution in art generated celebrations of landscapes, colorful impressionists and stately portraiture, and survived through the twentieth century's own revolutionary abstractions.

A homage to the classics, a love affair with the human, a dream of education-induced piety—these were the goals of the Renaissance geniuses. Their heritage remains to captivate us as well as to stimulate us to new achievements.

FOR DISCUSSION/REFLECTION

One hears the term *secular humanism* quite a bit in today's society. Just what is secular humanism? We have discussed secular as being worldly and humanism as being concerned with the human aspect of life. Is this a bad term? Should we be concerned about things on a divine level? Is the human realm more important than the reign of God? Have worldly pleasures taken the place of spirituality? Is there room in today's world for both?

Discuss how one's human talents can be a source of spiritual development. Must singers sing only religious songs? Must painters paint only religious pictures? Must teachers teach only religion? How can we do what we are interested in and still lead a good life?

Did Renaissance artists paint only for the Church or did they paint what they wanted to? Could this repeat itself today? Are we involved in a renaissance?

FOR FURTHER READING

Gilmore, Myron. *The World of Humanism*. New York: Harper and Row, 1952.

Toward a Fresh Vision of Human Dignity— Connecting to Our Times

Renaissance artists and writers celebrated the human. They were humanists in the best sense of the word, viewing the person directly and boldly but always within a world of faith and God's presence. We style them "Christian humanists." They echoed the human idealism of Greece and Rome

FOR DISCUSSION/REFLECTION

For some humanists the Renaissance, with its belief in the dignity of human persons, gradually took on secular overtones. They said that worship of God served only to distract humanity from developing its own powers and creativity. Do you think that belief in God promotes immaturity? How does an authentic Christian humanism promote maturity?

The Renaissance was a time when human reason was praised. Many suppressed the supernatural. Did the Church of the Renaissance achieve a balance between these two? Does society today favor one over the other?

but within the context of a community of faith.

Once again in our own day there is a recovery of interest in the distinctly human. Our biblical scholars ponder the human side of the composition of the Bible. What were the human problems addressed by the biblical authors? What was the human history that shaped their insights and attitudes? Our theologians look at faith "from below" to meditate on the human side of the divine-human encounter. In religious education we explore human experience, its psychological stages and the social and cultural setting in which our students come to the table of word and sacrament. Our missionaries have become sensitive to inculturation, alert to the unique cultural patterns of the people they serve.

The doctrine of the Incarnation engages us today because we want to contemplate the humanity of Jesus as the door and window onto his divinity. We also do this because we wish to hold onto our human dignity in a culture that could easily treat us as a number, a thing, a category rather than a person. The threat to human dignity which the preoccupation with sexuality today poses must move us to probe more deeply that dignity and all that it entails.

The Renaissance began with much the same insight about the human and eventually framed it artistically in the works of Michelangelo, Palestrina and many others. We are only at the threshold of this perception about our human value. We can confidently anticipate that poets, playwrights, artists and sculptors will capture this for us in glorious new ways within the context of the faith.

23. Council of Trent

Winter Light at Trent: A Diary Entry
(December 4, 1563)

Eight inches of snow greeted me this morning as I prepared to attend the closing session of the Council of Trent. This won't disappoint my nephews, who made the eighty-mile trip north to Innsbruck for a ski weekend; the winds were taking the storm in that direction. The weather may be chilly, but I feel a warm glow of satisfaction in knowing I have been part of one of the greatest achievements in the history of the Church.

I have often wondered why it took so long to call a council in the first place. Why, I believe it was twenty-five years between Luther's break with the Church at the Diet of Worms and the opening of the Council of Trent. Apparently politics had a lot to do with it. One of the old cardinals told me that Pope Clement VII was more interested in settling the financial problems of his Medici relatives in Florence than in facing the Protestant question.

Francis I of France was hostile to any idea of a council, but Charles V of Spain was eager to see it come about. The German Catholics were interested, but they wanted a council that unreasonably limited the role of the pope in the proceedings.

Still, I know some work was done to reconcile Rome with the Protestants. I have reports on ecumenical meetings between Catholic and Protestant theologians. I mustn't forget the ecumenical conference at Ratisbon. Young John Calvin was there, as well as all the princes of Germany, the Emperor himself and a papal ambassador. What a shame it failed. The two sides were no longer able to communicate.

I was in Rome for the election of Pope Paul III. What excitement he generated when he told the cheering throngs that he would devote all his energies to calling a council. How disappointing to note that he first used his energies to find a comfortable royal position for his son, Pierluigi, and then to expend himself in making sure that his grandson married the daughter of Charles V of Spain.

When he did get around to calling a council, he met troubles on all sides. The cardinals said no. The French king said no and refused to let his bishops attend. I myself bore the personal invitation of the pope to the German Protestants. But matters were too far gone; they would have nothing to do with it.

Somehow, Pope Paul overcame all immediate obstacles and announced that the Council would open at Trent on November 22, 1542. Three papal legates arrived, but found no

FOR BACKGROUND

One of the most important decisions the Council of Trent made was to commission the writing of a Catholic catechism. This was the first time that the Church officially sought to present the truths of Catholicism in a comprehensive and systematic way. Completed in 1566 and popularly known as the *Roman Catechism*, it was intended to serve as a guide for clergy in instructing the faithful.

The *Roman Catechism* presented a positive and nonpolemical account of the teachings of the Catholic Church. It did not dwell on condemning Protestant errors, but addressed them by stating exactly what Catholics believe and teach. Given the heated and antagonistic spirit of the times, the *Roman Catechism* was a model of calm and confident proclamation. Its extensive use of Scripture enabled Catholics to see more clearly the biblical basis of their faith.

With its authority resting on the fact that it was decreed by an ecumenical council and approved by the pope, the *Roman Catechism* proved to be enormously influential. It went through 817 editions in four centuries (the first known English one was published in 1829). The renowned English theologian, John Cardinal Newman, spoke highly of it: "I rarely preach a sermon, but I go to this beautiful and complete catechism to get both my matter and my doctrine." As late as 1960 Pope John XXIII was still recommending it.

▼

FOR DISCUSSION/REFLECTION

For the everyday life of the Church, Trent's reform of the Mass was a significant achievement. Trent abolished *simony*, the selling of Masses as well as the selling of ecclesiastical posts. Trent unified the texts of the Mass, eliminated the superstitions surrounding the Mass and put priests under strict notice to follow the rubrics perfectly and avoid any fanciful or eccentric additions. Historical understanding of the evolution of the Mass was still at a primitive stage. Common opinion at the time traced the Catholic way of saying Mass back to Saint Peter. Below you will find some value judgments flowing from Trent's treatment of the Mass. What is your reaction? Discuss.

The universal Latin Mass, the same all over the world, was good because it emphasized the clarity, stability and universality of Catholic teaching and identity.
 Good___ Bad___ Don't know___

This unchangeable Mass made people feel the Church was unchangeable.
 Good___ Bad___ Don't know___

Trent felt it could not put the Mass in the vernacular because that would prove the Protestants right in saying the Church has no claim to divine authority.
 Good___ Bad___ Don't know___

one there. By spring of the next year, about a dozen bishops had assembled, but in the meantime war had broken out between France and Spain, so the meeting was closed until the war ended.

Eventually, the Council did open. It was on December 13, 1545. Thirty-one bishops and forty-eight *periti* (theologians, canon lawyers and other religious experts) gathered that day. Reginald Pole, the English cardinal, gave the opening speech. He said it was clerical sin that had brought religion to such a sad state of affairs. He made a passionate plea for sincerity in the task that lay before us.

Our first problem was one of procedure. We settled on three different kinds of gatherings: Each new matter would be first debated by the experts, with the bishops listening in on the discussions. Then the bishops would take up the matter themselves in private session. Finally, when they had hammered out a satisfactory statement of the case, it would be presented for a vote at a public session. Their decree would be read out as a Council conclusion.

I'm rather glad that all the bishops didn't attend. It was much easier to get work done. We ranged in attendance from thirty-two to two hundred and twenty-eight bishops. The majority were from Italy, but there was no unity of opinion among them. Italy was divided into the Kingdom of Naples, the Papal States and the Venetian Republic. Charles V controlled Naples. The pope set the tone for the bishops from his domain. The Venetian Republic held its own maverick position.

The Dominican Order wielded a deep influence on our proceedings. Twenty-three of the bishops and twenty-eight of the theologians were from the Order of Saint Dominic. That is why the teachings of Saint Thomas Aquinas were so central to our deliberations.

We had two vast areas to cope with: namely, the question of discipline and the clarification of doctrine. Every reformer, both Catholic and Protestant, had cried out about the abuses in the Church. Trent heard the complaints and did something about them.

Take the question of benefice. This was just another word for a source of income such as a diocese, an abbey or a parish. The problem arose when one person gained control of a large number of benefices and thus became mainly interested in the funds and not in the spiritual welfare of the people. Scandals arose when sales, trading and shady transactions concerning benefices made a mockery of religion and nursed the greed of the beneficiaries.

Another abuse was the custom of the absentee landlord. For example, the Bishop of Parma might also be the Abbot of Palermo. If he lived at Parma, he might never see Palermo even though he collected income for being abbot there. Milan hadn't seen its bishop for over a hundred years!

A peculiar variation of this, which happened in my uncle's family, was the custom of delaying the consecration of a bishop. My fourteen-year-old cousin was named Bishop of Pisa. From the moment of his appointment he began to receive income from the diocese. He put off ordination to the priesthood and consecration to the episcopacy until he was twenty-four. At that ripe age, he fell in love and decided to marry. He simply renounced his right to the mitre of Pisa, but meanwhile had ten years of income in his savings account.

Needless to say, at Trent we legislated a stop to all this. From then on, we allowed only one benefice to one man. We abolished absentee landlords. We insisted that a man be consecrated within six months of his appointment as bishop.

We also decided to eliminate the practice of fund-raising through the sale of indulgences. Luther had raised strong objections to this years before, and we could only agree that it was a custom that caused much mischief and misunderstanding among the people.

Our second task was the doctrinal one. We attempted to clear up key issues rather than give full expositions of the doctrines discussed. We tried to put forward the traditional teaching of the Church in such a way as to avoid confusion. A good part of our work was devoted to the doctrines of justification and the Eucharist.

Luther had taught that a person is justified by faith alone. What he meant was that the act of faith alone made a person a friend of God; good human deeds did not merit divine friendship. We said that both were needed: the act of faith and good human deeds. Thus God becomes our friend both through our faith and the human acts that please God. I realize that Luther knew the importance of good behavior in Christian life. But it's amazing to me that he couldn't see how it merited friendship with God, at least in some way.

As to the Eucharist, we preferred the term *transubstantiation* as the way of describing the mystery. The very substance or reality of the bread and wine change into the substance and reality of Jesus at the Mass. We further argued that Jesus is totally present under each species. There is, therefore, no necessity to receive him under the form of both bread and wine at Mass.

In speaking of the Mass as a sacrifice, we made clear that there was only one true sacrifice, that of Jesus at Calvary. The Mass simply makes that same sacrifice present in our own time and place.

At our closing session the Bishop of Catania asked the fathers of the Council, "Are you agreed that the Council should be closed and that the pope should be asked by the legates in the name of the Council to ratify all the decrees and definitions accepted under the three popes: Paul III, Julius III and Pius IV?"

All agreed. Cardinal Guise then said, "May we all confess the faith and observe the decrees of the most holy ecumenical Council of Trent!" The fathers replied, "We shall always confess that faith and observe those decrees."

The cardinal went on. "That is the faith of all of us. We are all united in it, we embrace it and subscribe to it. That is the faith of Peter and the apostles. That is the faith of our fathers. That is the right faith."

The hostile spirit of the times prevented Catholics from admitting that Protestants could be right about anything.
Good___ Bad___ Don't know___

Trent's failure to give people a sense of participation in the Mass forced them to run after extra-liturgical devotions so they could have a sense of participation in the worship of the Church.
Good___ Bad___ Don't know___

Then we sang the *Te Deum*. We had tears in our eyes. I saw many bishops who had fought and argued with each other these long years now embrace and kiss each other. I believe that we have produced a brilliant achievement with God's help and the endless goodwill of our participants. I leave the winter light at Trent with hope for the Church we have tried to renew.

FOR DISCUSSION/REFLECTION

The Council of Trent unified the Church after the Reformation had landed some serious blows. The Mass is a central part of Catholic life and the Eucharist is the central part of the Mass. Some of the reformers made the Bible the most important part of worship. Trent said that the celebration of the Mass had to be universal, meaning that it must be the same no matter where you were. It made the Church seem unchangeable.

Latin was the official language of the Church. Have you ever attended a Latin Mass? Why would the Church want to have the Mass said in a language that most people do not understand? What languages is the Mass said in today? Is it still the same? Does the language change what is going on there?

How much participation would you have in the Mass if it was only said in Latin? How much participation do you have in the vernacular (the language of the people)?

How has the ritual of the Mass changed since the Council of Trent?

Many of the laws introduced at the Council of Trent were changed or modified at Vatican II. It is interesting to note how laws and rules change but essential doctrines or beliefs never do. We believe the same things now as Christians did in the apostles' time.

Do you know the present day laws that pertain to fasting before Communion, Lenten fast and abstinence, wearing hats in church, Saturday night liturgies?

Council of Trent—Looking Back

This imaginary diary of a bishop at the last session of the Council of Trent stresses several items: (1) why it took nearly twenty-five years to get the Council going; (2) the disciplinary decisions of Trent; (3) the theological issues faced at this Council.

Political intrigue and selfish motives kept the Council from being a reality for nearly a quarter of a century. It's obvious that we should lament this. It is a pleasure, however, to report that the Church had the wisdom and good grace eventually to face up to the problem and bring about a stunning reform of its internal life along with a theological statement that served as the backbone for religious faith and thought up to our own days.

The disciplinary measures dealt with the Church's economic policies and the training of seminarians. Through abuses, churchmen were gathering benefits from places where they did not labor. Trent struck firmly against absentee landlords, the appointment of unsuitable men to the episcopate and the strange custom of "delayed consecration." While our diarist doesn't mention the reform of the seminaries, it should be noted here that the general principles Trent enunciated for seminary education and training have endured to our own time.

The doctrinal statements faced the Lutheran challenge of justification by faith alone, the matter of the real presence and the sacrifice of the Mass. Since the rhetoric of Luther seemed to exclude human free choice in justification, the Church spoke strongly on this matter. Because the Protestant position seemed to dilute the doctrine of the real presence and the sacrificial character of the Mass, the Council of Trent took up the language of transubstantiation to explain the meaning of the real presence and emphasized the continuing re-presentation of the sacrifice of Christ in each Mass.

Today's ecumenical discussions are clearing up many of the misunderstandings that developed at the Reformation, but many divisions still remain. The gulf opened by four hundred years will not be healed in a day.

Enduring Impact

The work of the Council fathers at Trent (1545-1563) produced a powerful and enduring impact on the Church. It helped shape the direction of liturgy, catechetics, theology, Church law and authority for the next four centuries.

Liturgy. Trent established an Order for the Mass that precisely outlined the rubrics, texts and behavior to be expected at liturgy. In its dogmatic coverage of the Mass, Trent stressed the Mass as a true sacrifice that made present the sacrificial event of Jesus at Calvary. Trent also insisted on good preaching at Mass and urged people to receive Communion on Sundays. Saint Pius V, the post-Tridentine pope who worked hardest on liturgical reform, established the Congregation of Rites, a clerical commission to watch over liturgical behavior in the Church.

Catechetics. The *Roman Catechism* was a product of the Fathers of Trent. It may surprise many, but it is a masterpiece of *kerygmatic* composition, that is, founded in biblical content and style. Its outline was creed, liturgy, law. Its theory was that religion begins with God. Hence the creed was a statement of God's work for humanity. Liturgy was the expression of this relationship with God experienced in the Mass and the sacraments. The law (the Commandments) was the outline of what people should do in the light of what God has done for them. Through the catechism Trent emphasized the need for all Catholics to have a good catechetical training.

Theology. Trent relied on the work of Thomas Aquinas for its theological expression. Most manuals of theology followed the same general outline: God, Trinity, Incarnation, Church, Sacraments, Morality, Last Things. The approach reflected the preference for clear statement of doctrine and the role of faith as firm agreement with Church teaching and fidelity to tradition.

Church law. Trent touched the day-to-day life of Catholics with laws about Communion fast, the Lenten fast, Friday abstinence from meat and extensive marriage laws. Since Vatican II Catholics have seen changes in these fast and abstinence laws. Marriage laws, especially those dealing with annulments, have been updated and revised in a newly published Code of Canon Law.

The magisterium. Because of the confusion generated by both the cultural chaos following the Black Death and the ecclesiastical chaos following the Reformation, it was important for Trent to make a strong case for the authority of the official teachers of the Church, particularly the pope and bishops. Without the kind of unity this would bring, there was no real guarantee that the hard work of Trent would last. Hence, in the following centuries the term *magisterium* applied mainly, if not exclusively, to this group within the Church.

It is popular among current Church reformers to look down on Trent. This is unfair: Trent provided a framework for the Church's operations that lasted four hundred years.

Why are Church councils good? Does the Church need one of these every so often? Why do changes upset some people? Do we equate change with weakness?

This has been a time of such disaster, and the malice of heretics so obdurate, that there is nothing they have not infected with error at the instigation of the enemy of the human race, even in what was clearest in our profession of faith or most certainly defined.

—Council of Trent

A REFORMING COUNCIL

In 1906, while secretary to Bishop Radini Tedeschi of Bergamo, the future Pope John XXIII came across the archives of Saint Charles Borromeo, the great Counter-Reformation saint who, some three hundred fifty years earlier, had been bishop of Bergamo. In these thirty-nine volumes Roncalli, whose scholarly vocation it would be to edit them, saw how Borromeo set about the reform of the diocese according to the decrees of the Council of Trent. Throughout his work as editor, Roncalli was heartened to discover that the Council of Trent was not an anti-Protestant council but a reforming one.

VIDEO

The Reformation. Encyclopedia Britannica (46 minutes).

From Protestant Challenge to Pastoral Concern—Connecting to Our Times

We have already made several substantial connections to the Second Vatican Council in this book. We must do so repeatedly because it stands as the turning point of the Church's history in modern times. So once again we draw a link between Vatican II and an event of the past, this time, the Council of Trent. The angle that engages our attention here is the contrast between a Trent that strove to respond to doctrinal and disciplinary challenges and a Vatican II which was primarily pastoral in nature.

The Council of Trent was born in an age of ecclesiastical controversy and necessarily had to deal with the Protestant Reformation. Vatican II was called to update the Church's pastoral responsibilities in the area of liturgy, Scripture, catechesis, priesthood and relations with other Christians and non-Christians, particularly the Jewish community.

Central to Vatican II's approach to pastoral mission was the understanding of the Church. At Trent the bishops stressed the eternal, hierarchical nature of the Church in the face of the Protestant emphasis on the Church's "invisible side." At Vatican II the bishops dwelt much more on the Church's spiritual nature as a mystery, as God's people, as the Body of Christ, as a temple of the Spirit, while not ignoring its institutional reality. This was embodied in the document *Lumen Gentium, Light of Nations.*

But the bishops went beyond this internal reflection. They also explored the Church's relation to the modern world. How can the Church minister to a new world with its global awareness, the information explosion, the scientific mind and the enormous social problems presented by the developing nations? They wrote their conclusions in *Gaudium et Spes, The Church in the Modern World.*

Ecumenical Councils intensely reflect a Church in historical progress. Through the lens of Trent and Vatican II we encounter a Church in action, living by the Spirit and ready to move forward.

24. The American Scene

Catholics came early to what would eventually be the continental United States. Spanish Catholics arrived in St. Augustine, Florida, in 1565 and penetrated California as early as 1542. By 1772 there were mission stations in San Diego, San Carlos (Carmel), San Gabriel (near Los Angeles), San Antonio and San Luis Obispo. Spanish Catholic activity in the Southwest was equally impressive. They founded Santa Fe in 1609 and, in 1630, reported baptisms of five thousand Indians in New Mexico.

French Catholics settled in the Louisiana Territory in 1699 and controlled the area until 1766, when the Spanish took over. In 1755 the French exiles from Acadia (see Longfellow's "Evangeline") added to the number of French Catholics in Louisiana. The Acadians are the ancestors of the Cajuns.

John Carroll

But the civilization that laid the foundations of the future United States was English and Protestant. England's continuing religious reformation in the sixteenth and seventeenth centuries affected the religious aspects of American colonization. First roots were struck in Jamestown, Virginia, in 1607. By that time England had definitely split with Rome. The Pilgrims came to Plymouth in 1620. They and their fellow Puritans founded the Massachusetts Bay Colony.

The Puritans represented the dissenting wing of England's reformation. Calvinist in their theology, they were resolutely opposed to Roman Catholicism and stoutly repudiated any Catholicizing influences in Protestantism; they would have nothing of the "papists." One reason they blocked any celebration of Christmas was because they identified such merrymaking as a papist creation—too Catholic.

Puritans firmly believed that Catholics had corrupted the gospel. They viewed Rome as "Babylon on the Tiber" and they believed the pope to be the anti-Christ of the Book of Revelation. Their recent historical experience gave them plenty of evidence that their religious judgments were unassailable. Catholic Queen Mary I ("Bloody Mary") had appeared to support the burning of three hundred Protestants between 1555 and 1558.

They read and reread John Foxe's *Book of Martyrs*, reminding them how Catholics had martyred Protestants. Vivid in their memory was the recent Gunpowder Plot of 1605, when Guy Fawkes and a group of Catholic subversives planned to blow up King James and the Houses of Parliament. On top of this, England's worst political enemies were France and Spain—both Catholic countries.

These English settlers barely had a foothold on the northeast coast of the United States. Not unreasonably, they feared the possibility of hostile action from Catholic New

FOR BACKGROUND

The New World was discovered in 1492 during the papacy of Innocent VIII. There was a scramble to see who would rule and who would settle the newly acquired lands. Pope Alexander VI sent the first missionaries and also set up the Papal Line of Demarcation in South America.

The Reformation came right on the heels of this discovery. The New World afforded a haven for many persons fleeing from religious persecution, both Catholic and Protestant. These groups who could not live in harmony in Europe eventually would do so America.

France to the north in Canada and Catholic New Spain to the south in Florida, Texas and Mexico. Protestant New England had skirmishes with the French and Indian alliance from Canada, and Protestant Georgia tangled with Catholic Floridians to the south. Religious and political poison soured the environment of the English colonies.

The Puritans set the pace for a strain of anti-Catholicism that became endemic to the American scene. In 1647 they enacted a statute against any priests who might appear. (Priests were automatically considered to be disturbers of the peace and enemies of the true religion.) If caught, a priest was to be put in jail for life. "If he escapes and is afterward retaken, he shall be punished with death."

Actual persecution of Catholics in the colonies was, in reality, relatively mild, mainly because there were so few of them. Despite the restrictive laws and unwelcoming atmosphere, some Catholics did arrive and settle mainly in Maryland, Pennsylvania, Virginia, New York and New Jersey.

The most predominant Catholic settlement was in Maryland. Catholics tried to keep a low profile religiously in colonial days, while at the same time building up their prosperity. They belonged to the social and political elite of the Maryland colony. They were pragmatic, rather than ideological, Catholics. Maryland governors were to "instruct all Roman Catholics to be silent on all occasions concerning matters of religion, and treat Protestants with as much mildness and favor as justice will permit."

Catholic backing of the American Revolution won grudging acceptance from the Protestant majority, and anti-Catholic prejudice, articulated powerfully by the Puritan intellectuals and divines, abated slightly. But it penetrated Protestant consciousness and would flare up again and again in American history. Catholics would live with the tension of proving to Protestants that they could be good Americans—and proving to the pope they could be good Catholics.

The story of Charles Carroll, cosigner of the Declaration of Independence, and of his cousin Bishop John Carroll is the first—and one of the more pleasant—chapters in the stormy relationship of American Catholics to American Protestants.

The setting for the imaginary dialogue that follows is the park in front of Independence Hall in Philadelphia a few years after the victory over the English. A prominent Catholic woman, Mrs. Thomas FitzSimmons, is engaged in a discussion with John Carroll, America's recently elected first Catholic bishop.

'For God and Country': A Dialogue
(c. 1791)

Mrs. FitzSimmons: I'm amazed that we have created a country that has separation of Church and state. That certainly wasn't William Penn's intention. Over our fireplace is an engraving of his theory of government: "Government seems to me to be a part of religion itself, a thing sacred in its institution and purpose."

Bishop Carroll: All the first colonists felt the same way. The Mayflower Compact of 1620 reflects the sentiments of your William Penn. The Pilgrims and others came here to establish religious states purged of the problems back home. Separating the state from religion was farthest from their minds. The Pilgrims were blunt in their intentions: "Having undertaken for the glory of God and the advancement of the Christian faith a voyage to plant a colony in the northern parts of Virginia, we covenant and bind ourselves in a body politic to further the needs of the aforesaid."

Mrs. FitzSimmons: The colonists created a new style of Church-state relations. They reduced the clergy's authority and would not let them be quasi-nobility. The laity managed the churches and introduced a democratic style.

Bishop Carroll: I think the best thing the colonists brought with them was the concept of freedom of religion. They practically invented the idea of freedom of conscience in religious matters.

Mrs. FitzSimmons: Except for Catholics and witches!

Bishop Carroll: Old prejudices die hard. The Salem witch trials of 1692 were a disgrace.

Mrs. FitzSimmons: I still resent the righteousness of the Puritans toward Catholics and other non-Puritans.

Bishop Carroll: Thank God for Roger Williams and Anne Hutchinson. They made Rhode Island the home of religious tolerance.

Mrs. FitzSimmons: Except for Catholics! It was a little pompous for them to say, "Let the saints of the Most High walk in this colony without molestation in the name of Jehovah." Just let a Catholic try it in those days.

Bishop Carroll: Still, the ideal of religious freedom was born there. I can appreciate their fear of Catholics. They still recalled too vividly the Catholic brutalization of Protestants in Europe.

Mrs. FitzSimmons: Anti-Catholicism lingers in our new republic. I am furious with New Hampshire for still forbidding Catholics to hold public office fifteen years after the Declaration of Independence.

Bishop Carroll: It will take time to convince Protestants we are coequal citizens. Massachusetts and Connecticut still make Protestantism the official state religion within their boundaries.

Mrs. FitzSimmons: I sometimes think it is only because of the

FOR BACKGROUND

The Councils of Baltimore were a series of provincial (meetings of the province of Baltimore) and plenary (including all archbishops and bishops) councils which met in Baltimore, Maryland, throughout the nineteenth century.

The First Provincial Council was convened in 1829 by Bishop John England of Charleston and discussed such issues as rising anti-Catholic prejudice, trusteeism and appropriate Catholic literature. Six more councils followed. In 1846, at the Sixth Provincial Council, Mary was chosen as the Patroness of the United States under the title of the Immaculate Conception.

The First Plenary Council was convened in May of 1852 and addressed the growth of the Catholic community, pastoral and parochial life, ritual, liturgy and Church finances. It decreed that parochial schools be built wherever possible, that catechism instruction be given to children and that seminaries be created in every diocese or province. The Second Plenary Council was held in 1866, soon after the Civil War, and was primarily one of consolidation.

The Third Plenary Council convened in November 1884 under the direction of Archbishop James Gibbons. Its decrees shaped the direction of American Catholicism until the Second Vatican Council. Its chief concern was education, mandating both the establishment of elementary schools within two years and the founding of the Catholic University of America. The Council's most notable achievement was the drafting of a uniform catechism for the United States: the *Baltimore Catechism*.

FOR DISCUSSION/REFLECTION

Protestants were a minority in Europe but became the majority in America. Catholics were generally not trusted by these Protestants, so Catholics did not participate in much of the secular society. Do you think that this religious discrimination is still alive today? Are Catholics welcome everywhere today? Can a Catholic run for office?

A generation or two ago this country had many ethnic churches. If an immigrant came from Italy or Spain or Poland or Ireland or wherever, he or she would join a parish of other immigrants of like background. Why did the Church have these ethnic parishes? Did these people feel more "at home" in these churches? What ethnic churches are found today? Who are today's immigrants?

The only Catholic to sign the Declaration of Independence was Charles Carroll, cousin of John Carroll, the first American bishop. Are many Catholics involved in public office today? Is it a conflict of interest to be Catholic and a political leader?

There has been only one Catholic President of the United States. Al Smith from New York was the first Catholic to run for president in 1928 but was defeated. Catholic John F. Kennedy won election in 1960. Why would people question the performance of a president because of his religion? Are there any religious groups that could not be elected? Why? What are your feelings on this?

Saint Elizabeth Ann Seton was instrumental in the beginning of parochial schools. Today there are Catholic schools from preschool to university. At

wealth of Catholics that we have any freedom at all.

Bishop Carroll: Money brings power. We have comparatively few Catholics in the United States, but many of us are big landowners or engaged in rich shipping enterprises like the Moylans.

Mrs. FitzSimmons: Why did we back the Revolution?

Bishop Carroll: The English kings favored freedom for Protestants, but not for Catholics. Even in our "Catholic" colony, Maryland, there was difficulty for Catholics.

Mrs. FitzSimmons: And don't forget my Quaker state. We could not worship in public, have voting rights or hold public office. Mr. Penn was for it, but not the king.

Bishop Carroll: Our Church was in a sorry state on July 4, 1776. We had only twenty-five priests in the thirteen colonies, mostly in Maryland and Pennsylvania. Virtually all of them were Jesuits, an order which had been suppressed in Europe. The priests could not look there for leadership.

Mrs. FitzSimmons: I felt we had no leadership. How could we when the Catholic bishop of London was in charge of us? How was he going to take much interest in a flock three thousand miles away?

Bishop Carroll: Chaos, that's what it was. No leadership. The Church needed organization. All twenty-five priests favored revolution.

Mrs. FitzSimmons: So did most of their parishioners.

Bishop Carroll: That is why my cousin Charles and I joined Mr. Franklin on a diplomatic mission to Canada to enlist the support of French Catholics for our revolution.

Mrs. FitzSimmons: So we joined the Protestants in fostering armed revolt. It was the first time Protestants looked at us as partners. We all had a vested interest in preserving freedom of religion.

Bishop Carroll: Not to mention our common economic interests. Political freedom would lead us to religious freedom and economic independence.

Mrs. FitzSimmons: Oh, how we joined in that fight! Washington made Moylan an aide-de-camp. John Barry put his ships at the service of the navy and became a hero.

Bishop Carroll: My Maryland produced the Maryland Old Line Contingent from St. Mary's County. They are very proud down there about their role in the protection of New York and the defense of Boston.

Mrs. FitzSimmons: Yes, the Protestants have warmed up considerably toward us because of our clear patriotism. Imagine that bigot Jonathan Boucher preaching a sermon on toleration for Catholics.

Bishop Carroll: Our best supporter was President Washington. They all knew my cousin Charles Carroll was right when he said, "Our blood flowed as freely in proportion to our numbers to cement the fabric of independence as any of our fellow citizens."

Mrs. FitzSimmons: Our courage has paid off. We have a Bill of Rights that guarantees religious freedom for Catholics and everyone else. and now we have our own bishop in you, my dear John Carroll.

Bishop Carroll: I cannot help but think that our American Revolution is part of God's plan. In a recent sermon I said, "Since the American Revolution, I have always thought that Providence was reserving an even more extraordinary revolution in the order of grace."

Mrs. FitzSimmons: Church and state are now separated. But Church and society are not. I believe that is how God's grace has touched us and I am convinced the old Church of Europe will see it our way one day.

all levels of education many non-Catholics attend these schools. Why? When might a non-Catholic feel out of place in a Catholic school? Many other denominations now have schools as well. Why does the country seem to be in need of religiously affiliated schools?

The American Scene—Looking Back

During the colonial period in America, the Catholic Church was generally outlawed. There was mutual distrust and fear between Protestants and Catholics. Protestants thought of the Church as a political power rather than as a religious community, while Catholics looked on the Protestant Churches as Christianity in various states of deterioration. As a result of these attitudes, the Protestant majority withheld from Roman Catholics both active and passive participation in colonial affairs. In 1776 Maryland and Pennsylvania were the first to pass a declaration of religious freedom which offered Catholics the opportunity to participate openly in the public life of the republic. After the Revolution, when the Constitution was being written, the authors thought that a declaration of religious freedom was the only possible solution to allow for the variety of beliefs that existed in the republic.

The First Amendment to the Constitution put the Church within the law and legally enabled Catholics to participate in government.

In spite of discrimination, Catholics did contribute to the formation of the American nation. Two outstanding Catholics noted for the part they played in this early period are John and Charles Carroll.

The Carrolls

John and Charles Carroll were cousins born during the colonial period to a wealthy, landowning family whose status raised them above the usual condemnation of "papists." Both boys attended a Jesuit school in Saint Omer, France. Charles returned to Maryland to become one of its wealthiest citizens and, after 1776, one of the most prominent public figures in the young republic. John went on to the Jesuit novitiate.

After ordination John taught in Europe until 1773 when the Jesuits were suppressed. At forty years of age, he returned to his mother's home in Rock Creek, Maryland, and assumed the duties of a parish priest while watching the mounting conflict between England and the colonies. Apparently there was no question in his mind on which side his allegiance lay. When the request came to accompany the

FOR FURTHER READING

Ellis, John Tracy. *American Catholicism.* Chicago: University of Chicago Press, 1969.

Hennesey, James J. *American Catholics.* London and New York: Oxford University Press, 1981.

FOR BACKGROUND

The prevailing reputation of Jesuits was such that former President John Adams wrote a letter of warning to President Thomas Jefferson in 1816 stating: "If ever there was a body of men who merited eternal damnation on earth and in hell, it is this Society of Loyola's. Nevertheless, we are compelled by our system of religious toleration to offer them asylum." Asylum was granted in part because of the Society's suppression in 1773 due to political pressures in Europe. The Jesuits were not fully restored as a religious order until 1814.

committee to Canada, John accepted the appointment although he had strong convictions about the inadvisability of clergy entering the political arena. Later, as first bishop of the United States, he converted this conviction into one of the guiding principles for the American clergy.

The public role of the Carrolls did a great deal to aid the social acceptance of Catholics. The well-known and staunch patriotism of Charles made the Carroll name respected throughout the colonies. Thus, the choice of a member of the Carroll family as the first Roman Catholic bishop of the United States did a great deal to bridge prejudice.

In 1790, John Carroll was consecrated the first bishop of Baltimore after having acted as vicar apostolic for a few years. For thirty years he did much to set the direction for the American Church. He forged a creative role for the Church in a new type of country rather than transmit a medieval institution to the infant republic. He requested of Rome the right for the American clergy to elect their hierarchy. (After he himself was elected, however, this privilege was withdrawn.) He also requested of Rome the right to use vernacular in the liturgy, but this was denied.

He set out to establish Catholicism in this young country and, to this end, he influenced the foundation of schools, the institution of new religious orders, the creation of dioceses and the repression of schisms. This work set the stage for a strong Church community and built a foundation on which the Church could grow.

John Carroll died in 1815, just prior to the arrival of waves of Catholic immigrants that would inundate and outnumber native-born Catholics. The newcomers brought with them new problems, but a secure foundation for the Catholic Church in the United States had already been laid.

During the administration of John Carroll, the uniquely American policy of separation of Church and state was inaugurated. To Europeans, this phrase seemed to mean that the new republic had made a conscious effort to eliminate religion as a force in public life. They interpreted it as a demeaning of religion. Yet this was not the American intention or meaning. The Declaration of Independence begins with a profession of faith in God, and the first article of the Bill of Rights prohibits the state from interfering with religion or its exercise. The American tradition, begun by the constituting body of the republic, put religion beyond the state, not the state beyond religion. It granted liberty to the Church, not exile from public life.

The Catholic Moment Has Come— Connecting to Our Times

The election of President John F. Kennedy marked a turning point in the acceptance of Catholics by the Protestant majority in the United States. Electing a Catholic president was the ultimate act of affirmation of the Catholic community. Now, affirmation is not the same as agreement. Nor does it imply that Catholicism will be immune from the bias and prejudice that was ordinary fare in American history from the days of the Puritans on. Catholic-bashing is still around.

But by and large Catholics can rest free and easy in American society as accepted partners in the great democratic experiment. In fact, Father Richard John Neuhaus, convert from the Lutheran Church, argues that the "Catholic Moment" has come. Until now, he explains, the American struggle to maintain and advance democratic values, virtues and ideals has been supported by the guidance of the Protestant churches. But with the weakening of the mainline Churches, there is need of a fresh and strong religious community, such as Catholicism, to take up the traditional role of fostering the virtues of participation, respect for others, family strength, education, faith and patriotism.

Neuhaus believes the Catholic Church is historically prepared, numerically significant (twenty-five percent of the population), spiritually vital and morally disciplined enough for this task. As he would say, "The Catholic Moment has arrived." He intends no hint of "takeover" or any intent to subvert the freedom of religion in our country. He is simply saying that what a vital Protestantism offered to the success of our democracy, Catholicism is presently able to continue. He is not saying that Protestantism no longer has anything to offer, or that Judaism and other people of good will will have no place in the public square. He observes that Catholicism has received a lot from America and should now shoulder responsibility equal to its gifts for the good of American society.

The tiny seed of Catholicism, born in colonial days, has now become an oak tree in the American garden along with the others. We have received much. We should now be givers more than takers.

FOR FURTHER READING

Crews, Clyde F. *American and Catholic: A Popular History of Catholicism in the United States.* Cincinnati: St. Anthony Messenger Press, 1994.

VIDEO

Catholics/Americans. Paulist Press (twenty-two fifteen-minute sections on six videocassettes).

Part Four
Modern Church

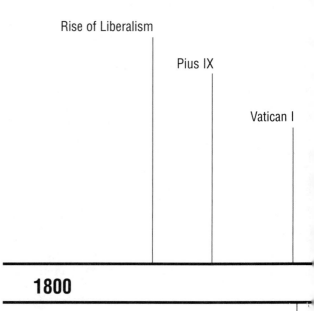

EVENTS IN THE CHURCH

Rise of Liberalism

Pius IX

Vatican I

1800

Franco-Prussian War

EVENTS IN SOCIETY

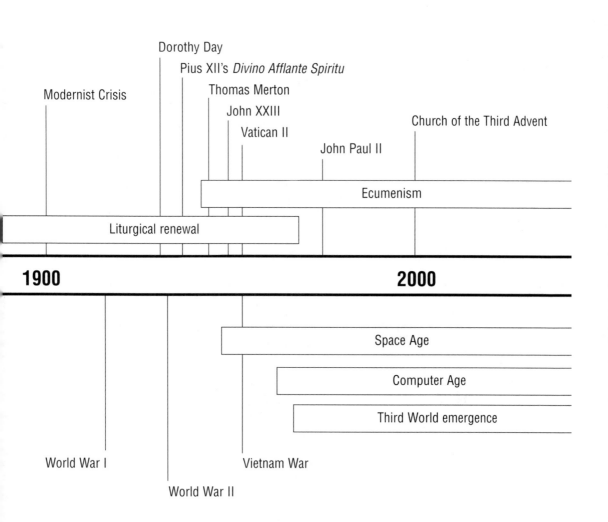

Dorothy Day

Pius XII's *Divino Afflante Spiritu*

Modernist Crisis

Thomas Merton

John XXIII

Vatican II

Church of the Third Advent

John Paul II

Ecumenism

Liturgical renewal

1900

2000

Space Age

Computer Age

Third World emergence

World War I

Vietnam War

World War II

25. On Guard Against Liberalism

Pius IX and the First Vatican Council
(1846-1878)

Pius IX

Pius IX was a charmer. A "people's pope," he loved strolling about Rome, chatting and joking with those he met. To him we owe the now common custom of large papal audiences. He wanted people from all over the world to come and see their Holy Father. He established the tradition of personal devotion to the pope.

Still, few popes have been more controversial; "Pio Nono" was hated as much as he was loved. Holding the longest tenure in the history of the papacy—thirty-two years—Pius had ample opportunity to dismay liberals and dash their hopes; he championed conservative causes right up to his death at eighty-six.

Things didn't start that way. Liberals cheered when they heard of his election. They misunderstood Pius from the beginning. At most an enlightened conservative, Pius was never a liberal. Admittedly, his first decisions had a liberal ring: He granted amnesty to political prisoners in the Papal States. He created some representative government in which the laity could have some jurisdiction over certain matters. He lifted censorship restrictions on political news (but not Church news). He retained absolute veto power, however. He did not approve of freedom of religion and forbade Jews in the Papal States political equality with Catholics.

Political developments soon drew Pius back from even these tentative enlightened measures. The leaders of the Risorgimento, a movement to unify the Italian states into one nation, were determined to remove northern Italy from Austrian control. The pope's parliament declared war on Austria, but Pius vetoed their decision. He would not allow a war against a Catholic nation.

The people were not pleased with his decision. Mobs rioted in the streets of Rome and an assassin killed his prime minister. Armed demonstrators surrounded the papal palace and aimed a cannon at it.

Pius disguised himself as a parish priest and escaped to Gaeta, where he took up residence in a small hotel. Risorgimento leader Garibaldi entered Rome and declared a republic. This happened in 1848, two years after the election of Pius IX.

A coalition of European diplomats met to find a way to return the pope to Rome. They backed a French expeditionary force which successfully recaptured Rome and gave it back to the pope. Whatever tender feelings Pius may have had for liberals, they no longer existed. As far as he was concerned, liberalism was synonymous with persecution of the Church.

Camillo Cavour and his Piedmont plan confirmed Pius's convictions. Cavour, leader of the liberals in the north Italian province of Piedmont, had abolished religious orders and stripped the Church of its control of education. Cavour envisioned uniting all of Italy under the leadership of the kingdom of Savoy. His conquest of Italy would begin by the seizure of the Papal States, though he planned to let the pope keep Rome.

By 1860 Cavour had taken the Papal States. (The French still held Rome for the pope.) Cavour asked the pope to renounce his right to the Papal States. In return the Italian government would recognize his right to the Vatican and the papal palaces and galleries; take a hands-off policy regarding the appointment of bishops and pastors; pay their salaries and provide the pope with funds to maintain his operations. The Church would have the freedom to teach and preach. (Cavour's proposal to Pius IX in 1860 was virtually the same as the one made by Mussolini to Pius XI in 1929—and accepted in the Lateran Treaty.)

One side of Pius IX agreed with the proposal: He did believe in the unification of Italy and was sympathetic to the goal of Risorgimento. But the other side of him prevailed in this dilemma: He could not bring himself to concede to a liberal ascendancy. It was too godless and too secular. Moreover, it seemed to him to be God's will that the Papal States remain in the hands of the pope. So he said no to Cavour.

A New Kind of Papacy

The twists of history benefited the Pope more than he knew at the time. At the very moment his political power virtually vanished, his spiritual power exploded. From being the temporal monarch of a small Italian principality, he emerged as a worldwide spiritual leader. In theory the popes always had this role; in practice this was less true. Local aristocratic bishops held great power in the various monarchies and checked papal influence on local diocesan affairs.

The decline of papal political power marked the rise of papal spiritual eminence. A trend called ultramontanism (literally, "beyond the mountain") contributed to this development. The movement centered in France, that country "beyond the mountain," north of the Alps. Ultramontanists were Rome-centered, pope-oriented Catholics. What motivated them? Many were political conservatives who viewed the pope as a defense against revolutionary ideas.

The move toward centralization had begun with the Concordat of 1801 between Pope Pius VII and France, which

FOR BACKGROUND

In the eighth century, when the popes needed protection from some barbarian tribes, Pepin the Short, King of the Franks, donated much conquered land to the papacy. On this land, known for centuries as the Papal States, was maintained a papal army to protect the pope. Little by little over the centuries, this land was ceded back to Italy. All that remains today is the Vatican and certain churches and palaces in Rome.

Pope Pius IX was pope longer than any other pope—thirty-two years. The Middle Ages were over and people were looking for more power within the Church. Pius IX kept the Church hierarchy intact.

[W]e teach and declare as a divinely revealed dogma that when the Roman pontiff speaks ex cathedra, that is, when, in the exercise of his office as shepherd and teacher of all Christians, in virtue of his supreme apostolic teaching, he defines a doctrine concerning faith or morals to be held by the whole Church, he possesses, by the divine assistance promised to him in blessed Peter, that infallibility which the divine Redeemer willed his Church to enjoy in defining doctrine concerning faith or morals.

—Vatican I

FOR BACKGROUND

The *Syllabus of Errors* characterized the papacy of Pius IX. Written in 1864, the *Syllabus* was appended to the encyclical *Quantra Cura*. It condemned eighty theses attributed to modern thinkers, including pantheism, religious freedom, rationalism, socialism's position on the right to private property, denial of the temporal power of the pope, subjection of the family to the state, freedom of the press and separation of Church and state.

Many Catholics and other committed Christians were disappointed with the *Syllabus*, which simply listed errors to be condemned and contained no explanation of their context. Lacking understanding of modern developments and their foundations, it only served to polarize liberal and conservative elements within the Church.

In his conclusion to the *Syllabus*, Pius IX refuted the notion that "the Roman Pontiff can, and ought to, reconcile himself and come to terms with progress, liberalism and modern civilization." Many would thus consider it the "charter" of conservative ultramontanism.

called for all the French bishops to resign. From that moment on, the pope could appoint his own men. They owed him their job, not the French king or some local baron. At the same time Pius IX encouraged the parish clergy to turn to him for help against their bishops' arbitrariness.

Suddenly the politically shorn Pius was the magnet for a host of new forces. He championed the conservatives who hated political liberalism, tied the bishops to him by the favor of his appointment and allied himself with the parish clergy (and in turn their parishioners). His audiences endeared him to thousands of pilgrims who went home with the good news that they had actually seen—maybe even met and touched—the pope.

Pius IX made the papacy an international spiritual force in a way no pope had ever done before. He became a single ruling figure, a holy and international force around whom the world's Catholics could focus their allegiance. In the very death of the old order, the pope led a movement of faith. One might call it a "triumphalism for the millions."

This papal role is so familiar to us we forget it was not always this way. In fact we owe this role to Pius IX's thirty-two years of shaping the posture of the papacy in this manner.

Vatican I and Papal Infallibility

In 1867 the Papal States were gone. Pius still had Rome, thanks to the French. International papalism was on the rise. Pius decided to call the First Vatican Council. It would celebrate the eighteen-hundredth anniversary of the martyrdoms of Peter and Paul. Pius intended to rally the Church against the liberal rationalism of the nineteenth century just as Trent stood against the Protestantism of the sixteenth century.

Seven hundred bishops gathered for the opening of the Council on the Feast of the Immaculate Conception, 1869. The bishops planned to study the nature of the Church, the roles of bishops and pope. As things turned out, the issue of papal infallibility quickly engulfed the Council Fathers. About eighty percent of the bishops favored making papal infallibility a dogma. The opposing twenty percent came from dioceses in Austria, Hungary, France and the United States.

The liberal bishops argued that the trend of history was on the side of freedom and that this doctrine would make the Church look too authoritarian. Conservatives countered that this new freedom constituted a grave danger to the Church's existence. Liberals worried that papal infallibility would give too much power to the pope and not enough to the bishops. Conservatives replied that it would temper the excessive independence of bishops, such as had occurred in France.

Despite the polarization, most bishops were of a moderate disposition. They sought a middle-ground solution. This was especially true of the Italian bishops, who made up a third of the assembly. They had not participated in putting infallibility on the agenda. But Pius IX backed the conservative intransigents. As the Council moved to a vote on the matter and it became clear that infallibility would pass, sixty bishops went home rather than go on record against it. On July 18, 1870, 535 bishops approved the doctrine. The weather report for that day indicates a violent thunderstorm swept the Vatican.

By the end of summer the Franco-Prussian War began. Vatican I recessed, never to open again. France pulled its troops out of Rome. The soldiers of the United Italy moved in. Pius retreated to the Vatican property and became the "Prisoner of the Vatican." Not until Vatican II was Vatican I's unfinished business about the Church and the bishops taken up. It may have been just as well. The mood of Vatican I did not seem to be one of readiness to speak of the Church as the "People of God" or to take up the issue of the bishops' collegial relationship to the pope, let alone matters of religious freedom and ecumenical dialogue.

Pius IX died in 1878. He left behind him a Church in siege as far as society was concerned: withdrawn, fearful, uninvolved. At the same time, life inside the Church was vibrant. Hundreds of thousands of men and women packed the convents and monasteries. New hospitals, schools and missions sprang up all over the world. Mass attendance percentages were probably the highest in history and the devotional life of the Church never had it so good. Catholicism became a world force to be reckoned with. The question was how anyone could open a dialogue. Ninety-two years later, John XXIII had an answer.

FOR BACKGROUND

Modernism describes an attempt by some early twentieth-century thinkers to bring Catholic teachings more into line with contemporary science, history, philosophy and Protestant biblical scholarship. Some of them altered Catholic doctrine to make it more acceptable to modern men and women. Pope Pius X condemned these errors in his decree, *Lamentabili*, and in his encyclical, *Pascendi* (both on September 8, 1907). Modernism's most extreme form questioned the divinity of Jesus, saw the Church in purely sociological terms, viewed Scripture as just literature and held that doctrine must change to suit the times. Some opponents of modernism became extreme themselves and had to be moderated by Pope Benedict XV (1914-1921).

Liberalism—Looking Back

The eighteenth-century Enlightenment, the French Revolution of 1789 and the bloodbaths of the Napoleonic wars devastated the Catholic Church, especially in France and its environs. Rationalist radicals oversaw the emptying of all the monasteries, the slaughter of priests and nuns, the pillaging of churches. Napoleon humiliated the pope and made puppets out of the bishops. People questioned the very existence of the Church.

In 1815, only twenty-five years after the French Revolution, an astonishing turnabout took place. Thousands of new recruits flocked to the monasteries and seminaries. Missionary orders suddenly flourished again. Intellectuals reevaluated the thinking of the Enlightenment and declared it was not as impressive as it first seemed.

New thinkers judged the Enlightenment's view of human nature too shallow. They repudiated its mechanized vision of nature and renounced its dogma of progress. Was the "reign of terror" progress? Were the Napoleonic wars that drained the blood of Europe's youth progress? Some progress! The new thinkers sought once again the values of

FOR DISCUSSION/REFLECTION

Respond to the following "forced choice" opinion sample. Discuss your answers:

Most Catholics are bothered by papal infallibility.
    Agree___ Disagree___

Most Catholics do not understand the limits of papal infallibility
    Agree___ Disagree___

It was unwise of Pius IX to encourage worldwide personal devotion to the pope, because this diminishes local loyalty to the bishop.
    Agree___ Disagree___

Pius IX was right in rejecting Cavour's proposal about the Papal States and accompanying concessions. Pius XI should have similarly rejected Mussolini's proposal in 1929.
    Agree___ Disagree___

It would not make much difference to us if the pope were still the ruler of the Papal States.
    Agree___ Disagree___

Lammenais should have swallowed his pride, accepted defeat and stayed in the Church.
    Agree___ Disagree___

Just as the Church finally accepted many of the liberal premises, so one day in the future the Church will accept many Marxist premises.
    Agree___ Disagree___

The study of the context of history excuses the decisions of people whom we think were wrong by our standards.
    Agree___ Disagree___

faith, mystery, reverence and regard for tradition.

Nevertheless, disenchantment with liberalism was not outright divorce. Many tenets of liberalism clearly were here to stay: The liberal agenda called for democratic government and the elimination of Church control of marriage and education. Reaction to the violent results of liberal philosophy meant that liberals would lie low but not disappear.

Between 1815 and 1830 Europe was in no mood for liberalism or any of its revolutions. Kings returned to their thrones with self-confidence, supported by the conservative backlash. The Church, accustomed to its traditional partnership of "throne and altar," was content.

Lammenais' Challenge

In 1831, new stirrings of liberalism were noted, this time inside the Church. A brilliant priest named Lammenais became the founder of Catholic liberalism. Together with the eloquent preacher Lacordaire and the scholarly historian Montalembert, he fought for the acceptance of liberal concepts within the Church.

His fundamental premise was that Church and state should be separated. He counseled the Church to examine more carefully the trends of history. He was convinced, correctly, that monarchies were dying. The Church should cut its ties with moribund forms of government and back the democratic wave of the future. At the same time, Lammenais advocated the concept of a strong papacy.

He believed in freedom of education and freedom of the press: One must trust in the power of truth to overcome error. And fifty years ahead of his time, he preached the right of every human being to have a vote. One should trust in the common sense of the people and their reserve of popular wisdom. Said he, "Let us not tremble before liberalism. Let us Catholicize it."

He could hardly have preached a more unpopular message. By no standards of the time was the Church ready for liberalism—even a Catholic one. The bishops preferred to tremble. They pointed out to him that such a plan would impoverish the Church overnight. Lammenais thought that was a splendid idea. At last the Church would be identified with the majority of humanity that was in fact poor, as well as with the Christ of Bethlehem and Calvary. He did not move them. Even the secular liberals repudiated him, especially his concept of universal suffrage. In 1831 they were not about to give the vote to the "ragged masses"—or to women.

Lammenais felt there was only one place to turn. Had he not supported the concept of a strong papacy? Surely the pope would listen to him. He misread Gregory XVI, the closed-minded authoritarian predecessor to Pius IX. Gregory probably felt he was, in fact, sufficiently strong. What more power did the papacy need? The papacy had survived the insulting behavior of Napoleon and lived to bury him.

But Lammenais and his two friends, Montalembert and Lacordaire, thought they could change Gregory's mind.

They wrote a memorandum explaining their views and set out for Rome as "pilgrims for God and liberty." They gave the pope their memorandum on December 30, 1831. They waited for his reply. And waited...and waited. No answer. Disillusioned, they returned to France. The pope waited six months to give them his answer: a thundering no! His encyclical *Mirari Vos* totally rejected their plan.

Lammenais was crushed. Still, he spent a year trying to gain some concessions. In a series of letters with the Vatican he hoped to pry open some corner where a dialogue could begin. The pope would not listen; he demanded obedience. Lammenais despaired when the pope supported the Orthodox Russian Czar's suppression of Catholic Poland's rebellion. Bitter and exasperated, Lammenais left the Church which had "divorced itself from Christ to fornicate with his torturers."

Why wouldn't the Pope bend a little? Why was the Church of the 1830's—and throughout most of the nineteenth century—so intransigent about liberalism? Perhaps a comparison with the twentieth-century Church's attitude toward communism may help.

The Russian communist revolution was blatantly atheistic and overtly anti-Church, not only in theory, but in practice. Communists used police-state methods to intimidate and destroy religion, however unsuccessfully. Pius XI and Pius XII were outspoken enemies of communism because of this atheism and hostility to religion. In the 1830's secularistic liberalism had attempted to destroy the Church in much the same way, provoking the same reaction. Pope Gregory XVI raged against the liberalism of the French rationalist revolution for much the same reason that Pius XII would fume about the radicalism of the Russian communist revolution. Lammenais did not have a chance of being heard.

By extension, Gustavo Guttierrez, today's Latin American advocate of liberation theology which "Catholicizes" Marxism, would have had no hearing from Pius XI or Pius XII; neither has John Paul II enthusiastically endorsed this approach. At the same time many of the liberal ideas advocated by Lammenais are now, a century later, accepted by the Church. If history repeats itself, some of us may live to see elements of Marxism accepted by the Church of the twenty-first century.

The story of Pius IX shows that Lammenais would have been no more successful with him. The events leading up to the election of Pius in 1846 reveal an uncompromising attitude within the Church toward liberalism, whether of the secular kind or Lammenais' Catholic version. To their credit, liberals did not lie down and die. They stayed and fought, inside and outside the Church. They have lived to see the Church accept much of their agenda, modified by time and reflection and adapted to continuity with Church tradition.

FOR BACKGROUND

The majority of bishops at Vatican I (1869-1870) wanted a solemn proclamation that the pope, when he taught *ex cathedra* (literally, "from the chair") on matters of faith and morals, was infallible due to the special grace of his office as the successor of Saint Peter. Henry Edward Cardinal Manning, Archbishop of Westminster in London, was the leader and articulate spokesman for this move.

A number of bishops, however, believed that the time was not right for such a declaration. Most of them were not opposed to the teaching, but just to the wisdom of promulgating it then. Even the great Father John Henry Newman of England, later a cardinal, held this position.

Nevertheless, the doctrine of papal infallibility was approved and proclaimed in *Pastor Aeternus* on July 18, 1870. The several bishops who voted against it later submitted to the teaching. Vatican II clarified the bishops' role in defining infallible teachings in collegial communion with the pope.

FOR FURTHER READING

Granfield, Patrick. *The Limits of the Papacy.* New York: Crossroad, 1987.

Teaching Authority and Infallibility in the Church, ed. Paul C. Empie, T. Austin Murphy and Joseph A. Burgess. Minneapolis: Augsburg, 1978.

Tillard, J. M. R. *The Bishop of Rome.* Wilmington, Del.: Michael Glazier, 1983.

Today's Liberal Agenda—Connecting to Our Times

Liberalism means different things at different times. In this chapter we saw that nineteenth century liberalism in continental Europe had this agenda: (1) Get rid of kings and install democracies; (2) call for separation of Church and state; (3) promote freedom of the press and free speech; (4) remove the Church's control of education and marriage. Churches could still have private schools and their own internal rules about marriage. That agenda eventually prevailed, as one can see in the nations of Europe and North America.

Liberalism today maintains vigilance over the agenda mentioned above. What are some of its new goals, especially in the United States? (1) Extend democracy to the developing nations. (2) Lobby for the empowerment of women. (3) Promote multiculturalism. (4) Advance the rights of such minorities as blacks, Hispanics and Native Americans. (5) Awaken nations to the importance of environmental concerns. (6) Increase the role of the courts in achieving social goals. (This is called judicial activism.)

Within the Church, liberals call for decentralizing authority, shifting it from the Vatican to local Churches. They advocate specific causes such as married clergy, women's ordination (despite Pope John Paul's letter denying its possibility), reinstatement of resigned married clergy and acceptance of artificial contraception as morally correct behavior. They also stress social justice causes.

The result is a division within our Church today between liberals and conservatives. Father Avery Dulles, S.J., distinguishes the extreme versions of these divisions (paleoconservatives and radical liberals) from more moderate forms of liberals and conservatives. He correctly believes that cooperation and mutual understanding is possible and desirable between the moderates of both persuasions. Civilized discussion and prayerful openness at this level can work. Responsiveness to the Church tradition is necessary for all. Staying with the extremes only results in revolt and schism.

26. Dorothy Day: Catholic Radical

In 1932, the third year of the Depression, when every fifth American was unemployed, Dorothy Day and Peter Maurin began the Catholic Worker Movement. Through its hospitality houses, farming communes, discussion groups, study clubs and publications, members of the movement spread the social doctrines of the Church and saved many lives from tragedy. The following is the first editorial in the first edition of their newspaper, *The Catholic Worker*.

Dorothy Day

'Our First Editorial'
(May, 1933)

For those who are sitting on benches in the warm spring sunlight.

For those who are huddling in shelters trying to escape the rain.

For those who are walking the streets in the all but futile search for work.

For those who think that there is no hope for the future, no recognition of their plight, *The Catholic Worker* is being edited. It is printed to call their attention to the fact that the Catholic Church has a social program.

It's time there was a Catholic paper printed for the unemployed. The fundamental aim of most radical sheets is the conversion of its readers to radicalism and atheism.

Is it not possible to be radical without being atheistic? Is it not possible to protest, to expose, to complain, to point out abuses and demand reforms without desiring the overthrow of religion?

In an attempt to popularize and make known the encyclicals of the popes and the program offered by the Church for the constructing of a social order, this news sheet was started.

The first number of *The Catholic Worker* was planned, written, and edited in the kitchen of a tenement on Fifteenth Street, on subway platforms, on the "L," on ferry boats. There is at present no editorial office, no overhead in the way of telephone or electricity; no salaries paid.

The money for the printing of the first issue was raised by begging small contributions from friends. A priest in

Newark sent us a dollar. Another generous friend sent in twenty-five dollars. The rest of the money needed the editors squeezed out of their own earnings, and at that they were using money necessary to pay milk bills, gas bills, rent and electric bills.

By accepting delay the utilities did not know that they were furthering the cause of social justice. They were, for the time being, unwilling cooperators.

We are asking our friends and sympathizers to help out towards the next issue by sending contributions and subscriptions and orders for bundles. The price of the paper is one cent a copy, in order to place it within the reach of all. And for the unemployed it is distributed free to those who wish to read it. Next month someone may donate us an office, who knows? It is cheering to remember that Jesus Christ wandered this earth with no place to lay His head. "The foxes have holes and the birds of the air their nests, but the Son of Man has no place to lay His head." And when we consider our fly-by-night existence, our uncertainty, we remember (with pride at sharing the honor) that the disciples supped by the seashore and wandered through cornfields picking the stalks to make their frugal meals.

Dorothy Day

The needs and problems of the 1930's are, in different forms, today's needs and problems. Now, as then, their solution lies in the concern and love for others that Jesus taught must be the way of his followers in every age. The exact shape of that response is seldom easy to decide, as the following excerpt from Dorothy Day's autobiography, *The Long Loneliness* (Thomas More Press, 1989), shows.

'War Is the Health of the State'
(1952)

One Christmas at the close of World War II, we received a card from the Rochester group saying that they liked *The Catholic Worker* much better before the pacifists got hold of it. Another letter came from Boston, from an elderly worker who had been responsible for the first house of hospitality in Boston. She too reproached me for the extremism of our revolutionary pacifist position. She was a good trade unionist and was thinking in terms of the immediate steps to be taken, while we tried to keep the vision of a new social order, brought about by peaceful means.

It struck me then how strange a thing it was; here we had been writing about pacifism for fifteen years and members of two of our groups were just beginning to realize what it meant.

We had been pacifist in class war, race war, in the Ethiopian war, in the Spanish Civil War, all through World War II, as we are now during the Korean war. We had spoken in terms of the Sermon on the Mount and all of our readers were familiar enough with that. We had lost subscriptions and bundle orders, but these cancellations came from those who frankly disagreed with us and the matter was settled at once.

But there were a very great many who had seemed to agree with us who did not realize for years that *The Catholic Worker* position implicated them; if they believed the things we wrote, they would be bound, sooner or later, to make decisions personally and to act upon them.

Union workers in steel plants, auto and airplane factories—many in industry and business would have to find other jobs, jobs not tied up with the war effort. And where could they get them? If they worked in the garment factories, they would have to fill government orders for uniforms. Mills turned out blankets, parachutes. Raising food, building houses, baking bread—whatever you did you kept the wheels of industrial capitalism moving, and industrial capitalism kept the wheels moving on war orders. You could not live without compromise. Teachers sold war stamps and bonds. Children were asked to bring aluminum pots and scrap metal to school. The pope asked that war be kept out of the schoolroom, but there it was.

We wrote as much as we could on the subject, and Father John J. Hugo wrote articles and pamphlets—"The Immorality of Conscription," "Catholics Can Be Conscientious Objectors," "The Weapons of the Spirit," "The Gospel of Peace." The last two were printed as *Catholic Worker* pamphlets under the imprimatur of the Archdiocese of New York.

In Europe, Father Stratman, a Belgian Dominican, wrote *The Church and War* and *Peace and the Clergy*, and Father Ude of Austria wrote a monumental book, *"Thou Shalt Not Kill."* Only the first two appeared in English. All of these set forth our stand.

What would you do if an armed maniac were to attack you, your child, your mother? How many times have we heard this. Restrain him, of course, but not kill him. Confine him if necessary. But perfect love casts out fear and love overcomes hatred. All this sounds trite but experience is not trite.

On one occasion an armed maniac did try to kill Arthur Sheehan, one of our editors, during the war. A victim of World War I, who had already assaulted several other men in the house and almost broken my wrist one day when I tried to turn off the radio in the kitchen, took a large bread-knife and a crucifix and announced he was going to kill Arthur. Another woman and I seized him, forcing him to drop the knife. We could not hold him, however, and after he had hurled a gallon can of vegetables at Arthur and smashed a hole in the wall, we restrained him long enough to allow Arthur to escape. We called the police and asked

FOR DISCUSSION/REFLECTION

Dorothy Day was considered a radical. She took a stand and refused to back down. Is it possible to go against the tide and still keep one's faith? Can a person demonstrate against the government and still be a member in good standing in the Church? What are the necessary ingredients to successful protest?

Even with the separation of Church and state do the two sometimes seem intertwined? Are people's religious convictions brought out into the open? Is this more true of Catholics? Does the "public" expect more from Catholics? Why or why not?

Because something is legal, does that make it good? Are there some laws of the land which are contrary to the laws of God? Which ones? What is the difference between the law and the spirit of the law?

Consider specific teachings the Church has concerning such things as:
— The worker
— A just wage
— Working conditions
— Civil disobedience
— Bigotry
— Racism

▼ ━━━━━━━━━━━━━━━━

FOR FURTHER READING

Allaire, James and Rosemary Broughton. *Praying with Dorothy Day*. Winona, Minn.: St. Mary's Press, 1995.

Day, Dorothy. *The Long Loneliness*. Chicago: Thomas More Press, 1989.

that Harry be confined to Bellevue for observation, but since we would not bring charges against him, the hospital released him the next day. Later we persuaded them to keep him for a month in the psychiatric ward. He was returned to the hospital, but at the end of thirty days he was out again, and continued to eat on our breadline during the war. Some time later we heard that he had shipped out on an oil tanker.

There were many other incidents that would have resulted in violence if moral force had not been substituted for coercion, which would have resulted in greater trouble.

David Mason was another pacifist member of our group. David came from Philadelphia, where he had been one of the leaders of the house of hospitality there, to work during the war in our New York house. A large stout man, forty-five at that time, with white hair and a peculiar short-stepping gait as though his legs were not properly matched to his big body, he was a paternal figure around the place when most of the young men were called. He served as one of the editors of the paper, took care of the mail, wrote articles, cooked meals. In fact, he was cooking the evening the FBI came to pick him up for failure to report.

I was away on a speaking trip at the time but I can imagine the picture. Two men drove up to the house at Mott Street and stalked in, looking very official.

"Where is David Mason?"

"Upstairs in the kitchen. Shall we get him?"

"No, we will get him," and the two agents went through the long hall, the courtyard, up the stairs, and found David, an apron around his large middle, making gelatine for the evening dessert.

"And that night we had gelatine at the Federal House of Detention," he said ruefully, "and it was like leather, not as good as mine."

They kept him only a few weeks, much to his regret. He was obviously not the physical material our infantry needs. "I wanted to write a book," he said as they released him. He came back to the soup kitchen and editorial office instead. Arthur Sheehan, who was exempt as a former tuberculosis patient, is now working for CARE and David for a new Catholic daily.

Younger men, such as Tom Sullivan from our Chicago house, who went to war and served in the Pacific, and Jack English, formerly of our Cleveland house, another veteran, will not call themselves pacifist, though Tom is an editor of our pacifist paper. Tom was brought up on the West Side of Chicago and his heart is always with the underdog. He would scoff at the idea of being called a mystic, but I can only explain his attitude toward war on mystical grounds. He agrees with the condemnation of the means used in modern war. He probably would never lift a hand to injure another man, but his attitude is that if other men have to suffer in the war, he will suffer with them.

He poses the question—how explain the two thousand years of Christianity during which time Crusades were preached, wars were fought with the blessing of the Church, and warriors were canonized?

"I do not consider myself strong enough to court martyrdom," he says, "and that is what it means if atheistic communism wins out. Since nobody seems to be using the spiritual weapons you are always talking about, we may have to use the material ones."

He says nothing about means and ends. He is leaving that to the theologians. And his is the general opinion of the rank and file in the Church today.

It is a matter of grief to me that most of those who are Catholic Workers are not pacifists, but I can see too how good it is that we always have this attitude represented among us. We are not living in an ivory tower.

Jack English suffered more in the war than the others. A gunner on a bomber, he was shot down and spent a year in a Rumanian prison camp. He was rescued by the Russians, only to go through the blitz in London. Jack has theologian friends whose opinions keep him away from the extreme pacifist position.

Tony Aratari, also from a prison camp, Charlie McCormick, Joe Monroe, members of the Catholic Worker group, and younger men in their early twenties just with us to help as long as the draft board permits, talk the issue over constantly. Can there be a just war? Can the conditions laid down by Saint Thomas ever be fulfilled? What about the morality of the use of the atom bomb? What does God want me to do? And what am I capable of doing? Can I stand out against state and Church? Is it pride, presumption, to think I have the spiritual capacity to use spiritual weapons in the face of the most gigantic tyranny the world has ever seen? Am I capable of enduring suffering, facing martyrdom? And alone?

Again the long loneliness to be faced.

FOR DISCUSSION/REFLECTION

In your own town or city there must be many leaders in the fight for equal rights. Equal rights affects all of us. No one group or minority should be treated in a lesser way. Dorothy Day took a stand for the worker, Cesar Chavez of the United Farm Workers for the migrant worker, Jimmy Carter in his work with Habitat for Humanity. Can you think of local persons who have made a difference?

How does the Catholic Church measure up in the struggles for equality for all Americans? What programs in the Church help? Is it the responsibility of all of us?

Throughout her life, Dorothy Day enthusiastically broke unjust federal laws. One time an IRS auditor met with her concerning delinquent tax payments. After some small talk she replied, "You figure out how much I owe you and I won't pay it. How's that?"

Dorothy Day—Looking Back

Dorothy Day was born in Brooklyn on November 8, 1897. Her father's career as a newspaper man greatly influenced her life, for it brought her with her family to California, Chicago and back to New York, and it gave her her life's profession. During that time she grew up, attended the University of Chicago on scholarship for two years and enrolled in the Socialist Party because she was greatly troubled by the impoverished masses.

In New York, indignant over the appalling poverty and the conditions that gave rise to it, she took her first job on the Socialist daily paper, the *Call*, where she worked for five dollars a week writing a column emphasizing the sordidness of slum living. During this period of her life, she discussed revolution with her friends, walked in picket lines, went on hunger strikes and was jailed. In order to make a more positive contribution, she worked for a year as a probationer nurse. Disturbed and frustrated by all she saw, Dorothy wandered through Europe, back to Chicago, to New Orleans and, finally, to New York. Here, two important events happened: She joined the Catholic Church and she met Peter Maurin. She and Peter formed the basis of the Catholic Worker Movement.

The initial step of the movement was the founding of *The Catholic Worker* newspaper in order to spread a vision of a society where justice and love are possible. In three years, its circulation increased to one hundred fifty thousand. Then houses of hospitality were begun so that mutual aid could supplant state aid because Peter Maurin taught that charity is personal and should not be the realm of the state. Next, farming communes were started to provide land and homes for the unemployed. Both of these projects sprung up rapidly all over the country.

Peter Maurin died in 1947. He has been likened to a Saint Francis of modern times, for he chose to live in poverty all his life. Because of his mission, he rejected honors, prestige and recognition.

Under the leadership of Dorothy Day, the Catholic Worker Movement continued to do good for those in need, to give vision to the worker and to bring forth a meaningful synthesis of gospel and social values.

The Importance of Social Ministry in the Church—Connecting to Our Times

Old Testament prophets such as Amos awoke the consciences of God's people to the needs of the poor. In his last judgment sermon (Matthew 25:31-46), Jesus said that we will be saved or damned on the basis of how we treated the hungry, naked, sick, helpless, lonely and imprisoned. What we do to them we do to Jesus. The Acts of the Apostles and the Epistles detail many examples of concern for the poor. In scriptural terms we speak of this as the prophetic tradition, meaning the call from God to heal both the symptoms and the causes of poverty—to seek and establish justice on earth.

Once we begin not to worry about what kind of house we are living in, what kind of clothes we are wearing, once we give up the stupid recreation of the world; we have time—which is priceless—to remember that we are our brother's keepers and that we must not only care for his needs as far as we are immediately able, but we must try to build a better world.
—Dorothy Day

Dorothy Day was an eloquent exponent of this. Her Friendship Houses were centers of hospitality for the poor, hungry, naked and dispossessed. In this way she ministered to the direct and personal needs of people. This is treating the "symptoms" of injustice and poverty. But she had a broader vision, one consistent with the social teachings of the Church. She also confronted public policies and laws that kept the poor from rising out of their poverty, policies that were intrinsically oppressive and kept people from escaping the cycle of poverty. Here she addressed the "causes" of injustice. In a special way her pacifism motivated her, for she believed there is no peace where there is no justice.

Enlightened Catholic parishes today have caught her

spirit. They have poverty outreach programs, social justice committees, specific goals for treating both the symptoms and causes of injustice. Parishes have opened their facilities to help those afflicted by drugs, alcohol, violence, incest and other baleful social ills of our time. Catholic social activists have sought to help refugees, oppose capital punishment, help AIDS victims, assist pregnant teens, support hospices and minister to a host of other public problems that exist in our times. Catholic Charities is the largest provider of social services after the federal government. Catholic Relief Services does much the same on a worldwide basis. In some countries, such as Eritrea, it is virtually running all social services.

AUDIO

Tales from the Catholic Worker, by Dorothy Day. Credence Cassettes.

27. Thomas Merton: Modern Monk

Not since Saint Bernard (Chapter 11) has a monk achieved such notoriety as Thomas Merton (1915-1968). His leap to fame came from his lucid autobiography, *The Seven Storey Mountain*. The book told of his wandering youth, his year at Cambridge, his first coping with the craft of poetry, his wild undergraduate years at Columbia, his conversion to Catholicism and his call to the Trappists.

His story was so inspirational that it drew countless hundreds of war veterans, students and even teenagers to monasteries all over the United States both as candidates and as retreatants. The following excerpt from *The Seven Storey Mountain* tells of Merton's journey to enter Gethsemani, the Trappist monastery in Kentucky.

Transition: An Autobiographical Excerpt
(1941)

It was nothing less than a civil, moral death.

This journey, this transition from the world to a new life, was like flying through some strange new element—as if I were in the stratosphere. And yet I was on the familiar earth, and the cold winter rain streaked the windows of the train as we travelled through the dark hills.

After Buffalo, we began to pass factory after factory, lit up with a blue glare in the rain, working all night on armaments: but it was like looking at something in an aquarium. The last city I remembered was Erie. After that I was asleep. We went through Cleveland and I knew nothing of it.

I had been getting up and saying the Rosary in the middle of the night, as a sort of a night office, for several months past. I asked God to wake me up at Galion, Ohio, so that I could do this, and so, in the middle of the night, I woke up, and we were just pulling out of Galion. I began to say the Rosary where our tracks crossed the Erie line, which was the way I had come there the first time, on my way to Gethsemani in the spring. Then I went back to sleep, rocked by the joyous music of the wheels.

At Cincinnati, where we arrived about dawn, I asked the Traveller's Aid girl the name of some Catholic churches, and got in a taxi to go to St. Francis Xavier's, where I arrived just as Mass was beginning at the high altar; so I heard Mass and received Communion and went back to the station and had breakfast and got on the train for Louisville.

And now the sun was up. It was shining on bare, rocky valleys, poor farmland, thin, spare fields, with brush and a few trees and willows growing along the creeks, and grey cabins, from time to time, along the line. Outside one of the cabins a man was splitting a log with an axe and I thought: that is what I will be doing, if God wills it, pretty soon.

It was a strange thing. Mile after mile my desire to be in the monastery increased beyond belief. I was altogether absorbed by that one idea. And yet, paradoxically, mile after mile my indifference increased, and my interior peace. What if they did not receive me? Then I would go to the army. But surely that would be a disaster? Not at all. If, after all this, I was rejected by the monastery and had to be drafted, it would be quite clear that it was God's will. I had done everything that was in my power; the rest was in His hands. And for all the tremendous and increasing intensity of my desire to be in the cloister, the thought that I might find myself, instead, in an army camp no longer troubled me in the least.

I was free. I had recovered my liberty. I belonged to God, not to myself: and to belong to Him is to be free, free of all the anxieties and worries and sorrows that belong to this earth, and the love of the things that are in it. What was the difference between one place and another, one habit and another, if your life belonged to God, and if you placed yourself completely in His hands? The only thing that mattered was the fact of the sacrifice, the essential dedication of one's self, one's will. The rest was only accidental.

That did not prevent me from praying harder and harder to Christ and to the Immaculate Virgin and to my whole private litany, St. Bernard, St. Gregory, St. Joseph, St. John of the Cross, St. Benedict, St. Francis of Assisi, the Little Flower and all the rest, to get me by hook or by crook into that monastery.

And yet I knew that if God wanted me to go to the army, that would be the better and happier thing. Because...that is the will of God. There is only one happiness: to please Him. Only one sorrow, to be displeasing to Him, to refuse Him something, to turn away from Him, even in the slightest thing, even in thought, in a half-willed movement of appetite: in these things, and these alone, is sorrow, in so far as they imply separation, or the beginning, the possibility of separation from Him Who is our life and all our joy. And since God is a Spirit, and infinitely above all matter and all creation, the only complete union possible, between ourselves and Him, is in the order of intention: a union of wills and intellects, in love, charity.

I stepped on to the platform of Louisville station in the glory of that freedom, and walked out into the streets with a sense of triumph, remembering the time I had come that way before, the previous Easter.

FOR BACKGROUND

Thomas Merton belonged to the Trappists—the Order of Cistercians of the Strict Observance (O.C.S.O.). This expression of monasticism has its origins in the seventeenth century and was centered at the Abbey of la Trappe (hence the name) in France. This reform aimed to recover the austerity of the earlier Cistercians and their interpretation of Saint Benedict's Rule. La Trappe emphasized renewal in monastic enclosure, silence and manual labor, expressing a spirit of apartness from the world and dedication to prayer and penance.

The reform movement spread and was adopted by the Cistercian community of Melleray in Western France. That foundation's continued growth made the establishment of a new community necessary. Friendship with the aged American Bishop Flaget of Bardstown drew them to Kentucky. On December 21, 1848, forty-five men from Melleray founded the Abbey of Gethsemani, which Thomas Merton entered in 1941.

Trappists say of themselves: "This search for God is the goal of our monastic day, a day composed of the *opus Dei*, *lectio divina* and manual work. Our Cistercian life is simple and austere, truly poor and penitential in the joy of the Holy Spirit. Through the warmth of their welcome and hospitality our communities share the fruit of their contemplation and their work with others."

FOR DISCUSSION/REFLECTION

In his many writings on social activism, war and peace, Eastern and Western mysticism, Merton struggled with the reality of censorship. Is there a value to or need for censorship today?

Is there a lesson to be learned from Merton's acceptance of censorship even when he did not agree with the reasons for it?

In discussing the basic dimensions of Christianity, monasticism is usually not included. It finds little support in apostolic times; its scriptural basis is slim to nonexistent. Jesus called everyone to a life of perfection, not just a select few. What do you see as the basis for monasticism? Does Merton provide any clues? What witness does monasticism provide to the Church? The world?

Supposedly living apart from the world and its concerns, how do you think Merton was able to sensitize himself to speak out for the civil rights movement and against the Vietnam War? Why was he so respected in his lifetime? Why is he so respected today?

The Bardstown bus was half full, and I found a somewhat dilapidated seat, and we rode out into the wintry country, the last lap of my journey into the desert.

When I finally got off in Bardstown, I was standing across the road from a gas station. The street appeared to be empty, as if the town were asleep. But presently I saw a man in the gas station. I went over and asked where I could get someone to drive me to Gethsemani. So he put on his hat and started his car and we left town on a straight road through level country, full of empty fields. It was not the kind of landscape that belonged to Gethsemani, and I could not get my bearings until some low, jagged, wooded hills appeared ahead of us, to the left of the road, and we made a turn that took us into rolling, wooded land.

Then I saw that high familiar spire.

I rang the bell at the gate. It let fall a dull, unresonant note inside the empty court. My man got in his car and went away. Nobody came. I could hear somebody moving around inside the Gatehouse. I did not ring again. Presently, the window opened, and Brother Matthew looked out between the bars, with his clear eyes and greying beard.

"Hullo, Brother," I said.

He recognized me, glanced at the suitcase and said: "This time have you come to stay?"

"Yes, Brother, if you'll pray for me," I said.

Brother nodded, and raised his hand to close the window.

"That's what I've been doing," he said, "praying for you."

Following *The Seven Storey Mountain*, Merton produced a volume of books, articles, poems and letters. In his writings, he condemned a society that rested content with a Harlem and the injustice and racism it represented for him. Over and over again he returned to the themes of social justice and announced his own pacifist convictions. He opposed the Vietnam War and stated that some student activists he met were truly modern monks.

The following selection from *Selected Poems of Thomas Merton* (New York: New Directions Paperbook, 1959) illustrates how deeply this monk was involved in the issues of the world he had left behind.

And the Children of Birmingham
(1959)

And the children of Birmingham
Walked into the story
Of Grandma's pointed teeth
("Better to love you with")
Reasonable citizens
Rose to exhort them all:
"Return at once to schools of friendship.
Buy in stores of love and law."
(And tales were told
Of man's best friend, the Law.)
And the children of Birmingham
Walked in the shadow
Of Grandma's devil
Smack up against
The singing wall.
Fire and water
Poured over everyone:
"Hymns were extreme,
So there could be no pardon!"
And old Grandma
Began the lesson
Of everybody's skin,
Everybody's fun:
"Liberty may bite
An irresponsible race
Forever singing,"
Grandma said,
"Forever making love:
Look at all the children!"
(And tales were told
Of man's best friend, the Law.)
And the children of Birmingham
Walked into the fury
Of Grandma's hug:
Her friendly cells
("Better to love you with.")
Her friendly officers
And "dooms of love."
Laws had a very long day
And all were weary.
But what the children did that time
Gave their town
A name to be remembered!
(And tales were told
Of man's best friend, the Law.)

Thomas Merton and the Protestant theologian Karl Barth died on the same day. The following selection is from Merton's *Conjectures of a Guilty Bystander* (New York: Doubleday Image, 1966).

FOR BACKGROUND

While studying at Columbia University, twenty-three-year-old Merton met a Hindu monk named Bramachari. The two discussed many religious topics. At this time Merton felt an attraction to Eastern mysticism (one he would in the end rediscover), but met an interesting response from the Hindu: "There are many beautiful mystical books written by the Christians. You should read St. Augustine's *Confessions* and *The Imitation of Christ.*" With amusement and appreciation, Merton remarks that he was told to study Christian mysticism by, of all people, a Hindu monk.

FOR DISCUSSION/REFLECTION

Thomas Merton sought to integrate the traditions of the East with his own Catholic, monastic heritage. This attempt was met by many with suspicion, confusion and at times rejection. Can Christianity learn anything from religious traditions other than its own without undermining itself?

Have you learned something from another religion which served not to diminish but strengthen your Christian faith?

The Paradox: Karl Barth

FOR DISCUSSION/REFLECTION

In Merton's story about Karl Barth and Mozart, we see Merton preoccupied by paradox, seeming contradictions that somehow fit together. What is the value of paradox? Does it help us to avoid extremes or oversimplifications? How?

Why do you think the Protestant Barth would listen to the music of a Catholic Mozart—a Mozart who thought "Protestantism was all in the head"? Why was it important for Barth to wake up the "child" inside him?

In light of World War I, Barth declared the liberal Protestant idea of progress bankrupt. His writings, most notably *Commentary on Romans* and *Church Dogmatics*, stress God's transcendence and humanity's judgment by the Word of God. It is important to stress the difference between God and humanity; Barth had seen religion used as ideology too often. But what might happen if the idea of God's transcendence and sovereignty is stressed too much?

Barth once said that religion is a human effort by which we seek to hide from God. Would you agree with that statement? In what ways does religion both hide and reveal God?

Karl Barth had a dream about Mozart.

Barth had always been piqued by the Catholicism of Mozart, and by Mozart's rejection of Protestantism. For Mozart said that "Protestantism was all in the head" and that "Protestants did not know the meaning of the *Agnus Dei qui tollis peccata mundi.*"

Barth, in his dream, was appointed to examine Mozart in theology. He wanted to make the examination as favorable as possible, and in his questions he alluded pointedly to Mozart's masses.

But Mozart did not answer a word.

I was deeply moved by Barth's account of this dream and almost wanted to write him a letter about it. The dream concerns his salvation, and Barth perhaps is striving to admit that he will be saved more by the Mozart in himself than by his theology.

Each day, for years, Barth played Mozart every morning before going to work on his dogma: unconsciously seeking to awaken, perhaps, the hidden sophianic Mozart in himself, the central wisdom that comes in tune with the divine and cosmic music and is saved by love, yes, even by *eros*. While the other, theological self, seemingly more concerned with love, grasps at a more stern, more cerebral *agape*: a love that, after all, is not in our own heart but *only in God* and revealed only to our head.

Barth says, also significantly, that "it is a child, even a 'divine' child, who speaks in Mozart's music to us." Some, he says, considered Mozart always a child in practical affairs (but Burckhardt "earnestly took exception" to this view). At the same time, Mozart, the child prodigy, "was never allowed to be a child in the literal meaning of that word." He gave his first concert at the age of six.

Yet he was always a child "in the higher meaning of that word."

Fear not, Karl Barth! Trust in the divine mercy. Though you have grown up to become a theologian, Christ remains a child in you. Your books (and mine) matter less than we might think! There is in us a Mozart who will be our salvation.

Thomas Merton—Looking Back

Thomas Merton was born in Prades, France, in 1915. His father was English and his mother American. His formative years were spent in France, Bermuda, England and the United States, where he received a Master of Arts degree in English from Columbia. As a young man, radically upset with the injustices of life, he joined the Communist Party, where he hoped to find a solution to these problems. Later, he teamed up with the Catholic Worker Movement. Not long after this, he joined the Catholic Church.

In 1941, Merton entered the Trappist monastery at Gethsemani, Kentucky. Since he was an author prior to his entrance, his superiors encouraged him to write. His first published book was his autobiography, *The Seven Storey Mountain*. It made the bestseller lists and has been in the standard repertory of paperbacks ever since. Thereafter, until his death Merton poured out an immense volume of poetry, essays and journalistic pieces on topics ranging on everything from Zen Buddhism to civil rights.

For several years Merton was appointed master of novices. After that he withdrew to a hermitage on the abbey property. He developed a growing interest in the contemplative life of the Far East. It was this that prompted him to journey to Bangkok, Thailand, for an ecumenical (Buddhist and Catholic) conference on East-West spirituality. He died while in Bangkok on December 10, 1968. He was fifty-three.

How Does Good Confessional Literature Help Us?—Connecting to Our Times

Contemporary America has become a "confessional culture." TV talk shows thrive on public confessions, especially those of the most sensational and bizarre kind. The shameless outpourings on TV and talk radio used to make ordinary mortals blush. Today these self-revelations make heroes out of victims, sometimes gain them big book contracts and certainly make the sponsors and hosts multimillionaires. Confessional behavior is big business. What was once confided to a priest, a therapist or a private diary is now a distracting public scourge. Most of this blather debases human dignity and has little moral or spiritual worth.

How different then is the confessional statement of Thomas Merton in his autobiography *The Seven Storey Mountain*. His self-revelation has proved to be far more enduring. As a gifted writer and poet, he expressed the story of his conversion to Catholicism in absorbing prose. It can be enjoyed on literary merit alone. But as a testimony of faith, Merton's autobiography ranks with Augustine's *Confessions*, as well as with the less literary but equally compelling Thérèse of Lisieux's *Story of a Soul*. No serious reader can come away from these confessions without feeling challenged to evaluate his or her spiritual state and the reality of faith itself.

Merton, along with C.S. Lewis, continues to be among the most widely read spiritual writers in the English lan-

"The teaching and example of Christ provide the foundation for the evangelical counsels of chaste self-dedication to God, of poverty and obedience. The Apostles and Fathers of the Church commend them as an ideal of life. They constitute a gift of God which the Church has received from her Lord and which by his grace she always safeguards....

"From the God-given seed of the Councils a wonderful and wide-spreading tree has grown up in the field of the Lord, branching out into various forms of religious life lived in solitude or in community.... This sacred Council gives its support and praise to men and women, brothers and sisters, who in monasteries or in schools and hospitals or in missions adorn the Bride of Christ by the steadfast and humble fidelity of their consecrated lives and give generous service of the most varied kinds." (*Constitution on the Church*, #43, 46)

[T]he real purpose of asceticism is not cutting off one's relation to created things and other people, but normalizing and healing it. The contemplative life...is simply the restoration of man, in Christ, to the state in which he was originally intended to live.

—Thomas Merton

FOR FURTHER READING

Merton, Thomas. *The Seven Storey Mountain*. New York: Harcourt, Brace and Company, 1948.

Simsic, Wayne. *Praying with Thomas Merton*. Winona, Minn.: St. Mary's Press, 1994.

Thomas Merton: Spiritual Master, ed. Lawrence S. Cunningham. Mahwah, N.J.: Paulist Press, 1992.

Waldron, Robert. *Thomas Merton: In Search of His Soul*. Notre Dame, Ind.: Ave Maria Press, 1994.

AUDIO

Seeds of Contemplation and *Life and Holiness*, both by Thomas Merton. Distributed by Ignatius Press.

Developing a Conscience, *The Thirst for God*, *True Freedom* and *The Search for Wholeness*, all by Thomas Merton. Credence Cassettes.

guage. Lewis himself wrote a short confession of his conversion in *Surprised By Joy*. Merton and Lewis were both masters of English prose and gifted with the ability to frame their spiritual lives in appealing, inspiring and faith-filled ways.

When we have become weary of talk-show pollution, we turn to Merton, Lewis, Augustine, Thérèse of Lisieux and Teresa of Avila for some fresh air, dignity and genuine self-improvement.

28. New Movements

The State of the Church on the Eve of Vatican II: An Analysis
(1870-1962)

On October 11, 1962, an old stream bubbled its last as a new fountain of Church life burst forth with the opening of Vatican II. For ninety-two years, Vatican I had cast a long shadow over the history of the Church. Yet within its protective arms, new movements in liturgy, Scripture and ecumenism blossomed. We shall see how these three aspects of renewal fared on the eve of Vatican II. But we shall begin with a remembrance of things past: the devotional life of the Vatican I Church.

Stations and Rosaries: The Devotional Church

Deprived of direct access to the Mass because it was in Latin and because the priest seemed so much in charge of it, Catholics developed a "people's religion." The Franciscans gave them the Stations of the Cross and the Christmas crib. The Dominicans countered with the rosary. Catholics fed on the cult of the saints, the warmth of the Sacred Heart, the thrill of pilgrimages and the miracles at Lourdes. They showed enthusiasm for Eucharistic processions, novenas, blessed medals, scapulars, holy water, relics, tuneful hymns, flowery personal prayers and similar forms of popular piety.

Many of these practices began in the Middle Ages; virtually all of them predated Vatican I. For the most part they were alive and well on the eve of Vatican II. Not everyone approved of this popular religion. Its critics judged the music too sentimental, the art tasteless and the emphasis on feeling vulgar. They hinted that such practices were barely a step away from superstition and deplored the excessive attention on Mary and the saints, claiming this diverted people from the proper attention to Christ.

The critics had a point, even if their judgments seemed snobbish at times and displayed too casual a judgment on the faith of the "people's religion." Vatican II heard the critics' complaints and did something. The Fathers put the liturgy in the vernacular and invited the laity to be active participants. Architects began to design spare, austere churches shorn of all those friendly statues and vigil lights. And when it was time to redecorate the old churches, a new, stripped-down look emerged.

Did popular religion die on the eve of the Council? Not quite. One million people a year still go as pilgrims to

"The religious sense of the Christian people has always found expression in various forms of piety surrounding the Church's sacramental life, such as the veneration of relics, visits to sanctuaries, pilgrimages, processions, the Stations of the Cross, religious dances, the rosary, medals, etc.

"These expressions of piety extend the liturgical life of the Church, but do not replace it. They should be 'so drawn up that they harmonize with the liturgical seasons, accord with the sacred liturgy, are in some way derived from it and lead the people to it, since in fact the liturgy is by its very nature superior to any of them.'" (*Catechism of the Catholic Church*, #1674-1675)

FOR BACKGROUND

Ritual and traditions are very important to Catholics. We have devotions that date back centuries. The practice of naming people as saints goes back to the very early Church. In the age of the martyrs these people were held up as models for others who needed courage. These saints are still with us today. The Second Vatican Council did not end old traditions and practices.

Many movements during the early 1960's seemed to want to do away with some of these devotions. But that was not the case. Our traditions are alive and well today and available in a sense to many more Catholics than ever.

Modern churches reflect the tastes of today's society, not the Renaissance; baroque art is no longer popular. Pilgrimages to holy places were on the rise in the 1990's.

Concern for restoring unity pertains to the whole Church, faithful and clergy alike. It extends to everyone, according to the potential of each, whether it be exercised in daily Christian living or in theological and historical studies. This very concern already reveals to some extent the bond of brotherhood existing among all Christians, and it leads toward that full and perfect unity which God lovingly desires.
— *Decree on Ecumenism,*
Vatican II

Lourdes, Rome and Jerusalem. Biblical rosaries and updated Stations hold their own. New books of saints are proving to be popular. And the music—ah, the music! While Catholics have begun to sing Protestant hymns of four hundred years' standing, they are also singing new songs, many of which are as sentimental as the old devotional ones.

Should popular religion die? Of course not. The liturgy has taken its proper and rightful place in the life of the Church, but there is plenty of room for spontaneous, popular piety. And plenty of people find it helpful for their faith growth. Charismatic renewal, Marriage Encounter and small group sharing appear to be new forms of "people's religion."

The Liturgical Reform

In the beginning liturgies were celebrated at home. House Eucharists were the norm for over three centuries, until the move to basilicas in the fourth century (see Chapter 5).

In the Western Church, the evangelization of the invading barbarians—non-Roman, non-Latin-speaking people—led to a situation where the majority of the new parishioners could not speak the language of the Mass. So the people watched and the priest did Eucharist. Then the people watched a little less and started doing things on their own. Celts developed penance prayers to keep themselves occupied. Gauls created prayers of affection to pass the time at Eucharist.

Sitting in silence, cut off from the altar and each other, the worshipers lost a sense of community at Mass. The "we" of community gave way to the "I" of personal devotion. The Protestants understood what was wrong and introduced vernacular liturgies and hymns that everyone could sing. Who knows but what the Council Fathers at Trent did look wistfully at the Protestants, but could not bring themselves to imitate them because that was tantamount to admitting their revolt was legitimate. What could one say then about their heretical teachings?

Trent reformed the liturgy by disciplining the priests to follow exact rubrics in a mechanical fashion. Trent put dignity into a liturgy that had grown sloppy. They froze an archaic form of worship that had stateliness and tradition going for it, but left no room for the pulse of the people.

Not until the nineteenth century did the seeds of liturgical reform really get going. German researchers at Tübingen published studies about early Church worship, showing it was a community affair that appreciated the liturgy's mysterious character. They remarked how the Church Fathers insisted that the Body of Christ (Eucharist) builds up the Body of Christ (Church).

Benedictine monks at Germany's Maria Laach produced studies about Lent and Holy Week. There Dom Odo Casel developed the rites for the Easter Vigil that we substantially follow today. The French Benedictines at Solesmes rescued Gregorian chant from the archives and made it available—in Latin, of course—for popular usage. Benedictine Abbot Marmion wrote books that showed how one could have a spirituality based on Christ as its center and a liturgy as its expressive outlet.

Pius X encouraged the use of Gregorian chant and called for the writing of new Church music in the spirit of the liturgy. He asked all Catholics to go to Communion frequently, thus drawing their attention to a sacrament as a major source of spiritual growth. Centuries of alienation from the Mass plus the false attitude developed by the Jansenists (who insisted one must go to confession before every Communion to be pure enough) had dulled the Catholic sense regarding the Mass. Mass attendance was reasonably good in many countries, but participation and reception of Communion was minimal. Pius X also lowered the First Communion age from twelve or thirteen to seven or eight so that young people could become accustomed to receiving the sacrament and its benefits from an early age.

Pius XII advanced the papal teaching on liturgy in his encyclical *Mediator Dei*, stating that active participation in the liturgy is the greatest source of the Christian spirit. He urged Catholics to go to Communion at Mass.

Little by little, in tentative ways, people were being drawn into the Mass. In the late 1950's many parishes had "recited Masses" in which the people communally recited parts of the Mass together. Simple chant arrangements of the Ordinary of the Mass made it possible for full congregational participation. Hymn singing increased.

National conventions dealing with liturgical reform and renewal became commonplace. St. John's Abbey of Collegeville published *Orate Fratres* (now *Worship*) magazine. A perusal of its old issues is a blow-by-blow account of how the liturgical movement gained momentum and final victory at Vatican II. In fact, the Council's first approved document was the one on the liturgy, and it was the least debated, criticized or opposed. Over a century of preparation, scholarship and hard work by farseeing and courageous people made that possible.

Catholics Open Their Bibles

Luther's attention to the importance of the Bible placed Protestants in the tradition of biblical faith. In reaction, Catholics concentrated on the tradition of doctrine, dogma and theology. Protestants knew their Bible; Catholics knew their catechism.

In the nineteenth century the new science of archaeology forced Protestant Bible scholars to take a new look at the Bible. Archaeologists had uncovered ancient pagan libraries, stories told by people who lived at the same time as Bible people. Scholars were astonished to find these stories similar to those in the Bible.

For example, the Babylonian epic of Gilgamesh has a flood story very much like Noah's. The Code of Hammurabi bore startling similarity to the Ten Commandments. Armed with a better command of ancient languages and a

FOR BACKGROUND

The understanding of the Church before Vatican II could be described in three words: clerical, juridical and triumphalistic. Bishop Emile De Smedt said as much in his response to the first schema on the Church at Vatican II, which was rejected and rewritten. The Church was hierarchical because the clergy possessed all the power and initiative. A pyramidal structure predominated, with authority descending from the pope through the bishops and priests down to the faithful. The laity played a passive role, living out the teachings of the hierarchy.

The Church was juridical because it placed great stress on law and penalty. Membership and its obligations were clearly defined. One knew who was or was not a "practicing" Catholic. Church ministry was also guided by the norms of Canon Law.

The triumphalistic Church dramatized itself as a body set against the powers of evil, whether foreign culture or foreign religion. The Church saw itself as alone having the fullness of the truth and discouraged contact with other religions. These were the days of Catholic isolationism, "ghetto Catholicism." This model of Church would undergo radical reassessment at Vatican II as the Council Fathers reconsidered the Church's understanding of authority, freedom and purpose in history.

FOR DISCUSSION/REFLECTION

Is the Church on the eve of a possible Vatican III? Do you see issues in the Church and the world today that necessitate calling another ecumenical council? Or do you think Vatican II is yet unrealized, awaiting full implementation?

Prior to Vatican II, Catholicism could be described as having four central concerns: authority, sin, ritual and the miraculous. What concerns do you think are characteristic of Catholicism today? Can the above concerns still be seen in the Church today?

more accurate appreciation of ancient literary styles and historical sense, the new scholars brought the Bible alive in an entirely new and fascinating way.

Previously most Bible studies had begun with the assumption that it is the word of God. Divine inspiration was the starting point. The new scholars approached Scripture from the other end, the human side. Less concerned with the divine author, they wanted to see what the human author was doing. The Bible as a human word captured their attention.

This unlocked many mysteries. Why are there two creation stories, contradictory in detail and perspective? Why is John so different from Matthew, Mark and Luke? Scholars probed the minds of the writers, reconstructed their social milieu and gave us a clearer understanding of the purposes behind the authors' approaches. Some scholars emphasized the human side at the expense of the divine part of the process. This resulted in works like Renan's *Life of Christ* (1888), in which Jesus is only a human moral teacher, not Son of God and savior.

Catholic scholars developed interest in the Protestant work. Pope Leo XIII approved the opening of a Biblical Institute in Jerusalem under the leadership of Father Joseph LaGrange, a Dominican. But the pope was cautious. "The sense of Holy Scripture can nowhere be found incorrupt outside the Church. One cannot expect to find it in faithless writers who only gnaw at the bark of Scripture and never attain its marrow."

The Catholic Scripture scholars had barely gotten started when the Modernist crisis hit the Church in the first ten years of the twentieth century. "Modernists" were the "modern" version of eighteenth-century Enlightenment rationalists who denied the reality of the supernatural or of divine inspiration. They viewed the Bible not as the word of God, but as merely a human work inspired by human ingenuity. Its miracle stories were seen as myths, not historically true. The Bible was a human book pure and simple.

Pius X worried that such theories would affect Catholic theology and Bible studies and harm the faith of the people. His condemnation of Modernism in his encyclical *Pascendi* (1907) severely curtailed Catholic scholars, who lived under the constant threat of being called heretics. They carried on nonetheless, with patience and in obscurity.

Liberation finally came in 1943 when Pius XII issued their Magna Carta, his encyclical *Divino Afflante Spiritu*. He spoke positively about the new biblical studies, and cautioned scholars to be faithful to the Church's teachings and have a pastoral concern for the Catholic people. He approved the research done on literary genres and called for fresh translations of the Bible.

Catholics could open their Bibles at last. Results of the new Scripture studies are much in evidence in the documents of Vatican II. The Bible ceased to be only a Protestant book and became a book for all believers.

Ecumenism: Church Unity Movement

The Church lost the Orthodox in the twelfth century and the Protestants in the sixteenth. For that matter, Christianity broke with Judaism in the first century and never had a chance to be in significant touch with the birth and burst of Mohammedanism in the eighth century. One God and so many divisions!

The Protestants who gave us the start on our biblical renewal also inspired us in matters of ecumenism. At the World Missionary Conference in 1910 they began the modern ecumenical movement, which came to flower in the World Council of Churches in 1948.

Inspired by this, Cardinal Mercier initiated ecumenical dialogue with the Church of England in the 1920's. The Graymoor friars and nuns (a converted Anglican order of monks and nuns) made ecumenism one of their principal ministries. Little by little the ecumenical movement took a stronger foothold in the Church until, on the eve of the Council, Pope John XXIII invited Orthodox, Protestant and Jewish observers to attend. John selected Augustin Bea, a German Jesuit biblical scholar, to oversee this development. Cardinal Bea gave ecumenism the visibility it needed. A Council document was written on the subject, as well as one on religious freedom prompted by Jesuit Father John Courtney Murray.

Since the Council there have been ongoing dialogues between Catholics and Anglicans, Lutherans and Orthodox, as well as special meetings with representatives of non-Christian religions. We are not at one yet. But at least we are talking with one another in a civil and faith-filled manner. We pray with Jesus "that all may become one" (see John 17:20-23).

The Time Was Ripe

Devotionalism, liturgical revival, biblical renewal and the ecumenical movement—these were the pieces simmering in the Church on the eve of the Council. For over a century and a half, the Church had fought off the liberal ideas of the eighteenth-century Enlightenment as well as the earlier positions of the sixteenth-century Protestants. But the time had come to stop debating, to start talking and to share legitimate common values. Vatican II provided the right platform at the right time.

Liberals and Protestants ceased to be seen as enemies of the Church. In the friendly, nuanced conversation that ensued, a multitude of good ideas and practices were incorporated into the age-old tradition of Catholicism. John XXIII opened a window.

FOR BACKGROUND

The first session of Vatican II convened on October 11, 1962. Through the large bronze door of St. Peter's Basilica came Pope John XXIII, carried above the delegates on the *sedia gestatoria*, the throne-like chair on which the pope sits. John soon left the chair, however, to walk through the ranks of the delegates to make his opening speech. John also wore a bishop's miter instead of the usual papal tiara—another sign of the equality and communion in which he held his fellow bishops. Today this attitude is termed *collegiality*.

VIDEO

Saint! Don Bosco Multimedia (30 minutes).

Art Shapes Faith Shapes Art, by Jean Morman Unsworth. ACTA Publications (two 50-minute videos).

Where Have All the 'Movements' Gone?— Connecting to Our Times

FOR BACKGROUND

"The substance of the ancient doctrine of the deposit of faith is one thing, and the way in which it is presented is another." With these words, Pope John XXIII expressed the need for *aggiornamento* (Italian for "updating"). Pope John's vision of *aggiornamento* stressed that the Church's duty was "not only to guard this precious treasure, as if we were concerned only with antiquity," but to respond to the modern world and be open to serve it.

The term, which quickly became common Catholic parlance, means interior spiritual renewal or external adaptation of the Church's teachings and structures to modern times. At the Council both meanings were applicable. *Aggiornamento* continues to be a process for a Church that struggles for historical and cultural sensitivity.

New movements have a way of becoming old movements—or possibly no movement at all. This chapter takes a fond look at four movements bubbling at the eve of Vatican II in 1962: devotionalism, liturgical reform, new Scripture studies and ecumenism.

In a strict sense, devotionalism was never a movement, for popular piety is as old as the Church itself, ever mutating in different cultures, always responsive to the faith tastes of a given age. The movements in liturgy, Scripture and ecumenism are no longer movements but established parts of Church life. Liturgists continue to refine ritual. Scripture scholars will never be without work to do. Ecumenists have a lengthy, unfinished agenda. Decades later we all realize that a movement, once accepted by the establishment, requires a long time and persistent effort to penetrate the faith-consciousness of millions. Liturgical, scriptural and ecumenical awareness has barely touched the surface of Catholic consciousness.

Georgetown University's Father Larry Madden believes there should be a "second liturgical movement" so that its real meaning gets beyond the two hundred to two thousand parishes he believes are really in touch with all that liturgy is designed to do. (The United States has twenty thousand parishes.)

Many claim that ecumenism is presently at a standstill or plateau. The Church of England's approval of women's ordination has set back Anglican-Catholic prospects of reunion. Theological dialogue continues at lofty levels, but movement to reunion among the Christian Churches appears as far away as ever. In the United States Protestantism itself seems newly divided, as mainline Churches weaken and evangelical-fundamentalist Churches—the Churches with whom there has been no significant dialogue—flourish.

Scripture study at the popular level is a real success story. Programs such as the Paulist's *Share the Word,* Liturgical Press's *Little Rock Bible Study,* St. Anthony Messenger Press's *Scripture from Scratch* and Our Sunday Visitor's *Popular Bible Study* prove that Catholics can have an enduring and active interest in faith building through prayer, study and meditation on the Bible.

Movements are a sign of life in the Church. The Spirit will make sure we always have them. They are God's way of saying. "Wake up and put some energy into your faith commitment."

29. John XXIII and Vatican II

The world into which Pope John XXIII came had plenty of kings and prophets. But what it needed most was a wise man. John was just such a man, rising up from a rich soil and a peasantry that gives birth to men who know reality and have deep faith. He never forgot that background and its wisdom.

This spirit was beautifully reflected on the night of his election in October, 1958. As *Time* magazine records the story:

> In Sotto il Monte the three remaining Roncalli brothers, Zaverio, 75, Alfredo, 69, and Guiseppe, 64, were having supper after a hard day's work when the big news came over their old radio. The rice soup grew cold while they listened; then as excited neighbors poured from their houses, the brothers hurried upstairs to dress up for the occasion. And in Sesto San Giovanni, a little town near Milan, Angelo Roncalli's sister Assunta was out buying bread when the news reached her. "My God, little Angelo!" she gasped. "What's the matter?' asked the baker, and Assunta explained: "My brother's just been elected pope. He will have to work so hard."

He did indeed work hard. He strove to make real the Pentecostal prayer that the Spirit would "make new" the face of the earth. He faced this task with his favorite maxim of government:

To see everything.
To turn a blind eye on much of it.
To correct a little.

FOR DISCUSSION/REFLECTION

Vatican II touched all Catholics' lives and still affects us today. Discuss the articles listed below and their value to your Church.
— Dialogue with other religions
— The laity's involvement in the liturgy
— A renewal of vocations
— The role of women in the Church
— Active participation in the parish
— Parish councils
— Religious education programs
— The support of parochial schools
— The Church's involvement in the "outside world"
— The role of the pope in the world today
— The role of the local bishop

How long did it take for the effects of Vatican II to become evident in the Church? How did people react when these changes took place?

'I See the Light of a New Creation': A Pope for All People
(1958)

It was the day after Christmas, 1958. Pope John astonished the people of Rome by paying a visit to Queen of Heaven Prison. In that gray light the first thing to catch his eye and visibly touch him was a beautiful crib made by the inmates.

A thousand prisoners, wearing their striped uniforms, stood before him. Pope John spoke to them as "dear sons

John XXIII

FOR BACKGROUND

The first Church council was held in the city of Jerusalem in or about the year 50. Peter himself was in attendance. There have been twenty-one councils since that time. They are generally named for the place that they were held. Vatican II was the second council held in the Vatican.

Each council was called for a specific reason:
— Nicea I: to formulate a creed
— Ephesus: to deal with early Church heresy
— Constantinople I, II, III, IV to reinforce the issues of faith
— Constance: to heal the Great Western Schism
— Trent: to deal with the Reformation
— Vatican I: to define papal infallibility

In addition to the initiating reasons for calling these councils, many other things were accomplished. This was also true of Vatican II, which was called to bring the Church into the modern era.

and brothers." Then he was taken on a tour of the cell blocks. The prisoners were lined up to receive his blessing. He shook hands with each one until he came to one prisoner who drew back.

"I am a murderer, Holy Father," the man said.

John said nothing, but rather reached out and gave him a brotherly embrace.

Barely able to speak, the convict managed to say, "This is the happiest day of my life."

"Me, too," replied John simply.

The remarkable warmth of Pope John XXIII comes through constantly in the accounts of his life. For example, a few days after his coronation, Pope John held a special private audience for his family. The Roncallis entered the splendid papal apartments with feelings of discomfort, fear and hesitation. Quite a change from their farmhouse at Sotto il Monte!

Bashful and confused, they stood before the pope. They were so nervous that they dropped their presents. Homemade bread and wine and sun-cured ham, wrapped in colorful handkerchiefs, fell to the floor. They stood embarrassed and dismayed. John was not above smiling at the comedy of the situation, but he was quick to make them feel at home.

"Don't be afraid," he said. "It's only me."

An especially powerful example of John's genius with the common touch occurred about three months before he died. He received in audience the daughter of Nikita Khrushchev and her husband, the editor of the important Russian newspaper, *Pravda*.

The pope received them cordially and passed the time talking about their family. He asked how many children they had and what their names were. On finding out that the youngest was named Ivan, his eyes lit up and he said,

"You must give my special love to Ivan, for I know that is the Russian name for John."

Before they were to leave, John asked if he might give them a blessing. The communist couple became a little embarrassed. "No, no, Holy Father. You see, we are unbelievers."

"Come now," said John, "won't you let an old man give you a blessing?"

They did so, and were deeply touched by this moving gesture from John. Just before they departed, John took into his own hands the hands of Khrushchev's daughter. He said: "When I look into your eyes, I think of the first chapter of Genesis where God said, 'Let there be light.' I know I see a light in you that speaks of a new creation."

That night John spent about forty-five minutes studying a Russian grammar book. Before he went to sleep he offered to God his life for the peace and conversion of "his dear people of Russia."

'I Will Call a Council': An Action Pope
(1959)

Pope John found plenty to think about as he read the Roman newspapers. He saw a picture of Russians in Red Square joyously celebrating a Sputnik triumph. He read of Charles de Gaulle's efforts to solve the Algerian crisis. Near the bottom of the page, he noticed an item about a bearded rebel, Fidel Castro, who stunned America by turning the island of Cuba into a communist fortress.

His diplomatic reports informed him of starvation in Asia, Africa and South America. If, indeed, the poor are always with us, never had so many been with us.

John looked at his world and wondered about the role of the Church.

"Is my Church a seed or pearl?"

"Is it only the pearl of great price to be preserved from all possible contamination?

"Is the Church also the seed that must burrow into the earth of the poor and bring them new hope? Should it not penetrate the soil of the rich and the mighty that their consciences might be touched by the gospel of Christ?"

John had heard critics complain that the Church was irrelevant, that its pageantry and preoccupation with past glories obscured the message of Jesus. They claimed that people had stopped turning to the Church for meaning. Instead of saving humanity the Church seemed intent on saving itself.

FOR FURTHER READING

Hebblethwaite, Peter. *Paul VI: The First Modern Pope.* Mahwah, N.J.: Paulist Press, 1993.

_____. *Pope John XXIII: Shepherd of the Modern World.* New York: Doubleday, 1985.

Sullivan, Francis A., S.J. *Magisterium: Teaching Authority of the Catholic Church.* Mahwah, N.J.: Paulist Press, 1983.

Vatican II: Assessment and Perspectives, ed. Rene Latourelle. Mahwah, N.J.: Paulist Press, 1988.

▼ ———————

VIDEO

The Mystery of Faith: An Introduction to Catholicism, by Michael Himes. Distributed by St. Anthony Messenger Press (ten 25-minute videos).

Third Millennium: Vatican II. Credence Cassettes (ten 25-minute videos).

John somewhat agreed with this criticism.

"Of course the gospel is precious. But if it is not allowed to take root in the lives of men, it will not be believed. If it is too protected, it will become like a museum piece—admired by tourists who give it a hasty glance. Men are saved by the living word of God, not by a lifeless trophy."

John decided that the Church as God's seed must be generously poured forth in the world. He would call a council to bring this about.

"The idea came to me," he said, "like a ray of blinding light. A council!"

On January 25, 1959, Pope John went to the Basilica of St. Paul Outside the Walls of Rome to celebrate the nineteen-hundredth anniversary of the writing of Saint Paul's Letter to the Romans. After the service, John gathered the eighteen cardinals who were present and talked to them about the state of the Church and the world.

"These problems must be faced. I intend to call a council of the universal Church. I would like to have your advice."

The cardinals were so surprised that they sat in mute astonishment.

John recorded in his diary his disappointment that they did not show at least some enthusiasm. "Humanly speaking, I could have expected that after hearing what I had to say, they would have crowded around me to express approval and good wishes. Instead there was an unbroken and impressive silence."

In the days that followed, John's advisers offered many objections. When all else failed, they used the tactics of delay.

"It may take as long as twenty years to get ready for so vast a gathering."

John had no intention of waiting that long.

"I am an old man. [He was seventy-nine.] You get the council ready within two years."

He overcame their resistance and swept aside their objections.

The planning committee chose October 11, 1962, as the opening date. They picked this date with an eye to pleasing the members of the Eastern Orthodox Churches: the feast of the Motherhood of Mary, recalling the fourth-century Council of Ephesus which declared that Mary is the Mother of God. Since this doctrine is held by the Orthodox Churches, it serves as a point of unity between Rome and the East.

The choice of this date was a gentle invitation to the Christians of the Eastern Churches to share in the new hopes of the council—and to reconsider the possibility of reunion.

In fact, the Russian Church did send observers to the council, though the Greek Orthodox Church was reluctant to do so. Several years later, Pope Paul was to have a historic meeting with the Ecumenical Patriarch of Constantinople, Athenagoras. The "good seed" was already at work on the task of Christian unity.

The Second Vatican Council opened amid the pageantry and splendor of St. Peter's, as it played host to the Church's leadership gathered from every corner of the world.

That evening, nearly a half million people poured into St. Peter's Square for a torchlight demonstration. John was overwhelmed.

"Dear children, dear children. I hear your voices. My voice is an isolated one, but it echoes the voice of the whole world. Here, in effect, the whole world is represented. You have come to open the Council, that God's treasures may be available to all men. He is on the wrong path who would limit himself to contemplating the luminous heavens and who keeps hidden the treasure that is the truth handed down by our forefathers. This Council will bring us to the right path."

On October 17, 1960, Pope John XXIII received in Rome about two hundred delegates of the United Jewish Appeal, the great American Jewish welfare organization. He welcomed them with open arms as he quoted the biblical passage: "I am Joseph, your brother." (Joseph was the pope's baptismal name.)

John XXIII and Vatican II—Looking Back

Pope John XXIII

Few people expected a seventy-seven-year-old man to be such an ambitious changer of Church history. The conventional opinion was that Angelo Roncalli would be a caretaker pope. Had they pondered more his unconventional career people might not have been so astonished. This most pastoral of popes had never had a parish. Virtually his entire life was spent in some form of administration. He was a desk priest, but one who never gave up his enjoyment of people.

His first ten years as a priest were spent in the service of Bishop Radini-Tedeschi, a first-rate diocesan planner. He worked with the bishop on the reorganization of the diocese while also teaching at the seminary. After a three-year service as an army chaplain in World War I, he took a post as national director for the Propagation of the Faith in Italy—a job similar to the one Archbishop Sheen held in the United States. He proved to be a successful fund-raiser, increasing annual contributions by four hundred percent in just four years.

Ordained a bishop in 1925, he served as chief papal representative in Bulgaria for nine years. He felt lonely in that strange country where an unfriendly Orthodox Church held sway. He also felt neglected, and recorded in his diary that he thought Rome was putting him on the shelf. Then one day a change came, an appointment as apostolic delegate to Turkey—further exile, in his opinion. For ten years he ministered to the tiny Catholic minority in a Muslim land.

None of this snuffed out his native love of people, regardless of religion or ethnic origin. In fact, his nineteen years in Bulgaria and Turkey broadened his outlook and fostered his sense of ecumenism. Finally, on his sixty-fifth birthday, just when many men plan on collecting their retirement benefits, he was offered a glamorous post: papal nuncio to Paris.

It was a nasty time to assume this distinguished post, for the anger of the French patriotic bishops was aflame against the cowardice of the Vichy collaborationist bishops. Roncalli used every wile he knew to put out the fire and heal the rifts in the French Church. He did exceedingly well and was awarded the red hat as well as the affection of the French, who loved him shamelessly.

In his seventy-second year he was at last given a genuine pastoral assignment. The pope made him Patriarch of Venice in 1953. Age did not wither nor custom stale his infinite energies. Vigorously, he set about creating and implementing a pastoral plan for his archdiocese, much in the manner of his early tutor, Radini-Tedeschi.

When he arrived in Rome in October, 1958, his seventy-seventh year, to participate in electing Pius XII's successor, he brought with him years of administrative, diplomatic and ecumenical experience. He also bore an ebullient love of people and a vision of what the Church needed. On the third day of the conclave, two cardinals went to his cell and told him they were convinced he was about to be elected. One of them, Cardinal Ottaviani, urged him to think of calling a council.

John's immediate reaction is not recorded, but his ultimate one is. One hundred days after his election, John XXIII announced to the cardinals and worshipers assembled at the Church of St. Paul Outside the Walls of Rome that he would call an ecumenical council for the renewal of the Church. The old man, the so-called transitional pope, undertook the breathtaking challenge of changing the course of history in the Catholic Church.

Pope Paul VI Completes and Implements Vatican II

From the early days of his priesthood, Father Montini (the future Paul VI) was introduced to the inside of Vatican affairs. His father was a prominent journalist involved in Italian politics—a fact that helped Montini gain a grasp of public affairs early on. With the election of Pius XII, Montini became one of two sub-secretaries of state. Before his death, Pius XII appointed Montini as archbishop of Milan. John XXIII included Montini among his first selection of cardinals.

During the first session of Vatican II, it became clear to Cardinals Montini and Suenens that an outline of a master plan was needed. Pope John had anticipated just one session and had not expected as much business as eventually arose. Montini and Suenens realized that the topics and positions for the Council were much more complex and open to debate than the preparatory committees envisioned. They approached Pope John and persuaded him to adopt their plan, at least in substance. As history would show, the acceptance of sixteen major documents on the topics actually discussed was virtually identical to their own plan.

Pope John died within six months after the close of the first session of the Council. Cardinal Montini was then elected pope and took the name Paul VI. He continued the work of the Council and was closely involved in its development over the next three sessions. If Pope John was the spiritual father of the Council, Pope Paul was its executor. His long years as secretary to Pius XII and his vast familiarity with Church affairs, Vatican policy-making and a worldwide Church served him well in his new ministry.

Paul's interest in world political and economic developments made him sympathetic to the thrust of the *Pastoral Constitution on the Church in the Modern World (Gaudium et Spes)*. The diplomatic and administrative skills acquired at the Vatican enabled him to move documents along. Experienced and bright, he knew more than most what was happening and why it would benefit the Church.

The hard years lay ahead after the Council. The implementation of the Council documents introduced changes that had a vast immediate impact upon every Catholic. The Mass was now in the vernacular. Priests faced the people and a new lectionary was published. Thousands of priests, anticipating permission for a married clergy, were disappointed by Paul VI's *Sacredotalis Celibatus (On Priestly Celibacy)* in which he refused to change the discipline. Ten thousand priests resigned in the United States alone.

The most difficult challenge Pope Paul faced in the postconciliar years was the decision he had to make about artificial contraception. He appointed a commission to study the matter. The majority judgment of the committee was that taking the birth control pill was not contrary to the purposes of marriage or the laws of God. Pope Paul agonized over this. Many called him a "Hamlet," after the hesitant figure in the Shakespeare plays who found it hard to make up his mind.

But finally the pope did decide, going against the findings of his commission and publishing his encyclical *Humanae Vitae*. The negative reaction of a great number of theologians, the ambiguous support of some conferences of bishops and the resistance of many laity, especially in Europe and North America, remained a severe trial for him for the rest of his papacy. Yet many others pointed out the pastoral wisdom of the encyclical and his prescience as to what a "contraceptive mentality" would produce.

The first years after the Council produced a certain euphoria that misled many to think most traditions would disappear, even perennial truths of Tradition itself. This caused a confusion about basic teachings and fundamental discipline. Pope Paul responded with a reaffirmation of Catholic faith in his *Credo of Paul VI*.

He followed this with *Mysterium Fidei (Mystery of Faith)*

to clarify and correct points of doctrine, especially on the Eucharist, that he believed were misleading in the widely popular *Dutch Catechism*.

Pope Paul VI had the unenviable task of holding the Church together after the Council. It was as though his arms were stretched to the breaking point. To his credit he succeeded with patience, calm and faith, intelligently illuminating what needed to be understood and peacefully addressing controversialists—or at least suffering in silence when he thought that was best.

All was not turmoil. He inaugurated the papal style of leadership fully embraced by John Paul II, making trips to Manila, Africa and Jerusalem. His embrace of the Ecumenical Patriarch Athenagoras signaled a new Catholic willingness to seek reunion with the Orthodox. He presided over the Holy Year of 1975, which brought millions of pilgrims to Rome. He piloted the Church through rough waters and set it on a sure course. He left behind him one of the most distinguished papacies in history.

The Council

John XXIII set as the Council's immediate task the renewal of the religious life of Catholics, the updating of the Church's teaching, discipline and organization. Its ultimate goal was the unity of all Christians.

The first period of the Council extended from October 11, 1962, to December 8, 1962. A number of the schemata were discussed but none was passed at this time. At the last general congregation, the already sick Pope John visited the Council to extend his thanks.

Pope John XXIII died on June 3, 1963. Shortly after his election, Pope Paul VI reactivated the Council proceedings, which had been suspended automatically at the death of the former pontiff.

The second period began on September 29, 1963, and lasted until December of that year. The fathers passed the *Constitution on the Liturgy* and the *Decree on the Media of Social Communication*.

The third period extended from September 14, 1964, to November 21, 1964. During this time, several parish priests were invited to participate in the general congregation as representatives of all parochial clergy. The fathers passed the *Constitution on the Church,* the *Decree on Oriental Catholic Churches* and the *Decree on Ecumenism.*

The final period extended from September 14, 1965, to December 8, 1965. The bulk of the schemata was passed during this period. It was also during this session that Pope Paul VI and Patriarch Athenagoras met and expressed their desire for unity between East and West.

On December 8, 1965, the last public session was held in the columned, majestic courtyard of St. Peter's Basilica. In solemn high pageantry, the leaders of the Catholic Church, along with representatives from eighty-one governments and nine international organizations, celebrated the accomplishments of this great ecumenical council. Practical hard work had produced and issued four constitutions, nine decrees and three declarations. In effect, the Council had brought about a turning point in the history of the Church.

What Do We Need, Reformers or Saints?— Connecting to Our Times

It has often been said that the Church needs saints more than reformers. Of course, many saints have been reformers, such as Teresa of Avila and Ignatius of Loyola. What the saying really means is that reformers who lack sanctity seem to be crabbed and negative improvers of the Church without the saving graces of love, holiness and persuasive witness. Pope John XXIII belongs to the saintly school of reform, a wise, holy, humorous and gentle pastor.

We could use a good dose of his approach again these days. Our Church has become politicized by the wranglings of divided camps within the community. Much of the arguing is dominated by a humorless and strident tone. The merits of the opposing positions become submerged by failures in courtesy, resorting to caricature and a sense that the quest for holiness is on the back burner. Reformers without sanctity are oppressive. Pietists who pay no attention to people's needs are irrelevant.

Vatican II sent out a loud and clear call to every Catholic to reach for holiness. It is not meant to be the preserve of an elite corps within the Church. The Holy Spirit excludes no one from this invitation. Actually, millions of Catholics are listening to the call.

Book publishers note that Scripture and spirituality are always at the top of their best-selling lists. The fact that so many people participate in daily liturgy, pray the Liturgy of the Hours (especially Morning and Evening prayer) and give themselves to regular sessions of centering prayer is a heartening and welcome sign that the search for holiness is alive and well.

John XXIII would be pleased. He prized the holy life above all else, as is evident from his diary, *Journal of a Soul*, and from Peter Hebblethwaite's wonderful biography of the pope. Those who wish to do something good for themselves, the Church and the world could not choose a better goal than to respond to the Holy Spirit's call to holiness.

30. The 'Third Advent'

The Church in the Year 2000: Tentative Predictions

FOR BACKGROUND

Pope John Paul II has brought the Catholic Church into the world culture. He has traveled throughout the known world. Not content to stay in the Vatican, he has given a human face to the Church for Catholics and non-Catholics alike. In 1994 he was named Man of the Year by *Time*. He shaped world events more than any other leader.

Catholics are found in every walk of life, in every town, in every city, in every job. Catholics are educated at every university, high school and grammar school in the nation.

Catholics think on their own within the teaching of the Church and feel free to voice their opinions. Catholics are not afraid to take a stand on moral issues like abortion and capital punishment. Standing for what we believe is part of our heritage.

What will the Church be like in the year 2000? That year will mark the beginning of the third millennium of Christianity, what John Paul II characterized as the "third advent" of Jesus Christ. While no one can predict with certainty what the Church of the Third Advent will be, there are trends one can cite. In this final chapter we will recapitulate some of the thrusts of history from Vatican I and Vatican II and see them as predictors of trends for the future. Our assumption is that the sweep of history points in these directions.

We will begin with some observations about culture and society with reference to their impact on Church history. We will then look briefly at the Church's recent past and future in terms of the papacy, theology and ministry.

Social Order: Farm, City, Globe

Rural Catholics. In 1870, the year of the First Vatican Council, about eighty percent of all Catholics lived on farms. The pope's constituents for the most part possessed a rural mentality.

Agrarian Catholics tapped the energy of fourteen million horses and twenty-four million oxen to pull plows, drag logs and do other heavy duties. They relied on the power of sun, water, wind, animals and people. They trusted the renewable sources of power. Forests supplied wood for stove and fireplace. Waterwheels and windmills turned millstones.

Very few people could read, or even saw the need to learn. If they did read, it was by daylight or candlelight. Most of them went to bed at sundown and rose at sunrise. They lived by the rhythms of the seasons and the cycles of nature. They were never far from the mystery of death and rebirth.

Little mail was sent or received. Town criers brought the news. People rarely traveled far from their local communities. Barring the fortunate few who lived near the "new" railroads, most people journeyed by foot or horse. It would be a treat to travel ten miles an hour. Their pace was slow, cyclical and predictable.

The industrial revolution had begun. Cities were growing. But eighty percent of the people still lived with the flow of the seasons, the cycles of night and day, birth and death, and the rural celebrations dating from the mists of memory.

Most Catholics of 1870 possessed a farmer's mindset. They prized the mystical, mysterious and transcendent. Most of them had never read Voltaire or Lammenais. While they felt the effects of the French Revolution and the Napoleonic wars, it is unlikely they knew about the liberal ideas that were changing society. Papal struggles with liberalism (Chapter 25) were battles among a tiny portion of the population.

Saints, miracles and mystics were the news fare for a rural Catholicism. Small wonder that the most celebrated saints of the age were a country priest, the Curé of Ars, and a shepherd girl, Bernadette of Lourdes. These rural Catholics were captivated by a mystical clergyman who wrestled with the devil and could read hearts and became the most popular confessor in France. They were charmed by a country girl who saw the Blessed Virgin and uncovered a spring where healing miracles could happen.

When the bishops of Vatican I assembled, they convened with the knowledge that most of their parishioners had what they liked to call "the faith of the Breton farmer." Theirs was still the world of aristocrats and peasants. The new society of the industrial revolution and liberal thought did not seem to merit much attention from them, except to deny and condemn.

Urban Catholics. Ninety-two years later, in 1962, the bishops of Vatican II faced a new world. Now eighty percent of all Catholics lived in cities and were citizens of the urban, industrial democracies in North Atlantic nations or the increasingly urban developing countries of the Third World. These urban Catholics could travel at speeds ranging from fifty-five miles per hour on the highway to faster than two thousand miles per hour on a Concorde jet. With the arrival of universal education, the bishops of Vatican II found themselves dealing with Catholics who had minds of their own and intellectual training often equal to—or superior to—their shepherds. The shepherds ruled an enlightened flock who made ninety-three billion phone calls a year, watched TV, drew energy from fossil fuels and were creating artificial environments.

Electricity had turned a rural day people into an urban night people, exiled from the rhythms of nature and the seasons. These urban Catholics now took trips to the country to see nature, as though it were a museum. They thought like city people. They had acquired the scientific mentality and were at home with the representative ways of democratic governments and the managerial styles of the industrial world.

Their saints were likely to be the Hindu Gandhi and the Baptist Martin Luther King, Jr., as well as Catholics like Dorothy Day and Mother Teresa—saints involved in the poverty and justice problems of an urban, industrial world. Impatient with the mystical and transcendent, Catholics in 1962 were problem-solvers; they liked being part of the act.

The Vatican II bishops responded accordingly to these

FOR DISCUSSION/REFLECTION

The Church has become increasingly involved in environmental issues. It seeks to promote all forms of life, including the whole of creation. To this end Pope John Paul II has said that "in many parts of the world society is given to instant gratification and consumerism while remaining indifferent to the damage which these cause." Do you see the Church helping to promote an attitude of ecological responsibility? Are you? What concrete acts can be done at the institutional and individual levels to protect the environment?

In the political realm, the Church traditionally has sought to avoid becoming identified with any particular government, political party or social movement. Has this always been successfully achieved? How should Catholic politicians balance their religious beliefs with their civic duty? Is there an essential link?

In the wake of Vatican II, the Catholic Church has attested to the positive value of culture. Do you see any tension between American culture and Catholicism? What gifts does American culture offer the Church? Where is American culture challenged by the gospel message?

According to theologian Avery Dulles, the richness of the Church's reality is expressed by a series of images or models: mystical communion, sacrament, herald, servant and community of disciples. The *Catechism of the Catholic Church* adds Temple of the Holy Spirit, Body of Christ and People of God. None of these models or images exhausts the mystery of the Church. Taken together, they form a

▼ ━━━━━━━━━━━━━━━

lovely tapestry that engages our contemplation and deepens our relationship to the Church. How many of these models and images touch you? How can you come to appreciate all of them individually and combined into one overview?

After a long period of a shortage of vocations, a number of dioceses are beginning to show a turnaround. In all cases the bishop is taking active leadership in recruitment. Parishioners offer prayer and adoration of the Eucharist. Younger priests and seminarians preach the call to priesthood as well as make personal contact with potential candidates. Several dioceses have established houses for college-age candidates who continue their education while becoming part of a priestly formation program on a residential basis. One diocese with eighty parishes already has forty-five seminarians. Continue to pray for an increase in vocations.

How do you see the role of women in the Church? How has the Church benefited from women's contributions? How, as a member of the Church, have you?

"Bishops, with priests as coworkers, ...are heralds of faith who draw new disciples to Christ; they are authentic teachers of the apostolic faith, endowed with the authority of Christ" *(Catechism of the Catholic Church, #888)*. Name some ways this teaching office strengthens our faith.

As the twentieth century draws to a close, Pope John Paul II sees the West embracing a "culture of death" with its emphasis on abortion, euthanasia and violence. He has challenged the Church and the world to support a "culture of life." What spiritual, moral and political

new urban Catholics. The Council's decisions about liturgy, the Church as People of God, collegiality, religious freedom, ecumenism and the need to dialogue with the world provided a conceptual framework for the Catholics of this new age, as well as guidelines for action in a fast-moving world.

Global Catholics. The wheel of history is turning again. The smokestack industries of the industrial revolution are dying; the world of the microchip has been born. Brain power is replacing brawn power. In little over a century we have moved from the horse to the engine to the chip, from the farmer to the laborer to the information worker. Welcome to the Age of Information!

A piechart of the workforce shows farmers at three percent; smokestackers at twenty percent; service people at twenty-eight percent; information industries at forty-nine percent—statistics which do not show the dependence all sectors have on information processing. The new society will produce information the way the old one mass-produced cars. In 1950 we created ninety-three thousand businesses a year. Today we invent over six hundred thousand.

The global village is here, wired with optic fiber, cabled from pole to pole and encased in satellites. The high-tech people of the Age of Information will need a Church that both appreciates the meaning of a high-tech life and responds to the high-touch needs of Catholics. In its community, structure and meaning, the Church already has a high-touch capability.

The community includes the Church's friendship network as well as the music, art, ceremony, eloquence, ministry, esthetics, asceticism and mystery of liturgy. The structure of the Church is made clear by the descriptions of roles, rights and duties of all the members in an open and free-flowing society. The Church's meaning system is a response to questions about the meaning and purpose of life. Community, structure and meaning—kept alive and updated—is an excellent high-touch response to the needs of high-tech Catholics of the age of the chip.

Images of the Church of Vatican I, the Church of Vatican II and the "Chip Church" all come to mind in viewing Pope John Paul II in Africa. Before him stand one million pre-industrial rural Africans, eager to hear this Vatican II presidential and collegial pope of the industrial age. Overhead a satellite from the chip culture hums, taking signals and beaming this scene to anyone on earth who cares to watch. Layers of culture come together in one quick insight—the receding past, the insistent present, the crashing-into-us future.

What does this picture of social movement mean for the sweep of history as it influences the image of the pope, the progress of theology and the development of ministry?

Pope: King, President, Pastor

The pope as king. On July 18, 1870, a storm shook the Vatican. Rain pelted the columns of Bernini; lightning sparred with the cross on St. Peter's dome while thunderclaps made street peddlers shudder. Inside the basilica, Pius IXd was reading the new dogma of papal infallibility aloud to the 535 bishops who had just approved it (Chapter 25).

The dogma achieved three goals: (1) to illustrate the Church's repudiation of liberalism; (2) to reinforce the authority of the pope; (3) to stay in touch with a rural constituency that was at home with a patriarchal figure in the shoes of the fisherman.

Above all the dogma accented the royal character of the pope. It crowned him king. This may have been out of step with avant-garde thinkers, but not with the customs of the times. Autocratic monarchs ruled Europe: Victoria in England, a Romanov tsar in Russia, a Hapsburg in the Austrian-Hungarian empire, a Bismarck in Germany and Bourbons in Spain.

The pope as president. Ninety-two years later the Church was ready to do without kings and elect a presidential leader. The Council document on the Church spelled out the collegial role of the bishops and the broad responsibility of all the "people of God" for the Church of God. Kingly popes had said, "I talk and you listen." Presidential popes showed willingness to listen as well as to talk.

It is important to note the role-modeling power of the pope because he exerts such influence on leadership styles in the Church. When the pope assumes a monarchical stance, then so can bishops, pastors, parents, school principals and other leaders. When the pope moves to a presidential role, so also do bishops, pastors, parents and so on.

The presidential style of recent popes opens up room for representative bodies in the Church such as synods for bishops, councils for the laity and boards for Catholic schools. Rule by fiat gives way to rule by consultation.

The pope as pastor. Will the popes of the Church of the Third Advent be more pastoral? One might hope so. The presidential popes give hopeful signals. The "September Pope," John Paul I, became famous for his smile. Before him, Paul VI was definitely a hugger, embracing both the Anglican Archbishop of Canterbury and the Orthodox Patriarch Athenagoras right in public. And speaking of public displays of affection, remember John Paul II kissing a woman on her forehead before the eyes of thousands in St. Peter's Square—the woman who was wounded the same day as he was shot by a would-be assassin. She and he recovered and met again in that fateful spot in a joyous sign of recovery and emotion.

Vatican I popes brought the world to the Vatican. But the new popes bring the Church to the world, as evidenced in the trips of Paul VI and John Paul II. Everywhere John Paul plays the crowds and eagerly shares himself with thousands. He affirms people and confirms the Churches. He sets the pace for the pastoral popes of the future, the kind of high-touch popes a high-tech world will need.

Theology: Faith, Reason, Discernment

Mystery without a problem. Catholic theologians in 1870

means should we espouse to enhance human dignity and protect human life from conception to the natural end of earthly life?

As the Church enters the third millenium, what pressing issues must it address? What challenges will it face in the years to come?

John Paul II

The Pope Forgives His Assassin

In the 1983 Christmas season, *Time* magazine put a startling picture on its cover. It showed a prison cell where two men sat on plastic chairs. One wore a white cassock, a white cape and a white skullcap; the other, a blue sweater, jeans and running shoes. *Time* reported the story this way:

"Last week in an extraordinary moment of grace, the violence in St. Peter's Square was transformed. In a bare, white-walled cell in Rome's Rebbibia prison, John Paul tenderly held the hand that held the gun that was meant to kill him. For 21 minutes the pope sat with his would-be assassin, Mehmet Ali Agca. The two talked softly. Once or twice Agca laughed. The pope forgave him for the shooting. At the end of the meeting, Agca either kissed the pope's ring or pressed the pope's hand to his forehead in a gesture of respect.

"What did they talk about? 'That,' said the pope as he left the cell, 'will have to remain a secret between him and me. I spoke to him as a brother whom I have pardoned and who has my complete trust.'"

Did the pope's visit influence Ali Agca? One year later Agca proclaimed that he was renouncing terrorism to become a man of peace. He traced his conversion to the pope's visit with him a year ago. After extensive reading of the Koran, Agca said he had become a devout Moslem with profound respect for Christianity. He promised that if he were freed he would become a preacher to all nations, proclaiming goodness and truth to all peoples.

faced rationalists outside the Church and supernaturalists inside the walls. The secular liberals preached the values of reason and the uselessness of faith. The great mass of rural Catholics loved the fire of faith and were chilled by all this talk about reason—if indeed they heard the talk at all. In such a situation Catholic theologians considered it their duty to rebuke the rationalists and console the believers.

Like their agrarian brothers and sisters, theologians were fond of the mystery of religion. Refreshed themselves by the life of faith and not in a mood to test the waters of rationalism, they did theology from faith's point of view. In so acting they left the impression of mystery without problem.

The rationalist-scientific mind saw life as a series of problems to be solved. The faith-motivated theologians viewed life as a mystery to be reverenced. How, then, did the theologians use reason? In doctrinal matters they found fresh ways to explain the old truths. They were keepers of the flame.

They were also guardians of the castle. Theologians polished their logic and argumentative skills in debates with Protestants and rationalists, proving them wrong and the Church right. In retrospect it looks like an age of innocence to us, though indeed all the combatants were earnest fighters. It must be said that even then some Catholic theologians thought the liberals and Protestants occasionally had a point. Liturgical and biblical scholars were among the first to benefit from the liberal and Protestant research. But on the whole, "mystery without a problem" is as good a phrase as any to capture the theological mood of Vatican I times.

Problem without mystery. The scrappy Catholic liberal theologians who served as *periti* (experts) at Vatican II were a new breed, not seen in Church circles for centuries. Now they were center stage in one of the most colorful Church events in history. They arrived armed with new freedoms and with the blessings of their bishops.

In a striking turnaround, the conservatives inside the Church were put on the defensive as invited Protestant, Orthodox and Jewish observers looked on within the very walls of St. Peter's. Did Pio Nono turn in his grave? Probably.

The new theologians were "city boys," products of an urban Church in a fast-paced society. Moreover, the revolution in communications arrived at the Vatican along with the bishops. Television, telephone, radio, jet planes, high-speed trains and all the other wonders of modern communication turned the basilica into a fishbowl. The stately secrecy of Vatican I crumbled before the up-front visibility and high profile of Vatican II.

Catholics worldwide had left the farm. Faced with the stress of the daily problems of urban life, they had become a problem-solving people. Not surprisingly, so also had the bishops and theologians—so much so that Vatican II theology was to reflect a new mood: problem without mystery. It's not that mystery was rejected. (Council documents, of course, reflect a proper attention to mystery—especially the constitutions on revelation, the Church and liturgy.) But energies were given to penetrating a seemingly endless agenda of problems.

Now freed to look at the Bible and dogmas "from below"—that is, from the human, rational, "people" side—theologians engaged with gusto in the fresh problems this approach suggested. Those studying moral issues found the problem-centered approach a natural one anyway. Already, however, one hears the plaint, "Is this all there is?" What does the future say?

Discerners. A "new" theology is growing up in the Third World. Especially in the Latin American theology of liberation, one notes a fresh angle. Latin American theologians have taken the Marxist theory and given it a Catholic slant. Like Lammenais in the 1830's, who said, "Don't tremble before liberalism. Catholicize it!" they do not tremble before Marxism. They take Marx's political and economic liberalism and integrate it with the Old Testament story of liberation in the Exodus and the New Testament story of liberation through the Paschal Mystery.

As North Atlantic theologians had taken intellectual liberalism and baptized it, Latin Americans have used economic liberalism and baptized it.

The African Church is growing at the rate of six thousand a day—and Africans are storytellers. Could it be that they will restore the role of storytelling in theology? Will they put life back in the parables? Will they prove that the teaching of Chicago's Father John Shea, the theologian of storytelling, is correct?

The Asian Church is growing fast in South India. Can we expect from this culture of mystical and aphoristic teachers new "books of wisdom" for the Church? Will they show us how to incorporate the revered books of Buddhism and Hinduism into the Christian perspective?

Poets, storytellers, aphorists—possibly the Third World will shake us out of the mystery-versus-problem cycle. They can offer thought forms which integrate the two—just as the Bible does. What, after all, is a psalm but a poem? Is not a parable a story? Are not the proverbs of Solomon aphorisms? A time of discernment lies ahead for the Church of the Third Advent.

Ministry: From Rural Pastor to Hi-Tech Priest

In pre-industrial times the parish priest shared the worldview of his parishioners. The largely rural Church stood in a world without much change. People rarely ventured beyond where they were born and raised unless forced to do so by wars or famine. From the time of the Council of Trent, priests were given much more education, especially with the introduction of the seminary system. This meant that the pastor was usually one of the few people in the parish with schooling. As a leader he was in touch with other leaders in the community and knowledgeable about social and economic opportunities. His spiritual prestige added to his other achievements. Hence, he was a major

FOR DISCUSSION/REFLECTION

A new millennium is upon us. The Church is moving into uncharted territory. If we look at the changes that took place in the past century and the speed with which these changes took place, we can only wonder what will happen in the future. How will Catholics deal with the future? Will the Church change a lot? Discuss the following situations:

— The computer age and the Church
— Genetic research
— The liturgy and participation
— The role of the pope
— The number of priests and
 religious
— The media
— The entertainment industry
— Religious observance

Make a joyful noise to the LORD,
 all the earth.
Worship the LORD with
 gladness;
come into his presence with
 singing.
 —Psalm 100:1-2

FOR FURTHER READING

The American Catholic Parish: A History from 1850 to the Present, ed. Jay P. Dolan. Mahwah, N.J.: Paulist Press, 1987.

Gjerghi, Lush. *Mother Teresa: Her Life; Her Works*. Maryknoll, N.Y.: Orbis Books, 1991.

Images: Women in Transition, compiled by Janice Grana. Nashville, Tenn.: Upper Room, 1976.

Pope John Paul II. *Crossing the Threshold of Hope*. New York: Alfred A. Knopf, 1994.

Spirituality in Ecumenical Perspective, ed. Glenn Hinson. Louisville, Ky.: Westminster/John Knox Press, 1993.

source of advice for his parishioners in both religious and secular matters.

The transitional period between the age of the farm and the emerging industrial revolution saw a vast population shift. People moved from farms to cities. They also migrated to America and to the colonies of the major European powers. Their priests moved and migrated with them. In the United States, the people of the immigrant Church found both comfort and stability in their ethnic parishes. The authority of the priest, inherited from rural times, remained as firm as ever. Moreover, the priest could and did use his prestige to help the parishioners politically and economically. The urban priest became the street-wise pastor who led his people through the strange maze of a foreign land. Some clergy became "labor priests" who fought for justice for the workers and gave legitimacy to the union movement.

After World War II, Catholics in America prospered. They went to college and left their old neighborhoods for the greener suburbs. The old dependency upon the priest for political and job-seeking assistance disappeared. The rise of a Catholic professional class meant that priests now ministered to educated peers. Like other Americans, the Catholic laity enjoyed participating in public life—political, educational, artistic and ecclesiastical. Vatican II's principle of subsidiarity and delegation soon found a friendly niche in parish life. At liturgy priests and altar boys were now sharing the worship event with adult laymen and laywomen and altar girls—as well as with lectors, Eucharistic ministers, music ministers and others. Parishes established councils to advise the pastor on all sorts of issues, such as the budget, religious education, social ministry outreach and the Catholic school. The rural patriarchal priest of old became a kind of CEO, the chief administrator of a complex operation. Younger clergy are armed with a knowledge of hi-tech and its potential for administration and service within a parish.

All this was accompanied by an increase of women in such ministerial roles as lectors and Eucharistic ministers. As the number of priestless parishes has grown, women often serve as pastoral administrators. Significant numbers of women have enrolled in degree programs in theology at seminaries as well as pastoral studies programs in Catholic universities. A fair number of parishes now have women as pastoral associates.

This has led many to hope for the possibility of women's ordination. But both Paul VI and John Paul II have concluded that "the Church is not authorized to ordain women to the priesthood." This has disappointed supporters of women's ordination, but has motivated them to seek ever more significant roles for women in the Church.

There is also a priest shortage in Europe and North America, due to large numbers of resignations and a drastic decline of vocations to the priesthood. Many argue that celibacy is the principle obstacle. They believe a married priesthood, with optional celibacy, is the most reasonable response to this crisis. A change of this magnitude, if it were to come at all, would be difficult to bring about. We shall have to see how the Holy Spirit moves the popes and bishops on this issue.

With the arrival in the United States of over twenty million Hispanics and thousands of Catholics from Vietnam, South Korea, Haiti and other countries, a new immigrant Church needs ministry. Unlike the old immigrants, these newcomers have not brought an ample number of priests with them. The Church in America must therefore find new ways to respond to this multicultural experience. This challenges the Catholics who have made it into the mainstream to be open and welcome to the newcomers. It also summons educators, priests and others to learn how to minister to them.

Intractable problems are nothing new for the Church, as our journey through its history demonstrates. It is important to keep a faith perspective, especially when pressing concrete difficulties beset the Church. Faith and prayer and trust in the Holy Spirit are more important when the details of daily life engulf us. The speed of the hi-tech age gives the illusion that all problems can be solved swiftly. This makes us impatient with life in general. The saints have spoken of "holy impatience," but they also taught and practiced the virtue of patience, in which we possess our souls. This does not impede action and progress. It gives it depth. In the long run we seek to do God's will, for only in this way will the Kingdom come.

AUDIO

The Sacred Feather, narrated by Waylon Jennings. Our Sunday Visitor (55 minutes).

Signposts for Pilgrims: An Inspirational Collection of Papal Quotes, narrated by Rev. Owen Campion. Our Sunday Visitor.

The Capacity to Hope Is One of History's Best Lessons—Connecting to Our Times

Up to this point we have been connecting past events to the present time. Since this chapter deals with the future, our connection is not with something that has already happened, but with a Christian virtue that orients us to the future: hope. Christian hope assures us that we are destined for eternal joy if we die reconciled to God and to others. It also tells us that we have an immortal soul that will survive our deaths and that our bodies will rise again to be rejoined to our souls at the general judgment and resurrection of the dead. We express this act of hope in both the Apostles' and Nicene Creeds.

This promise of future joy should make us hope-filled in the present time no matter how much pain, darkness or difficulty we may be experiencing. Of course, we are doing more than hoping in a time span. Our hope is rooted in the call we received to enter into covenant with God at our Baptism. It is founded on our identity with Jesus Christ, who has saved us from our sins and filled us with peace, joy and grace. He has risen bodily from the dead, the first fruit of all who will also participate in the resurrection unto glory. Lastly, our hope flows from the Holy Spirit, whose temples we are, whose dwelling place is within us when are open to divine forgiveness and sanctification. Hope proceeds from the trinitarian love directed toward us.

Because this sense of hope can sometimes be hard to hold onto by ourselves, we have the benefit of the hoping community, the Church. We have the local parish family where support, love and trust can and should be available. We have the diocesan and universal Church as the wider society of hope that inspires us to look beyond present troubles to the sun that lies behind the clouds.

People of hope whom we can see, hear, touch and feel can walk with us. They are transparencies of the invisible loving Persons of the Trinity as well as the Communion of Saints, the angels and the Virgin Mary, our Blessed Mother. Church history is full of very dark moments when a sense of hope was hard to maintain. Yet God's people joyfully marched on, filled with hope in Jesus. We study history to learn many lessons. The capacity to hope is one of the best of all lessons.

VIDEO

Jesus in My Life Today. Brown-ROA (15 minutes).

John Paul II: Biography of a Statesman of Faith. A & E Productions (50 minutes).

Roses in December. Ave Maria Press (56 minutes).

Sister Thea: Her Own Story. USCC Publishing Services.

This Land of God. Our Sunday Visitor (60 minutes).

The Vatican: Fortress of Christianity. Films for the Humanities (39 minutes).

Work of Love, Our Sunday Visitor (30 minutes).

Pentecost to the 'Third Advent'— Epilogue

We finish now our journey from Pentecost to the year 2000. We have witnessed the ups and downs of the "Old Lady," Holy Mother Church. It's an astonishing story by any standards. No novelist would dare to invent plots as circuitous and involved as has been the history of the Church. The truth of the matter is far stranger than any fiction—and far more enchanting, enraging, lovable, hateful, captivating, frustrating and, in the last analysis, homelike.

The story is full of triumphs and disasters, mean endings and happy ones. Jesus promised that the gates of hell would not prevail against the Church. He also said that he would keep the Holy Spirit close to it, and that he himself would abide with it all days. He must have kept his promise. When one ponders all the dead ends the Church slid into and then rebounded with the bounce and grace of a youngster, one can only conclude that a lovable divine force is at its center, a divine forgiveness in the face of all the Church's follies, a spiritual peace underneath all the storms.

Surely the old hymn is absolutely right: "The Church's one foundation is Jesus Christ our Lord."

Amen to that.
And thanks be to God!